THE
EXPERIENCE
OF
SCHOOLING

THE
EXPERIENCE
OF
SCHOOLING

EDITED BY

Melvin L. Silberman
Temple University

Holt, Rinehart and Winston, Inc.

New York   Chicago   San Francisco   Atlanta   Dallas
Montreal   Toronto   London   Sydney

Preface

This book of readings brings together for the first time a group of educational writers who share a common concern—what schooling does to children. In their view, the school experience raises critical problems for students. They face such difficult tasks as learning to live with teacher favoritism, preserving their individuality in a crowded classroom, adjusting to frequent personal evaluation, and accepting the pervasive authority of teachers and school administrators. Coping with these demands leaves them confused, afraid, and resentful.

Until recently, these problems have been largely overlooked in examinations of school life. The common practice has been to view schooling as an essentially academic experience. Few have sensed how much schooling is also an intensive experience in institutional living. However, the failures of our schools (especially in the inner city) and rising student unrest have begun to alter our sensibilities. There is a growing penchant for describing the school experience as it really is.

This book has some special features which are designed to make it a more meaningful and enjoyable experience than is usually the case with books of readings. Although the contents deal essentially with the psychological quality of the school experience, the contributors to the book include not only educational psychologists, but also educational sociologists, anthropologists, philosophers, and teachers. Almost half of the readings are either excerpts from books or articles which were later incorporated into books. Many of the selections contain descriptions of actual classroom experiences, while those with statistical data demand minimal technical knowledge on the part of the reader. There is also a discussion after each group of articles. This is a departure from the typical practice of providing introductions to each set of readings. The purposes of these discussions are to integrate material from each section of the book and to raise questions and draw implications concerning the matters discussed. They also help to unify the entire book.

Although a good number of readings are critical of the ways in which schooling affects children's lives, the book should not be considered as an indictment of schools. Actually, evidence is presented throughout the book that the nonacademic experiences children undergo in school are seldom planned. It might be preferable, instead, to view this collection as an examination of the unintended consequences of widely accepted school practices and conditions. Hopefully, such an examination will increase our awareness of these school experiences and encourage a wider inquiry into their impact on children.

I am grateful to the authors and publishers who gave me permission to have their material reproduced. I also wish to express appreciation to my colleague, Jerome S. Allender, for his insightful comments on the manuscript, to my wife, Shoshana, for her valuable help in compiling and writing the book, and to my secretary, Geraldine Ball, for her dependable and efficient clerical assistance. Above all, I wish to acknowledge my indebtedness to my former teacher, Philip W. Jackson, for sensitizing me to the institutional aspects of schooling and for encouraging me to undertake this project.

Temple University   M.L.S.
October 1970

Contents

Introduction

It is generally believed that the main concern of schools is instruction. But schooling is a much broader experience than being taught what is contained in textbooks. Students learn not only facts, skills, and concepts but also rules of membership in a social institution. For well over a thousand hours a year, students are urged to follow routines and procedures, to get along with each other, and to respect adult authority. Every day, students' actions are praised and criticized, their movements are directed, and their values and beliefs are shaped. Often these experiences in institutional living may have greater impact on students' ultimate well-being than do those we commonly identify with the academic curriculum.

By and large, students' efforts to come to grips with the institutional aspects of school life have been overlooked in favor of attending to their struggles as learners; this has not been entirely intentional. One reason why students' experiences in coping with the school as an institution have gone unnoticed is that our official educational planning does not consider these experiences. Consequently, their significance has been treated casually in comparison to the academic activities for which we require school attendance. Fortunately, these unstudied aspects of the school experience are currently receiving increased attention from educators. For example, the Association for Supervision and Curriculum Development held a conference in 1969 entitled "The Unstudied Curriculum: Its Impact on Children." A steadily growing number of writers are also beginning to concern themselves with what the school as an institution does to children. Some of the contributors to this discussion are impassioned critics of our schools, while others are better labeled as neutral observers. All of them, however, indicate through their writing that the nonacademic outcomes of schooling should be given greater weight than they presently are. This book of readings brings together most of these

1

writers in the hope that a clearer picture of the psychological quality of schooling will emerge.

The book begins with the argument that a "hidden" curriculum exists in schools. Its content is a set of rules, routines, and procedures designed to mold individual behavior to the requirements of institutional living. The hidden curriculum is made necessary by the fact that personal interests can rarely be accommodated in schools. Students must often yield when their own wishes and plans inconvenience people or interfere in other ways with the efficient operation of the school. But, acquiescing to these procedural rules is a painful process for most students, especially when the rules are numerous and rigidly applied. Mastering the hidden curriculum is also made difficult by confusion as to what is expected when demands contradict each other. Despite these obstacles, students have little choice but to find ways to conform to institutional expectations since they are typically presented as moral imperatives rather than as functional procedures which can be disregarded when they have little use.

Beyond the learning of rules and procedures which govern personal action, membership in a school requires a set of psychological adjustments. The next four sections of the book discuss these demands to adapt to the institutional world of the school. One of these adaptations is learning to live in school without the assurance of the adult acceptance that children take for granted at home. The problem is that teachers cannot be as intimate and patient with every one of their students as parents can be with each of their children. Their energies are severely taxed by the several roles they perform simultaneously for many students. It is not surprising, then, that students who teachers feel will make their job difficult or simply unrewarding are treated very differently from their classmates, even though few teachers consciously intend such differential treatment. Naturally, these ignored or rejected students find it difficult to become involved in school, because to do so would require them to counteract the negative expectations held by their teachers.

A second demand made in schools is that students manage their lives in a highly congested social environment where materials and activities must be shared. This means that students are required to do things together most of the time.

Individually, they have little opportunity in the classroom for private action. Personal pursuits sooner or later conflict with the teacher's rules or the wishes of classmates. Even when the chance to be alone arises, it is virtually impossible for a student to go about his business without being interrupted or distracted. As a result of these crowded conditions, a sense of privacy and individuality is difficult to achieve. In an environment which is essentially unresponsive to individual differences, one student is practically indistinguishable from another.

Schooling is, thirdly, an experience in withstanding continual evaluation of one's words and actions. Probably in no other setting is one so often judged as a person. To make matters worse, these judgments are typically voiced before an audience of peers. Consequently, classroom praise and criticism, although intended to help the learner, may threaten him instead. To cope with this threat to their self-respect, many students find it necessary to devote their mental energies to strategize how to avoid failure and shame. Saving face becomes more important to them than learning and thinking.

A fourth condition to which students must adjust in school is the pervasive authority of school personnel. Students must learn to follow procedures and obey regulations even when their purpose is unclear. They are also asked to conduct meaningful lives with few rights, privileges, and opportunities for responsibility and choice. Most administrators and teachers, of course, do not consciously try to be autocratic but few know how to avoid it. They rely on their authority to demand and restrict in order to carry out their educational functions. In response, students give up any sense of autonomy. They come to feel that their education is largely out of their hands. More important, they come to believe in the school's definition of their capacity for freedom and responsible decision-making.

One of the collective effects of these psychological demands is to make students overly concerned about their personal well-being in school and thus insensitive in their relations with each other. This book, therefore, turns to an examination of the peer tensions and antagonisms which are encouraged in schools. For example, it is common for teachers to ask students to evaluate each other and thus magnify the threat which classroom evaluation poses for students. They also invite de-

structive competition among students by dominating social interaction and thereby becoming the sole source of recognition
in the classroom. Furthermore, teachers influence the formation of peer cliques by their expression of differential attitudes
and expectations for different children. In most cases, the an-
tagonism, competition, and social exclusion engendered in
classrooms are unintended. Hence, the tension among classmates in schools often goes unrecognized and untreated.

Of course, the meaning of these nonacademic school experiences would be unclear without documentation that students
are affected by them. The book closes, then, with a report of
students' views of their schooling. At all age levels, students
are as much, if not more, touched by the institutional side of
school life as they are with its academic aspects. Their sense of
what schools are for is greatly biased by their experiences in
coping with institutional demands. As a result, their perceptions of schooling are confused and at times cynical. They do
not understand the contradictions in the school's goals and
expectations and have only two ways of viewing them. One is
to have the faith that school personnel are doing what is good
for them even if their actions are not fully comprehensible.
This is how younger children tend to feel. But, as they grow
older and spend more time in school, students develop serious
doubts about the value of schooling.

As the reader can readily sense from this overview of the
book's contents, schooling presents challenging problems to
children. They must contend with a morass of institutional
rules and regulations, the personal preferences and biases of
their teachers, and the crowded social conditions of the classroom. They must also learn to live with frequent public evaluation and limited rights and privileges. What children experience
when confronted with these demands is difficult to pinpoint
and doubtlessly varies from student to student. The testi-
mony presented in this book suggests, however, that students'
feelings fall into such negative categories as uncertainty, fear,
and resentment.

How concerned we are about the psychological conditions
under which children live in schools depends, perhaps, on how
necessary we feel unpleasant experiences are to a child's
growth and development. Our concern might also depend on
the extent to which we tolerate these conditions in our adult

lives, in our responsibilities at work, and in our relations with the major institutions of society. It might be more helpful, though, to assess the psychological quality of schooling by asking what kind of images of themselves children develop as a result of going to school. Does their schooling help them to believe in themselves, that is, to see themselves as competent, resourceful, capable of altering some parts of their environment? If we are to compel children to live at least ten years of their lives in schools, we owe it to them to explore seriously the answer to this question. If children do not form positive views of themselves as a result of their schooling, we are obligated to rethink how schools can be organized so that children will view them as a valuable resource in their lives.

Part I

THE HIDDEN
CURRICULUM

The Student's World*

PHILIP W. JACKSON

And I have seen dust from the walls of institutions,
Finer than flour, alive, more dangerous than silica,
Sift, almost invisible, through long afternoons of tedium,
Dropping a fine film on nails and delicate eyebrows,
Glazing the pale hair, the duplicate gray standard faces.
Theodore Roethke, "Dolor"†

Prehensile sophomores in the tree of learning
Stare at the exiled blossoming trees, vaguely puzzled.
John Malcolm Brinnin, "Views of the Favorite Colleges"‡

When you were a child, how many times did you find yourself cornered by an adult, usually a strange aunt or uncle, who opened the conversation with that oldest of all gambits: "Well, how do you like school?" As an adult how often have you been left alone with someone else's child and, not knowing what else to say, found yourself falling back on some variant of the standard query: "How's school?" If you have not had both of these experiences, and each of them several times, you must be something of a recluse, for talk about school, when the dialogue is between an adult and a child, is almost as popular a social maneuver as talk about one's health or the weather.

Yet such talk, despite its popularity, rarely yields much information about what life in school is really like or how that life is experienced by the student to whom we are speaking.

* *The Elementary School Journal*, 66, 1966, 345–357. Copyright © 1966 by the University of Chicago. Reprinted with the permission of the publisher and the author.
† "Dolor" copyright 1943 by Modern Poetry Association, Inc., from *Collected Poems of Theodore Roethke*. Reprinted by permission of Doubleday & Company, Inc. This is published in Britain by Faber and Faber Ltd.
‡ Reprinted with the permission of John Malcolm Brinnin.

There seem to be two major reasons why this is so. First, in most instances neither the child nor the adult takes the query seriously. Both know that questions about school, like questions about personal health, are polite social gestures and usually are not intended to be answered fully or honestly. Thus, when asked about his classroom experiences, the fourth-grader who is having a miserable time with long division and who hates his teacher with a deep and abiding passion knows that he is expected to respond in much the same way as the victim of a migraine headache whose health is inquired into. Custom requires both sufferers to grin and say, "Fine, thank you."

A second limit to what we can learn about school life by talking to students arises from the fact that students may themselves not be acutely aware of what is happening to them in the classroom. Or, more precisely, they may never have tried to express the vague feelings and intuitive knowledge engendered by that experience. School life, like life in the military service, is not easy to describe to outsiders. You have to have been there.

But even being there is not enough, for when fellow students, or army veterans, discuss their common experience they often overlook or fail to mention some of the obvious and pervasive aspects of that experience. And often it is these familiar and seemingly trivial features of life that are the most revealing when it comes to capturing the flavor or unique quality of membership in a social institution. Accordingly, the remainder of this essay will focus on some aspects of school life that students rarely talk about in the presence of adults or even, in all probability, in the presence of other students.

The subjects to be discussed are not dramatic, or even intrinsically interesting, though I shall do my best to keep them from becoming deathly dull. What is more important, they concern things we all know, even though we do not think about them too much. My only justification for asking you to attend to such mundane matters is my hope that a consideration of these trivial but neglected events will deepen our insight into the character of the student's world and, hence, might lead us to ask new questions about our responsibility for establishing and maintaining that world.

Two warnings are necessary. First, I do not bring words of uplift and inspiration. In fact, some of the things I am going to say about schools and schooling will not be pleasant. They may even sound harsh. But I am convinced that educators are ready for such talk, provided it stems from good intentions, and that they prefer frankness, even though it may hurt, to the sticky sentiment and clichés that have come to characterize educational discussions from college courses to in-service workshops. Second, I am not going to present a plan of action for your consideration. Indeed, I am going to raise many more questions than I shall answer. Here again, I believe that more and more teachers are becoming tired of hearing experts, whether from the university or the central office, hand out the latest panacea for eliminating our educational woes. For a change, therefore, I will ask you to do nothing but think. If there are practical implications that follow from what I have to say, it is up to you to find them.

The Social Traffic of the Classroom

Anyone who has ever taught knows that the classroom is a busy place, even though it may not always appear so to the casual visitor. Indeed, recent attempts to describe that busyness have yielded data that have proved surprising even to experienced teachers. For example, we have found in our studies of elementary-school classrooms that the teacher engages in as many as a thousand interpersonal interchanges each day. No comparable data are available for high-school teachers, but there is reason to believe that the interpersonal demands are equally severe at that level. A look at these and other demands is instructive as we try to understand what life in the classroom is really like.

First, consider the rapidity of the teacher's actions. What keeps her hopping from Jane to Billy to Sam, and back again, in the space of a few seconds? Clearly much of this activity is done in the interest of instruction. In most classrooms the teacher acts as a gatekeeper who manages the flow of interaction. When more than one person wishes to say something (a common condition in educational gatherings), it is the teacher who decides who will speak and when. Or we might turn our observation around and say that it is the teacher who determines who will not speak, for usually the number of students who want to say something exceeds the number who are granted the privilege.

Supply Sergeant

Another time-consuming task for the teacher, at least in the elementary school, is that of serving as a supply sergeant. Classroom space and material resources are limited, and the teacher must allocate these resources judiciously. Not every student can use the big scissors at once; only one child at a time can look through the microscope or drink from the drinking fountain or use the pencil sharpener. Again, it is important to recognize that the number of students who want to use these resources at any given moment is often greater than the number that can use them.

Closely related to the job of doling out material resources is that of granting special privileges to deserving students. The teacher frequently must decide whether a student is to be allowed to hand in his homework paper late or make up a quiz that he missed or have an extra day to finish his laboratory assignment. In elementary-school classrooms it is usually the teacher who assigns coveted duties, such as serving on the safety patrol, running the movie projector, or clapping the erasers. Students soon learn that in school, as in life in general, many are called, but few are chosen.

Official Timekeeper

A fourth responsibility of the teacher, and one that calls our attention to another important aspect of classroom life, is that of serving as an official timekeeper. The teacher sees to it that things begin and end on time, more or less. He determines the proper moment for switching from discussion to workbooks, or from spelling to arithmetic. He decides whether a student has spent too long in the washroom or whether those who take the bus may be dismissed. In many schools the teacher is assisted in this job by elaborate systems of bells and buzzers, but even when the school day is mechanically punctuated by clangs and hums, the teacher is not relieved of his responsibility for watching the clock. School is a place where things often take place not because people want them to, but because it is time for them to happen.

Our concern here is with the student and the quality of his life in the classroom. Therefore, the frenetic activity of the teacher, as she goes about calling on people, handing out supplies, granting privileges, and turning activities on and off, is of interest to us only insofar as the student experiences that behavior. We are interested, in other words, in what it is like to be on the receiving end of the teacher's action.

To begin, it is safe to say that for most students, some of the time, and for some students, most of the time, the classroom is a great place to be. When new insights are formed and mastery is achieved, when the teacher's queries can be answered with confidence, when privileges are granted and praise bestowed, when natural interests and desires coincide with institutional expectations—at such moments (and such moments do occur more or less regularly for many students) life at school must be extremely satisfying. A sufficient number of such experiences might well create the desire for further education and could set the stage for a lifetime of scholarship and academic pursuits.

But it is probably also true that for most students, some of the time, and for some students, most of the time, the classroom comes close to resembling a cage from which there is no escape. When activities are dull and repetitious, when the student is not called on even though he has signalled the desire to be heard, when privileges are not granted and blame, rather than praise, is bestowed, when natural interests and desires are antithetical to the demands of the institution—at such moments (and such moments probably occur more or less regularly for many students) life in school must be extremely irksome.

The important point is that these unpleasant aspects of school life are experienced not only by those who are failing in their schoolwork (although students with low achievement might receive more than their share of these discomforts). Nor are they simply a function of the cantankerousness or maladroitness of particular classroom teachers (although poor professional preparation and psychological disorders of teachers may well add to the student's burden). It would seem, in other words, that much of the pain of school life is a natural outgrowth of the problems of institutional living and the management of social traffic. Given the arrangement in which one person is chiefly responsible for serving the educational needs of thirty or thirty-five others and for articulating the demands of this group with those of several other groups in the same building, three of the most salient features of school life—delay, denial, and interruption—are almost inevitable.

Delay

Consider for a moment the frequency of delay. When we examine the details of classroom life carefully, it is surprising to see how much of the student's time is spent in waiting. In the elementary school, the students often line up for recess, for lunch, and for dismissal, and they frequently have to wait for the lines to be straight before they move. During individual seat-work they wait for the teacher to come around to their desk to inspect their work. When the whole class is working together, there is the waiting for the slower pupil to finish the work that the faster ones have completed. During discussion there is the waiting for fellow students to answer the teacher's query. When motion pictures or slides are shown, there is usually a delay as the room and the equipment are made ready. As time for the bell approaches, students are waiting for it to ring, even though they may still have their eyes on the teacher.

No one knows for sure how much of the student's time is spent in neutral, as it were, but it is certainly a memorable portion. How many of us who have lived thousands of days in schools can remember waiting anxiously for the minutes to tick away until the dismissal bell freed us? How many of us whose lungs are lined with chalk dust can recall the hours spent looking out the classroom window as we waited for the group in which we were imbedded to move sluggishly along? How many of us respond sympathetically to the following image of school life presented by George Santayana, as he describes his student days at Boston's Boys Latin School: "No blackboard was black; all were indelibly clouded with ingrained layers of old chalk; the more you rubbed it out, the more you rubbed it in. Every desk was stained with generations of ink-spots cut deeply with initials and scratched drawings. What idle thoughts had been wandering for years through all those empty heads in all those tedious school hours! In the best schools almost all schooltime is wasted."[1]

Idleness, unfortunately, is only part of the picture, and perhaps not even the most important part. Waiting is not so bad and may even be beneficial when the things we are anticipating ultimately happen. Indeed, Longfellow was probably speaking with the voice of wisdom when, in his *Psalm of Life*, he advises us to "Learn to labour and to wait." But he was just a shade too optimistic when, in another poem (the title of which ironically is *The Student's Tale*), he promises his reader that "All things come round to him who will but wait." At least it is doubtful that Longfellow was referring to things that go on in classrooms, for there the waiting is sometimes in vain.

Denial

The denial of desire is a commonplace in school, and likely it has to be. Not everyone who wants to speak can be heard, not all the students' queries can be answered to their satisfaction, not all their requests can be granted. It is true that, considered individually, most of these denials are psychologically trivial; but considered cumulatively, their significance increases. Part of learning how to live in school involves learning how to give up desire as well as waiting for its fulfilment.

Typically, things happen on time in school, and, as a result, activities are often begun before interest is aroused and terminated before interest wanes. Once again, there is probably no alternative to this unnatural state of affairs. If we were to wait until students requested a history class on their own, as an instance, we would have a long wait. Similarly, if we allowed students to remain in their physical education classes until they

[1] George Santayana. "The Latin School" in *Unseen Harvests*, p. 487. Edited by Claude M. Fuess and Emory S. Basford. New York: Macmillan, 1947.

grew tired of the game, there likely would not be time for other things. There seems to be no alternative, therefore, but to stop and start things on time, even though it means constantly interrupting the natural flow of interest and desire for at least some students.

Interruptions

But interruptions in the classroom are not confined to the beginning and ending of subject-matter periods. There are also more subtle ways in which activities are broken into. The irrelevant comment during class discussion, as an instance, often breaks the spell created by the relevant remarks that have preceded it. When the teacher is working individually with a student while others are present—a common arrangement in elementary-school classrooms—petty interruptions, in the form of minor misbehavior or students coming to the teacher for advice, are the rule rather than the exception. In countless small ways the bubble of reality created during the teaching session is punctured, and much of the teacher's energy is spent in patching up the holes, just as much of the student's energy is spent in attempting to ignore them. Students are constantly "turning back" to their studies after their attention has been momentarily drawn elsewhere.

Here, then, are three of the unpublicized features of school life: delay, denial, and interruption. As educators what do we make of them? Or better, what should we make of them? Let's dispense with extreme reactions first.

On the one hand, there is the temptation to ignore these aspects of classroom experience. After all, delay, denial, and interruption are features of life in several other settings. Why pay particular attention to these petty annoyances when they occur in school? Students themselves do not seem to be too upset by these occurrences, the argument continues; therefore, it is probably safe to ignore them, with perhaps a passing cluck of disapproval, and move to more pressing educational problems.

On the other hand, there is the temptation to magnify these undesirable events until they become all that can be seen of school life. This alternative, which might be called the school-is-hell approach, seems to be dominant on many of our college campuses these days. It is the credo of the new undergraduate religion: anti-establishmentarianism.

The trouble with these extreme positions, as with most, is that they can be maintained only by choosing to ignore certain salient features of our educational scene. Defenders of the optimistic leave-well-enough-alone point of view preserve their calm by remaining blind to the fact of widespread discontent in our schools. Defenders of the school-is-hell point of view must keep the edge on their fury by failing to acknowledge that there is massive satisfaction as well as massive dissatisfaction in our classrooms.

A more dispassionate point of view, although one that is unlikely to capture newspaper headlines, might lead us to examine the strategies that students develop to adapt to these mundane features of school life. What must be done, in other words, if the student is to live a large portion of his life in an environment in which delay, denial, and interruption are inevitable? Further, how do the strategies for adapting to these demands combine with, complement, or contradict the strategies for acquiring knowledge and developing intellectual mastery?

Patience and Resignation

The quintessence of virtue in an institutional setting is contained in the single word: *patience*. Without that quality life can be miserable for those who must spend time in our prisons, our hospitals, our corporation offices, and our schools. But virtue can become soured if tested too severely. And the conditions that lead to the development of patience can also, if carried too far, set the stage for the development of resignation —a much less virtuous condition. Indeed, the distinction between the patient person and the resigned person is not always easy to make on the basis of surface appearances, even though there is a world of difference in the psychological strength of the two.

While the patient person maintains a firm grasp on his own plans for the future and, hence, retains a sense of integrity, the resigned person does not. Resignation involves an act of psychological surrender in which one's own desires, plans, and interests are abandoned and action is taken on the basis of the desires, plans, and interests of others. The resigned person has not only given up hope, he has given up many other linkages between his motives and his actions. Resignation involves, in other words, a loss of feeling and a sense of no longer caring about what happens.

Returning to the situation in our schools, we can see that if students are to face the demands of classroom life with equanimity—rather than with disappointment, anger, and rebellion —they must learn to be patient. This means that they must be able to disengage, at least temporarily, their feelings from their actions. The hope is that the disengagement will not become permanent, that patience will not fade imperceptively into resignation. Yet in expressing this hope we acknowledge a real danger, for the one condition lies just beyond the other, along the same path. The problem, for the teacher, is to help students become uninvolved when conditions demand it, but not too uninvolved. We want students to be calm in the face of some of the frustrations caused by collective life in an institution, but we do not want them, in the jargon of adolescence, to "cool it."

Masquerade

The second-grader who groans with disappointment when an enjoyable classroom activity is terminated, and the fourth-grader who zestfully waves his hand while his classmate is struggling to answer the teacher's question, both will likely be transformed by the time they reach high school or college into the jaded "professionals" of the classroom—those living ink-blots whose enigmatic silence and languid slouch effectively mask both the presence and the absence of enthusiasm for educational affairs. Which ones are merely being patient, and which resigned? It is sometimes hard to tell.

Students also know that teachers like to see evidence of enthusiasm and involvement, and this knowledge causes alertness and other signs of interest to be worn as masks in much the same way as signs of indifference. Classroom courtesy demands that you keep your eye on the teachers and frown intensely at appropriate times even though your mind may be miles away. Again the teacher is faced with the problem of deciding which students are really with her as she goes about her work and which ones just appear to be with her.

The business of faking involvement and of masking withdrawal is not limited to the simple procedure of showing signs of attention when class is in session. These are not the only strategies by which students adapt to classroom demands. Nor are delay, denial, and interruption the only unpleasant aspects of school life with which the student must cope. The classroom, it must be remembered, is an evaluative setting in which the student must learn not just to comply with commands, but to comply in a way that yields a positive evaluation.

Thus arises the common practice of giving the teacher what she wants on written assignments and test questions, even though the assignments seem meaningless and the questions inane. Along with this practice goes the technique of disguising ignorance, of responding to the teacher's queries with sufficient ambiguity or with only thinly veiled flattery so that she will not discover and no longer care whether the student knows anything or not. (When I was a high-school student, this ploy was known as giving the teacher a "snow job." I do not know what name it goes under these days, but I am fairly confident that it is still being practiced.)

These forms of student behavior may be laughed off as harmless pranks, and sometimes they are nothing more than that. But all these acts of detachment and deception, each of which might be considered harmless, or even "cute," when used in moderation, grow out of attempts to deal with institutional constraints. When used excessively and in combination, they are the marks of the educational con-man, the student who has learned to size up teachers and give them what they want with all the shrewdness and feigned sincerity of a dishonest second-hand car dealer.

The Two Curriculums

Much that has been said up to this point can be summarized by suggesting that every school and every classroom really has two curriculums that the students are expected to

master. The one that educators traditionally have paid the
most attention to might be called the official curriculum. Its
core is the three R's, and it contains all of the school subjects
for which we produce study guides and workbooks and teaching materials. It is the curriculum that all the curriculum re-
form groups are shouting about these days.

The other curriculum might be described as unofficial or
perhaps even hidden, because to date it has received scant
attention from educators. This hidden curriculum can also be
represented by three R's, but not the familiar one of reading,
'riting, and 'rithmetic. It is, instead, the curriculum of rules,
regulations, and routines, of things teachers and students must
learn if they are to make their way with minimum pain in the
social institution called *the school*.

The Reward System

Two or three important observations might be made about
the relationship between these two curriculums. One is that the
reward system of the school is tied to both. Indeed, many of
the rewards and punishments that sound as if they are being
dispensed on the basis of academic success and failure are
really more closely related to the mastery of the hidden curriculum. Consider, as an instance, the common teaching practice
of giving a student credit for trying. What do teachers mean
when they say a student tries to do his work? They mean, in
essence, that he complies with the procedural expectations of
the institution. He does his homework (though incorrectly), he
raises his hand during class discussion (though he usually
comes up with the wrong answer), he keeps his nose in his
book during free study period (though he does not turn the
page very often). He is, in other words, a "model" student,
though not necessarily a good one.

It is hard to imagine any of today's elementary-school
teachers failing a student who tries, even though his mastery of
course content is slight. And elementary-school teachers are
not alone in this respect. At higher levels of education as well
rewards go to the solid citizen as well as to the budding
scholar. Surely many of our valedictorians and presidents of
our honor societies owe their success as much to institutional

conformity as to intellectual prowess. No doubt that bright-eyed little girl who stands trembling before the principal on graduation day arrived there at least partly because she typed her weekly themes neatly and handed her homework in on time.

This manner of talking about educational affairs may sound cynical and may be taken as a criticism of teachers or as an attempt to subvert the virtues of neatness, punctuality, and courteous conduct in general. But nothing of that kind is intended. The point is simply that in schools, as in prisons, good behavior pays off.

Just as conformity to institutional expectations can lead to praise, so can the lack of it lead to trouble. As a matter of fact, the relationship of the hidden curriculum to student difficulties is even more striking than is its relationship to student success. Consider, as an instance, the conditions that lead to disciplinary action in the classroom. Why do teachers scold students? Because the student has given the wrong answer? Or because, try as he may, he fails to grasp the intricacies of long division? Not usually. A student is more likely to be scolded for coming into the room late or for making too much noise or for not listening to the teacher's directions or for pushing while in line. The teacher's wrath, in other words, is commonly triggered by violations of institutional regulations and routines rather than by the student's intellectual deficiencies.

Even with the more serious difficulties that clearly entail academic failure, the demands of the hidden curriculum lurk in the shadows. When Johnny's parents are summoned to school because their son is not doing too well in arithmetic, what explanation will be given for their son's poor performance? More than likely blame will be placed on motivational deficiencies in Johnny rather than on his intellectual shortcomings. The teacher may even go so far as to say that Johnny is *un*-motivated during arithmetic period. But what does this mean? It means, in essence, that Johnny does not even try. And not trying, as we have seen, often boils down to a failure to comply with institutional expectations, a failure to master the hidden curriculum.

There is a further question that must be asked about the relationship between the official and the unofficial curriculums in our schools: To what extent does the mastery of one interfere with the mastery of the other? In other words, how do the demands of intellectual achievement relate to the demands of institutional conformity? Are they complementary or contradictory?

We have already seen that many features of classroom life call for patience, at best, and resignation, at worst. As the student learns to live in school, he learns to subjugate his own desires to the will of the teacher and to subdue his own actions in the interest of the common good. He learns to be passive and to acquiesce to the network of rules, regulations, and routines in which he is imbedded. He learns to tolerate petty frustrations and to accept the plans and the policies of higher authorities, even when their rationale is unexplained and their meaning unclear. Like the inhabitants of other institutional settings he learns that he must frequently shrug and say, "That's the way the ball bounces."

But the personal qualities that play a role in intellectual mastery are of a very different order from those that characterize the Company Man. Curiosity, as an instance, that most fundamental of all scholarly traits, calls forth the kind of probing, poking, and exploring that is almost antithetical to the attitude of passivity that has just been described. The productive scholar must develop the habit of challenging authority and of questioning the value of tradition. He must insist on explanations for things that are unclear. The scholar must certainly be a disciplined man, but his discipline is developed in the service of his scholarship, rather than in the service of other people's wishes and desires. In short, intellectual mastery calls for sublimated forms of aggression rather than submission to constraints.

Docile Scholars

These brief descriptions exaggerate the real differences between the demands of institutional conformity and the demands of scholarship, but they do serve to call our attention to points of possible conflict between the two sets of demands. Can both sets be mastered by the same person? Apparently so. Certainly not all our student council presidents and valedictorians are academic Uriah Heeps. Some have clearly managed to retain their intellectual aggressiveness while at the same time acquiescing to the laws that govern the social traffic of our schools. Apparently it is possible, under certain conditions at least, to breed docile scholars, even though the expression might appear at first glance to be a contradiction in terms. But how are these successes achieved? At what cost? And how many fail to achieve the synthesis of the so-called well-rounded student?

A Social Price

The cost of scholastic success must be measured not only in terms of the intellectual energy expended or the non-academic gratifications denied. For many students there is also a social cost. The students who accede willingly and sincerely to both the intellectual and the institutional demands of the school run the risk of being perceived as defectors by their peers. At the lower levels of education these students are likely to be called *goody-goodies, tattletales,* and *teacher's pets*; at the upper levels they are called *greasy grinds, eager beavers,* and *squares.* In the eyes of many of their classmates the students who receive the highest praise from the authorities of the school are the ones who have sold out to the system. For many students this kind of name-calling, which is often correctly perceived as reflecting envy, is not difficult to endure and is a small price to pay for the admiration of adults whom they respect. For other students it is more important to appear to be a "regular guy." Many would rather be seen as a "buddy" than as a "brain."

The number of failures in our schools is much larger than the number of students who do not come up to snuff on our achievement tests or final exams. The failures include an untold number who seemingly succeed but who turn off their intellectual motors when the dismissal bell rings. These children have learned how to give the teacher what she wants all right, but in the process they have forgotten how to use their mental powers to give themselves what they want when the teacher is not around. This group includes the students who make the honor rolls and the dean's lists during the school year but who do not know what to do with themselves during the summer vacation. It includes the thousands who, after their formal schooling is finished and diploma hung on their wall, will never again be stirred by the quest for knowledge. It includes the millions for whom a childhood of teacher-watching is followed by an adulthood of television-viewing, with hardly a change of posture or facial expression to mark the transition. One almost expects them to raise their hands and ask Johnny Carson if they can go to the bathroom. Adequate as students? Yes. Adequate as adults? No.

Two Worlds

And who is to blame for these failures? The schools? The society? The individual? All three share the responsibility, I suppose, but it is the school's role with which we are particularly concerned at present. The school, it would seem, asks the student for a commitment to two worlds—the world of the institution and the world of scholarship. Unfortunately, it often succeeds in obtaining only a feigned commitment to either one.

What about our own commitment to these two worlds? How have we partialled out our own loyalty? How much have we ourselves become Company Men, more interested in an up-to-date register than an up-to-date idea, more concerned with straight lines than with straight thinking? After all, we too, like our students, are rewarded for doing things neatly, and on time, with a minimum of fuss and bother. How often have we received compliments from our principals for the surface show of scholarship, for the attractiveness of our bulletin boards rather than for the vigor and imaginativeness of the ideas we present to our pupils? Nor are our administrators the villains of the piece, for they, in their turn, are caught in the same bind. The public wants its institutions to be run quietly, efficiently, and economically. The best-attended school-board meeting is almost always the one at which the budget is discussed. And who is this elusive public but the very people we educators had yesterday in our classrooms. So the circle is complete. No one is responsible, yet everyone is.

What, then, is life like in school? It would seem to be a life of contradictory demands and competing tendencies, a life in which discovery and disappointment go hand in hand, where the unpredictable and the routine are combined daily. These monotonous settings of desks and blackboards and books provide a stage for the cyclic enactment of a dull drama, a play that is at once boring and exciting. No wonder our young friend only says, "Fine!" when we ask him how things are going in the classroom. School is a puzzling place, and the puzzles are not all intellectual ones.

School Demands*

ANTON BRENNER
HELMUT HOFMANN
RACHEL WEDDINGTON

The purpose of this paper is to determine the nature of the demands that confront the child in the classroom situation. Such a study could help identify what a pupil is considered responsible for achieving during a particular period of his school career and also what he is considered responsible for already having achieved before the period in question. It is the latter with which we are concerned here.

We have chosen for analysis observations made by a single observer in the same classroom for a period of eight months.[1] The observations are running descriptions of behavior.

Thirty-three such descriptions based on observations made in a first-grade class of a private school[2] were categorized by each of three coders according to specified definitions of demands.[3] We recognize that the reliability of the descriptions is a function of observational bias and that, lacking specified pre-orientation, the observer was subject to the totality of a classroom situation and recorded the activity according to his own perspective. Nevertheless, the coders emerged with high agreement among themselves.

[1] The observations were made by G. T. Kowitz, who at the time was co-ordinator of the Child Development Research Program for the Greenfield Village Schools, Dearborn, Michigan. His observations were made from September, 1954, to May, 1955.

[2] The observations were made in the classroom of Aura Dietz, teacher of first grade in the Greenfield Village Schools.

[3] The three authors coded the demands. L. P. Lewandowski assisted in the validation of categories.

* *The Elementary School Journal*, 64, 1964, 261–264. Copyright 1964 by the University of Chicago. Reprinted with the permission of the publisher and the authors.

For our analysis we defined *school demand* as a requirement specified in the school program, a requirement that is evidenced explicitly by the teacher's words or acts, or implicitly by the situation. Every child in the group is expected to conform to or participate in the indicated activity.

School demands were classified as explicit or implicit on the basis of the following descriptions:

Explicit Demand

A statement (in the observations) that identifies the proposed activity as one intended for participation by all the children. Routine requirements are included.

Example: "The children are told to draw a picture about a story they heard."

Implicit Demand

A statement (in the observations) indicating indirectly through the teacher's involvement (through action or words or both) with one child or a few children that the behavior is expected of all pupils, though at the time of the observation all pupils were not participating in the particular situation.

Example: "John does not close the door. The teacher asks, 'John, don't you have doors at your house?' John nods and goes to close the door."

Subsumed under the definition of *demand* were some variations of school requirements that for the sake of clarity we further identified. Examples of each variation are provided.

Expectation

An implicit requirement by the classroom teacher; pupils have some leeway in complying with it.

Example: "Teacher talks to Tom about being a good helper. He can do the work easily and could help the others."

Request

A desire expressed by the teacher; pupils' compliance is entirely optional.

Example: "Teacher criticizes Ann for 'hanging on to people. . . . Every time I see you, you are hanging on to someone.'"

Suggestion

A presentation of ideas, activities, or materials, or all of these (in or out of the classroom) by the teacher for pupil participation; participation is considered enriching, though choice of participation is completely optional.

Example: "She then raises her hand. When the teacher calls on her she says: 'I have a book about that.' The teacher says, 'You can get a record too.'"

These subclassifications were not categorized separately; they are identified here to further define our use of the term *demand.*

Analysis of the demands according to the classifications defined yielded 718 demands in the 33 observations. Of the 718 demands, 210 were explicit, and 508 were implicit. On the average, there were about 22 demands during each observation. The ratio of explicit to implicit demands was 1 to 2.4.

To further identify the nature of classroom demands, they were classified according to their content. The categories used were the four major classes—emotional, mental, physical, and social—used in the larger study in which influences on readiness were being explored.[4]

Because a single demand could be classified in more than

[4] The present study is part of a long-term research project on readiness for school. The principal investigator is Anton Brenner, of the Merrill-Palmer Institute of Human Development and Family Life. The project is being carried out in co-operation with the Department of Pediatrics, Henry Ford Hospital, Detroit; the Greenfield Village Schools, Dearborn; and other schools in and outside Michigan. At the time that this article was written Helmut Hofmann was co-ordinator of research at the Greenfield Village Schools, and Rachel Weddington was research associate at the Merrill-Palmer Institute of Human Development and Family Life.

one of these content areas, the totals of the several categories are greater than unity. Data on the frequency of demands in each of the content areas are presented in Table 1. For purposes of comparison, the per cent that each content area contributed to the total was determined on the basis of the 718 instances. These per cents are presented in the last column of the table.

Of the total demands made, 47.49 per cent had content of a mental nature and 47.21 per cent had content of a social nature. Emotional content characterized 35.10 per cent of the demands, while content of a physical nature comprised 10.44 per cent.

When the demands were analyzed in the classifications of explicit and implicit, differences in the proportions in the sub-categories were marked. Of the explicit demands, the greatest proportion was mental (54.28 per cent), followed by social demands (40.95 per cent). Among the implicit demands, social demands, which made up 49.80 per cent, exceeded mental ones, which accounted for 44.68 per cent. Emotional demands constituted a larger proportion (41.73 per cent) of implicit demands than of explicit demands (19.05).

TABLE 1
Classification of 718 School Demands

	EXPRESSION OF DEMAND					
	Explicit n=210		Implicit n=508		Total n=718	
Content of Demand	Fre-quency	Per Cent	Fre-quency	Per Cent	Fre-quency	Per Cent
Emotional	40	19.05	212	41.73	252	35.10
Mental	114	54.28	227	44.68	341	47.49
Physical	35	16.67	40	7.87	75	10.44
Social	86	40.95	253	49.80	339	47.21

We could assume that the behaviors for which a teacher makes implicit demands are behaviors that can be taken for granted, rather than new learnings. Whether or not these actually represent behaviors developed before entrance to first grade, they may be judged as representing what the teacher assumes that the child brings to the situation and so indicate conditions of readiness expected in the particular situation.

In contrast, we might assume that the teacher's explicit demands represent behaviors that she considers new learnings which require specification and clear presentation for development.

The assumption seems supported by the fact that there were more implicit demands than explicit demands and by the fact that the proportion of mental content was higher for explicit demands than for implicit demands.

It appears that most of these demands represent developmental tasks for age six and first grade. A smaller number of demands represent the idiosyncratic expectations of the teacher.

This analysis and the accompanying speculations suggest a means of determining what is expected of the child in the school situation. For greater effectiveness, more rigor is needed in the observational techniques and in the analysis.

One finding is of special interest: the large proportion of social and emotional demands made of the child in the school situation. A large proportion of these behaviors are assumed to be developed by the time the child enters first grade. To the extent that such behaviors are undeveloped, the child is unready for first grade.

To determine whether readiness varies with the idiosyncrasies of teachers would require that comparable observational techniques be applied in various classrooms. Such a study would differentiate between common demands and demands that vary from situation to situation.

Uncertainty:
An Aspect of Teachers'
Classroom Communication*

ROBERT H. KOFF
RICHARD L. WARREN

Schools today are deeply engaged in problems of dislocation, dysfunction, and fragmentation created by rapid technological change and social crisis. To an increasing degree schools are being assigned the responsibility for resolving such problems. This responsibility focuses ultimately on teachers and students and on the kind of meaningful relationships between them which enhance both personal commitment and productivity. In this paper we are concerned with a particular form of teacher-student interaction—a category of classroom communication which appears to frustrate or delay meaningful interaction. The phenomenon which we will discuss may be best characterized as a type of disharmony or incongruity but which we choose to label as uncertainty. The starting point for our inquiry is reflected in two traditionally different approaches to examining the problem of learning.

The first approach is concerned with the question of how and why we learn. Principal investigators of this question are experimental psychologists such as Thorndike, Tolman, Guthrie, Hull, and Skinner. Inherent in this approach is the assump-

* A revised version of "Uncertainty: A Premetric Aspect of Classroom Communication," a paper presented at the American Educational Research Association Meeting, Chicago, Illinois, February, 1968, as part of a symposium entitled "Classroom Ecology: Studies in the Logic of Communication." Reprinted by permission of the authors. The authors wish to acknowledge helpful suggestions made by Roger E. Wilk and Richard E. Snow.

tion that a human subject has no significant aversion to learning itself, and thus research ought to endeavor to isolate those
conditions under which learning is best accomplished.

The second approach centers around the question of how
and why we do *not* learn. Principal investigators of this question are clinicians such as Redl, Bettelheim, Erickson, Harris,
and Masserman. This approach assumes that no matter how
favorable conditions for learning might be, (in terms, for example, of incentive and capacity) something is interfering with
the inner learning mechanisms of the student and is preventing
satisfactory learning.

Both of these approaches believe that students need to be
motivated and that learning proceeds best when students are
motivated. Motivation, according to Hilgard (1956), can be
thought of as basically two kinds: to obtain a pleasurable reward, or to avoid pain. Numerous studies have demonstrated
that students learn to seek pleasurable learning situations and
learn to avoid painful ones. Thus, given that motivation toward
pleasure and away from pain is powerful enough, pupils, given
the capacity, can learn to seek or avoid almost anything. However, when students do not have sufficient information at their
disposal to determine whether or not their behavior will have a
pleasurable or painful outcome, they are in a psychological
state which we choose to call "uncertainty."

The purpose of this paper is to describe the phenomena
that we have labeled "uncertainty." For the moment we are
defining uncertainty as psychological conflict—a conflict directly related to whether or not one's behavior in a given
situation will have a pleasurable or painful outcome. Students
are consistently forced to reexamine their conception of what
behavior is expected of them. Such reflection does have its
positive attributes, but when students become uncertain about
how to think or behave "the next time," they have no performance criteria upon which they can determine whether their
behavior will have a pleasurable outcome.

Uncertainty is, we feel, a function of inconsistency. For the
present the definition of inconsistency is reflected in the terms
changeable and contradictory, and for purpose of description
and simplification, we will focus on inconsistency in teacher
behavior—behavior that thwarts, we feel, the efforts of even
the most sophisticated student to gain the information neces-

sary to make decisions about what action he can take to obtain a pleasurable outcome. Inconsistency, of course, also has temporal attributes. That is, it may occur once or many times, or at a particular traumatic moment.

Inconsistency, and hence uncertainty, probably has a greater impact on the student when he first enters school. The centrality of the early years in laying the foundations for later developments in cognitive, affective, and social behavior has been well established. Uncertainty, therefore, is a phenomenon which we postulate constitutes an "invisible curriculum," and it grows out of an intricate network of the kind of experiences in classrooms which tend to turn students away from the process of schooling.

Certainly, students must learn that there are certain activities and certain conditions where it is important to remain uncertain—that old solutions may not work in dealing with new problems. But this "cognitive" conceptualization is *not* the uncertainty that we are describing. Cognitive uncertainty concerns the question of whether a specifiable level of uncertainty is a necessary or sufficient condition for school success. Our concern is to understand the ways in which pupil-teacher interaction fosters doubt about whether a behavior, or a set of behaviors, will have a pleasurable or painful outcome for students. Teachers generate uncertainty when they are sufficiently inconsistent in their behavior so as not to provide students with the "data" they need to evaluate or predict under what conditions their behavior might have a pleasurable or painful outcome.

Studies by Getzels and Thelen (1960), Jackson and Lahaderne (1966, 1967), Kounin (1967), Biddle and Adams (1967), Bellack *et al.* (1966) and others have begun to examine the manifold forces operative in the classroom. In particular, they describe the multiple decisions that teachers make while "under fire." These decisions are characterized by their spontaneity. In short, the classroom has been described as an interactive environment where the great majority of decisions that are made by the teacher during the course of a school day cannot be preplanned. It is this aspect of teacher behavior with which we are particularly concerned and for purposes of further clarification we want to offer very briefly some examples from observations in an elementary school of behavior that we are theorizing can be categorized as either eliciting uncertainty itself or as contributing to a sense of uncertainty. The observations were made in a first-grade classroom over a three-week period at the beginning of the school year. Our concern was to observe teacher-initiated communications which seemed potentially capable of eliciting in the students a sense of uncertainty. These communications are, obviously, the most accessible kind of relevant phenomena and the first grade, at the beginning of the school year, was a logical place to begin.

We do not at this point propose to say how esoteric or commonplace our illustrative materials may be, nor do we want to make any claims about how typical or atypical this first-grade teacher is. The setting is typical; the family background of the pupils is characterized neither by poverty nor by extreme affluence. In this school there are four first-grade classes and this particular teacher is rated by the principal as the most competent of the first-grade teachers. She is in her late thirties, married, and has had approximately twelve years of teaching experience. The data were gathered through naturalistic observations. The anecdotes presented here are selected from extensive field notes.

There were a number of behavioral norms which the teacher sought in the first few days to impose on the class and which, it appeared to us, seemed to create for the pupils a sense of uncertainty. One of these norms dealt with friendship; the teacher wanted the students to develop friendships within the class and with children from other grades. When the children came in from recess one day, she asked them what they had been doing. "How many of you used the swing?" "How many of you got a drink?" "How many of you saw a big brother or sister and hung around them during recess?" She paused and then went on, "Now let the older brothers and sisters play with their friends and you play with your friends in the first grade. You are growing up now and don't need to be watched over so much by an older brother or sister. It is time for you to make new friends." She paused again and then went on, "Anyone without a friend?" "Anyone who is really new?" One girl and one boy raised their hands. The teacher said, "All right, the rest of you in the class will want to become friends with them." This is one message about "making friends."

But it was not the only communication they received with regard to peer relations. As they became more engaged in school work, they were confronted with a different norm. On the second day she handed out coloring sheets on which there were a ball and a boat. The instructions were to color the ball red and the boat blue. She reminded them that they were not to look at their neighbor's work but to simply draw and color on their own sheets. As she walked down the aisle looking at the work, she said, "Someone is drawing the ball the wrong color. I'm not going to say who, though. Now, don't look at your neighbor. Don't look at your neighbor," she repeated, "because he doesn't know what's right." The next day the teacher arranged another coloring exercise and introduced it by saying,

> I'm going to give you a paper to color. Now, when you start coloring, don't look at your neighbors. I can't tell how well you're doing if you're looking at your neighbors, so if you are not certain, show you're not certain on your paper, and remember, if it's too messy, I'll throw it away.

When they had a similar kind of exercise several days later, and had begun to work, she suddenly said, "Janie, look at Janie's paper. Bobby, cover up your paper so that Janie can't see."

The children are asked to make new friends in the classroom, but these friends, especially if they are deskmates, are to be treated under certain circumstances with suspicion and avoidance. The teacher's behavior is characterized, it appears to us, by a sense of urgency—to socialize the children into patterns of behavior functional for what she feels are impelling pedagogical and administrative demands of classroom life. Contradictions inherent in such demands are not resolved through patience but acerbated through haste and inconsistency.

Teacher instructions created for the children other dilemmas, developing, for example, out of the interplay between academic responsibilities and family relations. When they first began learning about the new math, about sets and the difference between a numeral and a number, she said,

Your mommy and daddy may not be able to help you on all of this work, for example, the difference between a number and a numeral. This is part of your math homework, but it's something your mommy and daddy may not have had; however, an older brother or sister will know, because they've had this kind of work. You must study hard and learn so that you will know it when you are parents.

Several days later, they received further instructions concerning what they might or might not expect from parents when doing homework. She asked them to look through old magazines and find pictures which began with the same sound as brown, black, and blue. She said, "When you cut out these pictures, cut them out as neatly as possible. It's better to have one really neatly cut out picture than a lot of messy ones. Remember, I'm asking *you* to do it, *not* your mother or father. Even if it's messy, if *you* do it, I won't be so mad."

The established norm with respect to parental attitudes toward children is that parents are there to love, guide, and help them. In these examples parents are presented as being either incompetent or ineligible to guide and help. Furthermore, criteria for neatness and messiness are confused with issues of parental assistance and the skill to be learned. It is probably obvious that this teacher exercises firm control in the classroom and is rather talkative—inclines to moralize at length about the kind of behavior she expects of her students. Nevertheless, our field notes indicate that these kinds of communications were manifest in other classrooms, if not characterized by quite so much verbiage.

Perhaps one final incident might be cited, one in which the pupils in this classroom were involved, but in which their teacher was only a spectator. The school was visited one day by a young lady from a nearby metropolitan zoo as a part of a county wide service provided by the zoo to elementary schools. She had brought with her five young animals: a baby lion cub, a baby goat, a baby chimp, a pygmy horse, and a tortoise. Immediately after lunch, the primary grades gathered in the auditorium, sat down in a huge circle, leaving room for the young lady to enter with her cages and exhibit the animals. She took the animals out one by one and walked them around the circle, showing them to the children, talking about them, and cautioning the children to be rather quiet so that they wouldn't scare the animals. She had finished with the chimp and the cub and had the goat out on a leash. By this time the children were ecstatic. Each new animal brought increased "Oh's" and "Ah's" and joyous laughter. While the young lady was walking the goat around the floor, he suddenly began to urinate. This brought loud laughter from the children and, after a respectable pause, the teachers began to smile. The young lady maintained her composure, said she had something for this kind of emergency and immediately picked up some sawdust from a box and spread it on the floor. No sooner had she finished doing this, than the goat began to defecate. The children screamed with delight and the teachers, even more out of character, began to laugh. The young lady, however, was not amused. She was running out of sawdust, and understandably, was concerned that the noise might scare the animal. She stamped her foot and told them to be quiet. "Grow up. Let's not be so silly about this sort of thing. After all, you're house trained and you can go to the bathroom, but these animals aren't and there's no reason why you should be so silly and act like a . . ." and here she paused. Apparently her outburst was running ahead of her fund of similes. Finally, she burst out, ". . . and act like a little old lady!"

Inconsistency, the substance out of which uncertainty is created, might be examined in these three general forms: the teacher makes an inappropriate diagnosis of a situation, but deals with it logically; the teacher makes an appropriate diagnosis of a situation but deals with it illogically; the teacher makes an inappropriate diagnosis of a situation and deals with it illogically. What we are suggesting here is the need to work out a more operational definition of inconsistency and a typology for identifying and classifying teacher behavior which may contribute to uncertainty. Such a typology must include elements of order, sequence, space, source, and impact. Without regard at this point to problems of methodology and design, we consider the following questions useful guides to further exploration: What teacher behaviors facilitate the acquisition of uncertainty? What are the effects of uncertainty on student cognitive, affective, and social behavior both within and outside the classroom? What personality characteristics best describe a teacher who generates uncertainty? and What are the ecological conditions that foster uncertainty?

This discussion has been directed toward understanding what are essentially problems of linkage between teacher and pupil behavior. Our illustrative materials are concerned with inconsistencies in teacher communication, those teacher-initiated and those in response to pupil behavior. We have noted that much of teacher communication in the classroom can be characterized as a spontaneous adaptation to the ebb and flow of the pupils' group and individual behavior—an adaptation that seeks to implement and reflect both the academic and social goals of formal education. In this regard the teacher's role is immensely complex. Our attention to inconsistencies in teacher communication is not intended to ignore such complexity but rather to suggest that a teacher become more sensitive to her own behavior, in short, that she "listen" to herself as well as to her pupils.

References

Bellack, A., H. Kliebard, R. Hyman, and F. Smith, *The Language of the Classroom*. New York: Teachers College, 1966.

Biddle, B., and R. Adams, "An Analysis of Classroom Activities." A Final Report, 1967, University of Missouri, Contract No. 3-20-002, Office of Education, Department of Health, Education and Welfare.

Cronbach, L., "The Logic of Experiments on Discovery," in *Learning by Discovery*, L. Shulman, and E. Keislar, (Eds.). Chicago: Rand McNally, 1966.

Getzels, J., and H. Thelen, "The Classroom Group as a Unique Social System," *The Dynamics of Instructional Groups, N.S.S.E. 59th Yearbook*. Chicago: University of Chicago Press, 1960.

Hilgard, E. R., *Theories of Learning*. New York: Appleton, 1956.

Jackson, P., and H. Lahaderne, "Inequalities of Teacher-Pupil Contacts." Paper presented at the American Psychological Association, New York City, September 1966.

Jackson, P., and H. Lahaderne, "Scholastic Success and Attitude toward School in a Population of Sixth Graders," *Journal of Educational Psychology*, 58, (1967), 15–18.

Kounin, J., "Observation and Analysis of Classroom Management," Paper presented at the American Education Research Association, New York City, February 1967.

The Impact of School Philosophy and Practice on Child Development*

BARBARA BIBER
PATRICIA MINUCHIN

In this presentation we plan to discuss the main points of a research study that assessed the impact of different styles of education on the psychological development of children. The history of this study goes back into the earlier years of the century when new and sometimes dramatic ideas were being introduced into the educational field. Influenced by new social forces and new psychological insights, some educators began to revise their vision of the educational process. They began to see the function and organization of a school in different terms, reflecting their new understanding of child development, the nature of motivation and learning, and the complexity of personality formation.

* Abridged version of a paper delivered at the ASCD conference on "The Unstudied Curriculum," held in Washington, D.C., January 1969. Published by the Association for Supervision and Curriculum Development in a booklet entitled *The Unstudied Curriculum: Its Impact on Children.* Reprinted with permission of the Association for Supervision and Curriculum Development and the authors. Copyright © 1970 by the Association for Supervision and Curriculum Development.

The study presented in this paper was supported by the National Institute of Mental Health (grant #M1075), and is reported fully in a recently published book entitled *The Psychological Impact of School Experience* by P. Minuchin, B. Biber, E. Shapiro, and H. Zimiles (New York: Basic Books, 1969). Some sections of this paper are taken directly from the book.

Such ideas, and the methods that followed from them, reg-
istered unevenly on the various schools of the nation. They
were unnoticed or rejected by many but absorbed or modified
and carried forth by others. The net result is that, at any given
moment of time, children of the same age going to school in
America may be having very different school experiences—and
this is true even within the group of white, middle-class children going to school in the same city. Though their schools
may share certain broad features, they may at the same time
differ basically in very important ways—in the ways they define education, the goals they have for the children, the methods they use to teach them, the relationships they maintain, the
way they organize the school day, the total atmosphere they
set up for teaching and learning. Some of these differences are
explicit; others are implicit, often unidentified, generally unstudied.

It was these pervasive differences in school philosophy and
practice that interested us and provided the impetus for the
study. The research was set up to analyze differences in school
environment and to assess the impact of different kinds of
schools on the children who attended them.

In this paper we will describe the school environments and
present a portion of the findings about the children. First,
however, it is necessary to state the nature of the study design,
provide a framework for the substantive material to follow,
and define the principal concepts of the study.

The Design of the Study

In designing the study, we decided to conduct an intensive
study in a limited number of settings; this would allow us to
look at the environment and the children in some detail and to
explore many facets of their functioning. We therefore selected
four schools that represented variations in educational philosophy and method. We conceived of these differences as occurring principally along a continuum of modern-traditional ideology and practice. This continuum constituted the independent
variable of the study and is defined in detail as follows:

The Modern-Traditional Orientation: Definitions

The *traditional* orientation has been conceived as centering on the socialization of the child, through known and standardized methods, toward generally approved forms of behavior and established levels of achievement. By this orientation, adults carry their authority role as one with fixed and unquestionable prerogatives for decisions of right and wrong and for the induction of the young into the established adult world. Child behavior is evaluated in terms of its external impact and its conformity to general standards, and individual differences are seen largely in terms of distance from or correspondence with these preconceived standards and levels of expectation.

The school, in this traditional framework, defines its task in the realm of intellectual growth. It conceives of an established body of knowledge as constituting the intellectual content of the culture and defines intellectual growth in terms of mastery of this subject matter. It assumes a relatively direct training to be the pathway to such mastery. It evaluates pupil progress in comparative and competitive terms, and it tends to foster competition among the children for the approval and recognition of achievement, regarding other aspects of peer interaction as distractions from concentration and learning. It sees the teacher as the fixed authority in whom resides both the content of learning and the judgment of progress.

The *modern* orientation draws its philosophy from relatively contemporary understanding of the complex and dynamic forces involved in human behavior, learning, and growth. It expects a more complicated, uneven, and personally determined growth process and it sets a different balance between the general requirements of socialization and the needs and tendencies of the individual child. It incorporates the general view that the child will make his own life, that he will grow into a world different from the one he was born into, and that he must be capable both of adapting to it in a personally meaningful way and of making his impact upon it.

In keeping with this orientation, adults attempt to carry their authority role in a relatively flexible way; they relate more intimately with children, tolerate more challenge, and though they do not conceive of themselves as abdicating their role or functioning as peers, they are more consciously geared to ceding authority gradually as it becomes appropriate, manageable, and constructive for growth. This philosophy evaluates child behavior in terms of its motivation and meaning, as well as its social impact, and sees the individual child primarily in terms of his own pattern of interests, needs, capacities, and rate of growth.

The goals of a school, in this modern framework, are relatively broad. They involve the intellectual growth of the child, the education of his capacity to live and work with others, and the fostering of his development as a confident learner, as a person of unique skills and interests, and as a mature human being. The modern school stresses intellectual exploration and a probing toward integrative principles and depth of knowledge as much as it stresses the mastery of subject matter. It tends to explore new methods, to base its curriculum on understanding of the dynamics of child development, and to offer a variety of pathways and media for the achievement of mastery. It evaluates pupil progress primarily against a profile of the individual's strengths and weaknesses and only secondarily against group norms. It regards the peer group as a vital force for growth and learning, to be nurtured as such, and sees the teacher-child relationship as pivotal in the learning process and as best enacted in a way that is informed, flexible, and relatively close to the children.

The study was conducted in a large city; three of the schools were chosen from the public school system. The choice of a modern private school as the fourth school raised some research problems, but it seemed imperative to include a school that would have had time and opportunity to develop a stable and clear version of modern education. The obvious candidates for this most modern end of the continuum lay within the group of private schools, which inevitably have greater leeway to pursue and consolidate new ideas.

We made two other important decisions early in the planning of the study. The first concerned the socioeconomic background of the children. Since the children of the modern private school came from middle-class and upper-middle-class families, it was essential to choose children for the rest of the study who came from similar homes. We therefore chose public schools for the study from among those that served predominantly middle-class populations.

The other important decision concerned the age level of the

children to be studied. We wanted to study children who had been in school long enough to reflect the cumulative effects of their school experience but who would not present the psychological complications of adolescence. For this reason we chose fourth-grade children—nine to ten years old. As the chart below indicates, there were 105 study children—57 boys and 48 girls, distributed in the four schools. The schools are identified by fictitious names and brief descriptions of their positions on the modern-traditional continuum:

TABLE 1
The Study Schools and Subjects

SCHOOLS	SUBJECTS OF STUDY		
	Boys	*Girls*	*Total*
Conrad—a small independent school which had, for many years, exemplified *modern* educational values	17	12	29
Dickens—a large public school, outstanding in adapting *modern* concepts and methods within the practical limitations of its operation	12	12	24
Adams—a large public school which had added a few elements of the modern approach to its fundamentally *traditional* concepts and practices	18	16	34
Browning—a small public school which, relatively unaffected by modern trends, valued and sustained *traditional* methods	10	8	18
	57	48	105

Research material was collected in four areas through the efforts of four research teams. One team studied the schools as social institutions, gathering material through observations and interviews. On the basis of selection criteria the schools had been assigned relative positions on the modern-traditional continuum (see Table 1). But we continued to study them over a two-year period, while the rest of the research was being conducted, as a way of understanding more fully what the school environment was like for the children.

A second team observed throughout the academic year in the fourth-grade classrooms from which we drew our subjects.

They took records in a variety of academic and non-academic situations, recording the events and processes of the classroom and the activities of the study children.

A third team gathered material from the parents of the study children. They administered a questionnaire and interviewed each mother, in a session of about an hour and a half that covered her views about her child and her child-rearing attitudes and practices. This material was meant to give us some understanding of the relative impact of home and school on the areas of psychological functioning we were investigating, or at least to provide data on areas where home and school influence appeared to interact with each other.

The fourth area of data collection concerned the children and was the crucial one. The main test of school impact, after all, lay in the internalized effects on the children—the attitudes and reactions that were becoming part of them as functioning personalities. We attempted to tap this kind of impact through a series of sessions with each child. The research team saw each child six times, interviewing him about his life and ideas and opinions, and administering a series of tests. These included tests of intelligence and achievement; a series of problem-solving tasks; projective techniques such as drawings and imaginative stories and a play session; and a variety of other psychological techniques that tapped the child's moral judgments, his aesthetic preferences, his attitudes about school and authority, his image of himself and his own development. (Discussion of the first three areas of data collection have been deleted in this abridged version of the original paper.)

Impact on the Children: Selected Study Findings

We come now to the question of impact on the children. What difference does it make in the life of a child to attend a modern or traditional school? What kinds of differences did we expect? What questions did we ask about the impact of the schools on the psychological growth of the children in our study?

The questions we asked and the predictions we made covered a broad range. We expected an impact on many facets of intellectual functioning, for example, on intellectual attitudes and style of thinking; and we predicted that the impact of school experience would extend further to the formation of attitudes that the children would hold about other people, about themselves, their society, and their developing roles. We started with the obvious knowledge, that the family and early experiences shape the child's personality and expectations profoundly by the time he enters school, and we attempted, as we looked at the data, to keep cognizance of this continuing family influence. But we considered that the child's experiences in school occupy much of his life space, during these years, and that from these complex and multileveled experiences he learns much and is partly formed as a person.

For purposes of this presentation we have chosen to concentrate on two aspects of the child data: the children's attitudes toward authority, control and justice; and several aspects of self-image or identity. These have seemed particularly pertinent to a conference on the unstudied curriculum, since the differences we found probably stemmed in part from those aspects of life and relationship in school that have often been unspecified and unstudied but which probably have considerable impact on the growth and orientation of children.

First, let us consider the findings concerning the children's conceptions of school authority and their developing codes of judgment concerning right and wrong, control, and justice. We drew our material in this area from interview, from a sentence completion test, and from simulated dilemma situations. The relevant items are presented in Table 2.

In evaluating the children's attitudes toward rules and the authority structure of the school, we considered their responses to the Sentence Completion Test, categorizing them as: rebellious, resentful, conforming, or rational. We found clear differences among the school groups—or at least between the children of Conrad (the most modern school) and those of the three other schools. Children of this school were the most rational and objective in their attitudes. They did not focus on control or discipline; did not see the authority figures or the structure of the school as threatening; and were less apt than children of the other schools to be resentful or to conform to the structure of things in a passive and automatic way. This was certainly consistent with their experience in school where there was considerable attempt to make rules functional and to apply them flexibly, to reduce adult-child distance, and to make children participants in the processes of the classroom.

TABLE 2
Methods and Material for Study of Children: Attitudes toward School Authority, Codes of Control, and Principles of Right and Wrong [a]

CHILDREN'S ATTITUDE TOWARD SCHOOL AUTHORITY

Sentence Completion Test
(a standard psychological technique, presenting incomplete sentences for the child to finish)
Relevant items:
"When the teacher leaves the room . . ."
"The day Betty (Ben) was late to school . . ."
"Waiting in the principal's office, Emily (Ed.) . . ."
"When visitors came to Mary's (Jim's) class . . ."
"Whenever the teacher asked for quiet . . ."

CODES OF CONTROL AND PRINCIPLES OF RIGHT AND WRONG

Sentence Completion item:
"I try not to . . ."
Interview Question:
"What's the very worst thing a child in your class could do?"
Interview Question:
"Can you think of something that you would call unfair?"
Dilemma Situation:
The children were asked to judge which of two children who were taking an important test did more wrong: the one who was seen by the teacher while looking at someone else's paper or the one who did the same thing but was not seen.

---

[a] The methods and items described on these tables refer only to material discussed in the presentation; they are selected and condensed from the much wider roster of techniques and measures used in the study.

In reacting to our questions about right and wrong, fairness and justice (see Table 2), the children of our study gave evidence of complex and interesting thinking, with considerable flux and conflict in their ideas. These nine-year-old children were, after all, in a transitional stage developmentally. They were emerging from the pervasive parental control of earlier years into a broader world; they faced the conflicting demands of allegiance to adults and to the increasingly important peer group, and they were beginning to move toward the forging of personal and independent codes that would govern their judgments and their behavior in interchange with other people. Most of these children were past the first stages of moral immaturity, as defined by Piaget and Kohlberg, but there was much variation in their reactions. We might summarize the differences in the school groups as follows:

Children from the traditional schools responded with more constant referral to the school world—its rules, regulations, and infractions (noise, fooling around, poor work, inattention) —and with greater involvement in the consequences that follow transgression. Children of the modern schools, particularly those of Conrad, were less concerned with school infractions and gave more evidence of early attempts to forge principles that transcended adult demands in the school society and had more generalized meaning. Their concepts of the restraints they should ask of themselves were not centered on school mandates for good behavior, and their ideas of a child's misdemeanors were less schoolbound than those of the other children. They evaluated the cheating dilemma in terms of the underlying principle and rejected both conditions as wrong. Children of the other groups were more apt to judge *undetected* cheating as the greater wrong, attaching the magnitude of the transgression to its consequences (that is, the misdeed is somehow greater if one "gets away with it").

Our findings in this area are somewhat tentative, but they seem to indicate that the Conrad children were moving toward a higher, more advanced stage of moral judgment. Such findings raise an interesting point. They suggest that when a school ties the child sternly to a disciplinary structure—when it presents the child with the task of keeping constant track of the rules of acceptable behavior—it may defeat its own goal of shaping a morally mature individual. It may hold him longer to a relatively immature level of conscience and evaluation, dominated, in the words of Piaget, by precepts of "adult constraint" and power. When the quality of authority in the school is more flexible and benign, and when the child group is active, powerful, and in constant process of negotiating its own rules for work and play, as it was in Conrad, the child may be moved, even at young ages, to a more generalized plane of thought and judgment about the meaning of behavior and the issues of human interchange.

Now, to consider our material concerning self-image and the child's sense of identity. Here we asked a series of questions about possible differences between modern and traditional school children, and they fall into three subdivisions. First: *self-differentiation.* Would the children differ in self-knowledge? Would they differ in the extent to which their self-concepts were differentiated, clear, and personalized? Second: *images of life stages.* Would they differ in their view of their current lives and their growth over time? That is, would they differ in the extent to which they were invested in present or future and in their sense of continuity between different life stages? Third: *social sex roles.* Would they differ in their images of social roles and possibilities—particularly their roles and possibilities as males and females? Would they differ in the extent to which they saw these roles as flexible and permeable, on the one hand, or polarized and set, on the other?

Out of our knowledge of the modern and traditional schools, we predicted that the children of the more modern schools would communicate more differentiated ideas and perceptions about themselves; that they would be more invested in the pleasures and values of the current stage of their lives; and that they would see their own development with more individualized possibilities and with fewer elements of pre-established social roles and limitations. We expected that children of the more traditional schools would describe themselves in more global and impersonal terms; that they would place greater value on the adolescent and adult future as a time of fulfillment, independence and status, and that they would see their roles as relatively polarized, in sex-typed terms, with pre-established expectations for appropriate behavior and characteristics.

To study these complex ideas, we used a variety of techniques, briefly indicated on Table 3:

As indicated on Table 3, we drew material concerning *self-differentiation* from two sources: a letter to an imaginary pen pal and the Stick Figure Scale. The former was a communication by the child about himself, generated on his own without guidelines. We analyzed these letters in terms of the range and

TABLE 3
Methods and Materials for Study of Children:
Self-Differentiation, Images of Life Stages, and Social Sex Roles

---

SELF-DIFFERENTIATION

Dictated Letter

(The child was asked to imagine that he had a pen pal in a foreign country to whom he was writing for the first time. He was asked to dictate a letter about himself and his life.)

Stick Figure Scale (10 items)

(The child was asked to describe or evaluate himself by placing himself on a series of continua, the two end points of which were described in contrasting terms, as illustrated in the following example:

"Here's a boy (girl)   "Here's a boy (girl)
who's pretty sure all   VS   who lots of times isn't
the kids like him, that   so sure the other kids
he's popular."   like him so much."

WHICH ONE IS MORE LIKE YOU?

IMAGES OF LIFE STAGES

Interview Question:

"What do you think is the best age to be? Why?"

Stick Figure Scale Item:

"Here is a boy (girl) who   "Here's a boy (girl) who
thinks it will be wonderful   VS   thinks it was really best
to be all grown up."   when he was a little kid."

WHICH ONE IS MORE LIKE YOU?

Children's Picture Story Test

(An adaption for the age level of the familiar TAT. It consists of 12 pictures depicting children alone, with other children, in school and with adults. The child was asked to make up a story for each picture.)

Sentence Completion Item:

"The best job in the world would be . . ."

Interview Question:

"Have you ever thought about being grown up?"
"What do you think you'll be or do?"

TABLE 3 (continued)

SOCIAL SEX ROLES

Interview Question:
  "Do you think it's best to be a boy or girl? Why?"
Stick Figure Scale Item:
  "Here's a boy (girl) who   "Here's a boy (girl) who
  thinks boys have the   VS   thinks girls have the most
  most fun and the best life."   fun and the best life."
              WHICH ONE IS MORE LIKE YOU?
Children's Picture Story Test
  (see description above)
Play Session
  (The child was presented with a wide variety of miniature toys—
  figures, animals, vehicles, furniture, blocks, and so on—and a large
  table on which to play out stories with the objects. The session was
  approximately half an hour.)

quality of ideas the child conveyed about himself. The Stick
Figure Scale presented a series of hypothetical alternatives,
describing particular qualities in children, and asking the child
to evaluate himself in these terms. There were ten items,
touching on interests, feelings, and self-judgment. We used
this test for several purposes, but what is relevant here is the
self-differentiation score, in which we assessed the child's sub-
tlety and gradations of judgment, as he matched his own tendencies to the series of illustrative models.

We found that children from the two modern schools included a significantly greater range of qualities, in writing
their letters and describing themselves, and were more apt to
touch on feelings, plans, memories, and other aspects that
went beyond descriptive accounts of their activities. They also
responded to the Stick Figure Scale in a more differentiated
way, using the possibilities for gradations of judgment with
greater variety and flexibility. In all, they communicated a
more differentiated and less global image of themselves. In
these reactions of the modern school children we may have
seen the fused effects of at least two aspects of the modern
school: its attempt to teach a probing, differentiated style of
thinking in general, and its relatively strong focus on the individual child as the center of his own life and a legitimate
object of knowledge.

The child's perspective on *different life stages* was another aspect of self-image we investigated. It seemed to us that the organization and orientation of traditional and modern schools were very different in ways that might well affect the psychological perspective of the children. The traditional schools were preparing the children for the future—training them with the skills and knowledge they would later need. They transmitted images and values concerning the successful adult and offered models they hoped and expected the children would emulate. Where these schools were training children toward established roles and effectiveness in the future, the modern schools were stressing the depth and meaning of the child's current experiences. The modern schools saw past and future as continuous with the present and the child's future development, therefore, as an individual process. This led us to predict that children from traditional environments would be more oriented to the future and that they would project images of the future that were more standardized and had less continuity with their own current experience.

We gathered data in several ways. We asked the children directly about their stage preferences in the interview and in the Stick Figure Scale. We also looked for the prevalence of themes about the future in their projective stories and tapped their images of adult life and the future in the Sentence Completion Test and in the interview.

There were, as predicted, clear differences among the children in their responses to the material. Traditional school children were more apt to think about the future as the time of independence, accomplishment, and arrival, and they looked ahead to adolescence and adulthood as preferred life stages. Images of adulthood and the future often took the form of pre-established roles that had no experiential meaning in the present but were conventional and status oriented: President, secretary, housewife, doctor, banker—or "to go into my father's business"—with no accompanying image of what that business really was. The modern school pattern was different; and it was particularly among the Conrad children that predicted effects of the modern environment appeared. These children were most consistently invested in their current life stage; they were least apt to carry an adult or future orientation into fantasy situations; they were most apt to project a future image developed from the realities of current interests and experiences: to be a puppeteer, dancer, cello player, or "champion swimmer," because these were current hobbies and pleasures, or to search for an occupation that combined their interests ("I like horses and I like to act. I don't know how to combine those two. Maybe in a circus . . . but not really"). This pattern of reaction was particularly striking in its appearance among Conrad girls, since the remaining girls of the sample were even more interested and full of fantasy about the future than the boys were and often apt to see discontinuous roles waiting for them in that future.

A similar pattern of findings appeared in relation to *social sex roles*. Here we tapped direct attitudes, again, through the interview and Stick Figure Scale (see Table 3) and we analyzed play sessions and projective stories as a way of assessing the extent to which their fantasies and reactions were sex typed—that is, typical, in some way, of the reactions and concerns and fantasies that are generally associated with boys rather than girls, or vice versa.

As a word of explanation about this latter point: there are certain conceptions of appropriate male and female behavior that prevail in the culture. Boys, for instance, are allowed and expected to be more aggressive than girls; girls are allowed and expected to be more dependent than boys and more centered on their families. As personality qualities these are considered sex typed, in the broad culture, and, in fact, considerable research has established over and over that these qualities and themes are associated more with one sex than the other. Allowing for the validity of this prevailing trend, it was still our expectation that the traditional environment fosters a polarization of roles and appropriate qualities more than the modern and that children of the modern schools might thus be less extensively sex typed in their reactions than children of the traditional schools.

Our findings here were also supportive of the predictions. Most children of this age have some degree of loyalty to their own sex and their own in-group, and some concepts of sex-appropriate role and behavior were absorbed and shared by all the children of our sample. Within this framework, however, there were clear differences of thought and emphasis. The more committed assertions of allegiance to the advantages of one's own sex came from the children of the traditional schools —especially the boys—and these children were characterized also by the more conventional images of role behavior and the more sex-linked themes of play and fantasy. More open attitudes, when they appeared, were generally found among children from modern backgrounds. In this, the girls from modern backgrounds were again notable. They were relatively open in role evaluation, least conventional in their role conceptions, and not apt to typify the dependent, family-centered interests and concerns expected traditionally of girls and actually exemplified by the girls of our study from more traditional backgrounds. In this area, however, we need to note that family home factors were certainly influential, particularly in the role concepts of the girls.

If we were to summarize the findings about modern and traditional school children in terms of developing identity and self-image, we might say that the traditional school children were characterized by more impersonal and global perceptions of themselves as people and by a tendency to look at their own development in terms of the goals and established roles waiting for them and toward which they were being trained. Modern school children were more apt to see themselves, their qualities and interests, in differentiated terms; to center their energy and attention on their current experiences; and to see their development partly as an individualized evolution out of their current interests and personalities. This pattern characterized the children of Conrad in particular, though some aspects describe the children of both modern schools.

The implications of such differences are many. Some are quite subtle, and the risks, problems, and conflicts are not all on one side. It seems to us, however, that these findings are interesting and that they point to important differences in development. They suggest that the impact of the school is indeed broad, going far beyond the academic material it may identify as its curriculum.

In this study we asked and pursued a broad question: would schools with different educational philosophies and practices have different effects on developmental processes in the middle years of childhood? A search of this kind activates certain broad questions about the impact of school experience which cannot be answered from the findings but which become more differentiated as a result of the research experience. We may have asked these questions before the study began but we ask them differently when the study is over.

We face the question, for instance, of whether it would be possible to trace specific effects to specific aspects of the school environments. To what extent would it be feasible to trace a simple cause-effect route between the mode of authority functioning in school—the way rules are made, who makes them, how flexible they are, how central in the whole scheme of things, and how much obedience has high priority as a virtue —and the children's internalized attitudes toward authority? It seems tenable to posit such a relation. The analysis of the total school environment, however, points to other experiences and relationships not literally tied to the school's discipline system yet probably potent as influences on the complex phenomenon of attitude toward authority.

One of these is the climate established around knowledge and intellectual mastery. When cognitive experience is thus dealt with nonabsolutely, with attention to relativity and conditioning circumstances, the children are being inducted into a less authoritative mode of thinking which becomes a significant component of their general attitude toward authority. In the modern orientation knowledge is not straight jacketed into a right-wrong framework; children are introduced early into how altering the perspective, visual, or conceptual, can change the face of reality. They are led to consider attenuating circumstance in designating right from wrong and helped to see opinion as an evolutionary process that can move and change as new facts come to light.

Looked at this way, each of the effects we see associated with either the modern or traditional orientation is multidetermined. We cannot, in this kind of study, arrive at a simple cause-effect line of relation, but we can come closer to understanding the way the constellation of factors interact as determining influences.

In another vein, one asks what happens when we project this study against two major currents in education today: innovations in curriculum geared toward emphasis on cognitive power and changes in method through introduction of technology claiming to support more individualized teaching. The effectiveness of innovations is, in the last analysis, dependent upon the total climate of the school. The use of new techniques will be conditioned by the dominant ideas and values of the institution as well as the motivation and competence of the teacher.

There is another complex factor to be considered: the relation between methods and goals. That methods do not have a tenable existence separate from goals is being more widely recognized now than has been true for the last few years. But the question of goals is not going to be easily solved. For instance, almost everyone agrees these days on one goal— namely, to individualize education. But the agreement is more verbal than real; the concept has diverse, often contradictory meanings. Obviously, the sense in which the modern-oriented schools in our study supported individualized learning has little, if anything, in common with the kind of individualized learning to be accomplished by programmed learning in a computerized system.

In the last analysis, the place of technology, and the value of educational alternatives in general, must be weighed against the major questions of our times and the broad goals of human development. Young adults, in our day, have presented us with their concern for a society that does not readily offer them experiences and potential for individual fulfillment and have expressed their wish to influence and change that condition. In evaluating the impact of educational systems we may need to ask what school experiences develop people who can arrive at points of view, as members of their society, through questioning and analysis, and who are motivated to make things happen in new and imaginative ways. The differences we have found between modern and traditional schools may be relevant to such goals and concepts.

Discussion

While institutions exist to serve people, they often must place their own needs first. To maintain themselves, institutions require their clientele to postpone and even give up certain gratifications. Schools are no exception. A group of students may want to finish a chemistry experiment but the school schedule calls for them to proceed to their next class. Or a request by students to rearrange their desks may have to be denied because, among other considerations, it would make it difficult for the janitor to sweep the floor. Principals and teachers, then, demand adherence to what Jackson calls a "curriculum of rules, regulations, and routines," in order to insure orderly and efficient use of the school's services.

School personnel have special reasons to insist on an elaborate code of behavior. For one thing, compared to many other social settings, schools operate under very crowded conditions. But more important, school personnel must contend with students who, compelled to be there, are not always clients to be served but sometimes inmates to be controlled. Without regulations and procedures, chaos would reign. The function of the "hidden" curriculum is to teach students how to behave properly in school.

Learning to live by the procedural rules of the school, though, can be an unpleasant experience. The hidden curriculum, as Jackson describes it, tries students' patience. Whether they want to be called on in class discussion, or request the teacher's help, or use materials in short supply, students usually must wait their turn. They must also wait for each other to be quiet or get to the right page before the teacher will proceed. In addition, countless instructions and directions must be endured, even though a good number of them, according to the study headed by Brenner, do not relate to the academic activity at hand. Finally, spontaneous desires must often be held in abeyance until the proper time and place.

The hidden curriculum also creates conflict in students. Jackson argues, for example, that the institutional requirements of schools confuse their educational goals. Students are expected to be passive and conforming and yet at the same time, intellectually curious and aggressive. Koff and Warren describe how teachers present institutional expectations which contradict each other, and as a result, leave students uncertain concerning what is expected of them. Unhappily, many teachers seem to be unaware of the bewilderment students feel in trying simultaneously to be active learners, cooperative group members, and model school citizens. For instance, the teachers that Koff and Warren observed were apparently not cognizant of the uncertainty their communications created. As the authors explain, classroom events happen so quickly that teachers have little time to reflect on what they are saying. Nonacademic expectations, in particular, escape attention because, as Brenner, Hofmann, and Weddington suggest, teachers take them very much for granted.

If teachers and administrators examine their rules for acceptable behavior, however, they can find ways to lessen the pain and uncertainty students experience. Procedural expectations exist in every school, but as Biber and Minuchin indicate, they can vary in quality and impact depending on why they are created and how they are applied. In "modern" schools, a great deal of thought is given to working out a viable accommodation between the institution and individuals attending it. By developing rules which are functional and applying them flexibly, teachers in these schools try to allow for the needs of different students. They also may lessen the tension some children feel about committing classroom infractions. In "traditional" schools, by contrast, less attention is given to how well the student and the institution meet each other's needs. By expecting and receiving unquestioned obedience to their directions, teachers in these schools rarely have the occasion to think how rules can be adapted to meet the needs of varied classroom activities. Thus, the danger exists that routines and procedures become entrenched over time rather than subjected to periodic review. When this occurs, students are forced to learn to accept "the structure of things in a passive, automatic way."

Whenever school personnel do not fully grapple with the problems of institutional living, they risk solving them in unsatisfactory ways. For example, students may be asked to line up before leaving or entering school even though less regimented ways of avoiding pushing and shoving are possible. One reason that alternative solutions are not explored is that current procedures appear to be necessary. Without giving the matter

much thought, administrators cannot conceive how to manage
students without recourse to the means they have instituted.
To compound the problem, classroom teachers may place an
even greater value on the procedures the school principal expects them to enforce. For instance, besides dismissing students by rows, teachers might choose the quietest row first.
Thus, obedience to rules of dismissal becomes a virtue in itself,
quite apart from its functional necessity. When this happens,
students learn to view conformity as morally right and nonconformity as morally wrong. They learn little about why rules
and regulations are necessary or how to determine when they
are unnecessary. In this regard, many teachers who have allowed brief experiments in classroom government report that
their students create extremely stringent and inflexible rules
for themselves. One of the implications of their remarks is that
children are not mature enough to handle self-government.
Quite possibly, however, the students are merely exaggerating
what they have been taught about classroom procedures.
Their efforts to control themselves reflect the same unquestion-
ing stance toward rule making that the school adopts. Little
attention is given to understanding when classroom conditions
require institutionalized procedures and how they can be
planned to avoid unpleasant consequences for individual people.

     School personnel do not deliberately create rules they do
not need or perpetuate routines that have outlived their use-
fulness. Nevertheless, they must take a close look at the ways
in which they regulate students' lives. The more hidden and
unstudied institutional regulations are, the more imperative it
is to examine why they are instituted and maintained. Their
impact, as Biber and Minuchin demonstrate, is far greater
than one might assume.

Part II

TEACHER
FAVORITISM

36 Children—
An Excerpt*

HERBERT KOHL

EDITOR'S NOTE: *Herbert Kohl's book,* 36 Children, *dis-cusses his experiences teaching in a sixth-grade class-room in Harlem. Two excerpts are provided here. In one of them, Kohl describes his first day of teaching there, while, in the other, he reflects on his feelings and actions that first day as well as other days early in the school year.*

My alarm clock rang at seven thirty, but I was up and dressed at seven. It was only a fifteen-minute bus ride from my apartment on 90th Street and Madison Avenue to the school on 119th Street and Madison.

There had been an orientation session the day before. I remembered the principal's words. "In times like these, this is the most exciting place to be, in the midst of ferment and creative activity. Never has teaching offered such opportunities . . . we are together here in a difficult situation. They are not the easiest children, yet the rewards are so great—a smile, loving concern, what an inspiration, a felicitous experience."

I remembered my barren classroom, no books, a battered piano, broken windows and desks, falling plaster, and an oppressive darkness.

I was handed a roll book with thirty-six names and thirty-six cumulative record cards, years of judgments already passed upon the children, their official personalities. I read through the names, twenty girls and sixteen boys, the 6-1 class, though

* Reprinted by permission of the World Publishing Company from *36 Children* by Herbert Kohl, 3–8; 18–21. Copyright © 1967 by Herbert Kohl.

I was supposed to be teaching the fifth grade and had planned for it all summer. Then I locked the record cards away in the closet. The children would tell me who they were. Each child, each new school year, is potentially many things, only one of which the cumulative record card documents. It is amazing how "emotional" problems can disappear, how the dullest child can be transformed into the keenest and the brightest into the most ordinary when the prefabricated judgments of other teachers are forgotten.

The children entered at nine and filled up the seats. They were silent and stared at me. It was a shock to see thirty-six black faces before me. No preparation helped. It is one thing to be liberal and talk, another to face something and learn that you're afraid.

The children sat quietly, expectant. *Everything must go well; we must like each other.*

Hands went up as I called the roll. Anxious faces, hostile, indifferent, weary of the ritual, confident of its outcome.

The smartest class in the sixth grade, yet no books.

"Write about yourselves, tell me who you are." (I hadn't said who I was, too nervous.)

Slowly they set to work, the first directions followed—and if they had refused?

Then arithmetic, the children working silently, a sullen, impenetrable front. *To talk to them, to open them up this first day.*

"What would you like to learn this year? My name is Mr. Kohl."

Silence, the children looked up at me with expressionless faces, thirty-six of them crowded at thirty-five broken desks. *This is the smartest class?*

Explain: they're old enough to choose, enough time to learn what they'd like as well as what they have to.

Silence, a restless movement rippled through the class. *Don't they understand? There must be something that interests them, that they care to know more about.*

A hand shot up in the corner of the room.

"I want to learn more about volcanoes. What are volcanoes?"

The class seemed interested. I sketched a volcano on the blackboard, made a few comments, and I promised to return.

"Anything else? Anyone else interested in something?"

Silence, then the same hand.

"Why do volcanoes form?"

And during the answer:

"Why don't we have a volcano here?"

A contest. The class savored it, I accepted. Question, response, question. I walked toward my inquisitor, studying his mischievous eyes, possessed and possessing smile. I moved to congratulate him, my hand went happily toward his shoulder. I dared because I was afraid.

His hands shot up to protect his dark face, eyes contracted in fear, body coiled ready to bolt for the door and out, down the stairs into the streets.

"But why should I hit you?"

They're afraid too!

Hands relaxed, he looked torn and puzzled. I changed the subject quickly and moved on to social studies—How We Became Modern America.

"Who remembers what America was like in 1800?"

A few children laughed; the rest barely looked at me.

"Can anyone tell me what was going on about 1800? Remember, you studied it last year. Why don't we start more specifically? What do you think you'd see if you walked down Madison Avenue in those days?"

A lovely hand, almost too thin to be seen, tentatively rose.

"Cars?"

"Do you think there were cars in 1800? Remember that was over a hundred and fifty years ago. Think of what you learned last year and try again. Do you think there were cars then?"

"Yes . . . no . . . I don't know."

She withdrew, and the class became restless as my anger rose.

At last another hand.

"Grass and trees?"

The class broke up as I tried to contain my frustration.

"I don't know what you're laughing about—it's the right answer. In those days Harlem was farmland with fields and trees and a few houses. There weren't any roads or houses like the ones outside, or street lights or electricity. There probably wasn't even a Madison Avenue."

The class was outraged. It was inconceivable to them that there was a time their Harlem didn't exist.

"Stop this noise and let's think. Do you believe that Harlem was here a thousand years ago?"

A pause, several uncertain Noes.

"It's possible that the land was green then. Why couldn't Harlem also have been green a hundred and fifty or two hundred years ago?"

No response. The weight of Harlem and my whiteness and strangeness hung in the air as I droned on, lost in my righteous monologue. The uproar turned into sullen silence. A slow nervous drumming began at several desks; the atmosphere closed as intelligent faces lost their animation. Yet I didn't understand my mistake, the children's rejection of me and my ideas. Nothing worked, I tried to joke, command, play—the children remained joyless until the bell, then quietly left for lunch.

There was an hour to summon energy and prepare for the afternoon, yet it seemed futile. What good are plans, clever new methods and materials, when the children didn't—wouldn't—care or listen? Perhaps the best solution was to prepare for hostility and silence, become the cynical teacher, untaught by his pupils, ungiving himself, yet protected.

At one o'clock, my tentative cynicism assumed, I found myself once again unprepared for the children who returned and noisily and boisterously avoided me. Running, playing, fighting—they were alive as they tore about the room. I was relieved, yet how to establish order? I fell back on teacherly words.

"You've had enough time to run around. Everybody please go to your seats. We have work to begin."

No response. The boy who had been so scared during the morning was flying across the back of the room pursued by a demonic-looking child wearing black glasses. Girls stood gossiping in little groups, a tall boy fantasized before four admiring listeners, while a few children wandered in and out of the room. I still knew no one's name.

"Sit down, we've got to work. At three o'clock you can talk all you want to."

One timid girl listened. I prepared to use one of the teacher's most fearsome weapons and last resources. Quickly white paper was on my desk, the blackboard erased, and numbers from 1 to 10 and 11 to 20 appeared neatly in two columns.

"We're now going to have an *important* spelling test. Please, young lady"—I selected one of the gossipers—"what's your name? Neomia, pass out the paper. When you get your paper, fold it in half, put your heading on it, and number carefully from one to ten and eleven to twenty, exactly as you see it on the blackboard."

Reluctantly the girls responded, then a few boys, until after the fourth, weariest, repetition of the directions the class was seated and ready to begin—I thought.

Rip, a crumpled paper flew onto the floor. Quickly I replaced it; things had to get moving.

Rip, another paper, rip. I got the rhythm and began quickly, silently replacing crumpled papers.

"The first word is *anchor*. The ship dropped an *anchor*. Anchor."

"A what?"

"Where?"

"Number two is *final*. Final means last, *final*. Number three is decision. He couldn't make a *decision* quickly enough."

"What *decision?*"

"What was number two?"

"*Final.*"

I was trapped.

"Then what was number one?"

"*Anchor.*"

"I missed a word."

"Number four is *reason*. What is the *reason* for all this noise?"

"Because it's the first day of school."

"Yeah, this is too hard for the first day."

"We'll go on without any comments whatever. The next word is——"

"What number is it?"

"——*direction*. What *direction* are we going? *Direction.*"

"What's four?"

The test seemed endless, but it did end at two o'clock. What next? Once more I needed to regain my strength and composure, and it was still the first day.

"Mr. Kohl, can we please talk to each other about the summer? We won't play around. Please, it's only the first day."

"I'll tell you what, you can talk, but on the condition that everyone, I mean *every single person in the room*, keeps quiet for one whole minute."

Teacher still had to show he was strong. To prove what? The children succeeded in remaining silent on the third attempt; they proved they could listen. Triumphant, I tried more.

"Now let's try for thirty seconds to think of one color."

"You said we could talk!"

"My head hurts, I don't want to think anymore."

"It's not fair!"

It wasn't. A solid mass of resistance coagulated, frustrating my need to command. The children would not be moved.

"You're right, I'm sorry. Take ten minutes to talk and then we'll get back to work."

For ten minutes the children talked quietly; there was time to prepare for the last half hour. I looked over my lesson plans: Reading 9 to 10; Social Studies, 10 to 10:45, etc., etc. How absurd academic time was in the face of the real day. *Where to look?*

"You like it here, Mr. Kohl?"

I looked up into a lovely sad face.

"What do you mean?"

"I mean do you like it here, Mr. Kohl, what are you teaching us for?"

What?

"Well, I . . . not now. Maybe you can see me at three and we can talk. The class has to get back to work. All right, everybody back to your seats, get ready to work."

She had her answer and sat down and waited with the rest of the class. They were satisfied with the bargain. Only it was I who failed then; exhausted, demoralized, I only wanted three o-clock to arrive.

"It's almost three o'clock and we don't have much time left."

I dragged the words out, listening only for the bell.

"This is only the first day, and of course we haven't got much done. I expect more from you during the year . . ."

The class sensed the maneuver and fell nervous again.

"Take out your notebooks and open to a clean page. Each day except Friday you'll get homework."

My words weighed heavy and false; it wasn't my voice but some common tyrant or moralizer, a tired old man speaking.

"There are many things I'm not strict about but homework is the one thing I insist upon. In my class *everybody always* does homework. I will check your work every morning. Now copy the assignment I'm putting on the blackboard, and then when you're finished, please line up in the back of the room."

What assignment? What lie now? I turned to the blackboard, groping for something to draw the children closer to me, for something to let them know I cared. *I did care!*

"Draw a picture of your home, the room you live in. Put in all the furniture, the TV, the windows and doors. You don't have to do it in any special way but keep in mind that the main purpose of the picture should be to show someone what your house looks like."

The children laughed, pointed, then a hand rose, a hand I couldn't attach to a body or face. They all looked alike. I felt sad, lonely.

"Do you have to show your house?"

Two boys snickered. *Are there children ashamed to describe their homes?—have I misunderstood again?* The voice in me answered again.

"Yes."

"I mean . . . what if you can't draw, can you let someone help you?"

"Yes, if you can explain the drawing yourself."

"What if your brother can't draw?"

"Then write a description of your apartment. Remember, *everybody always* does homework in my classes."

The class copied the assignment and lined up, first collecting everything they'd brought with them. The room was as empty as it was at eight o'clock. Tired, weary of discipline, authority, school itself, I rushed the class down the stairs and into the street in some unacknowledged state of disorder.

The bedlam on 119th Street, the stooped and fatigued teachers smiling at each other and pretending *they* had had no trouble with their kids relieved my isolation. I smiled too, assumed the comfortable pose of casual success, and looked down into a mischievous face, the possessed eyes of the child who had thought I would hit him, Alvin, who kindly and thoughtfully said: "Mr. Kohl, how come you let us out so early today? We just had lunch . . ."

Crushed, I walked dumbly away, managed to reach the bus stop and make my way home. As my weariness dissolved, I only remembered of that first day Alvin and the little girl who asked if I liked being "there."

My first teaching experience was in a private school for schizophrenic children. The children were considered unreachable and actually excluded from the public schools (as they still are, despite passage of a new New York State law requiring public education for severely disturbed children. The New York City Board of Education claims that these children are "mentally ill," not "emotionally disturbed," and therefore are medical, not educational, problems). The teachers at the school didn't have sophisticated medical and educational backgrounds and hence didn't know a priori what was impossible for the children to do. They knew the children as individuals and couldn't believe in children being "unreachable," only "unreached." Over a five-hour day they forgot that the children were "disturbed" and could see them as different and unhappy. At times they succeeded in reaching and teaching those children, in helping them laugh and cry, and become curious about the world.

I knew that, did it, yet when I first began teaching in the public schools, in classes for "normal" children, the sight of a child not working or the sound of a defiant tongue made me nervous, angry, and guilty. The child was "fresh," "wasting time," "defiant," "disturbed," even—there were any number of self-protective labels I found myself using to stigmatize a child who couldn't conform in my class. I couldn't let things be, allow a child not to work or walk out of the room. I couldn't throw an insult off or reply playfully; rather I treated it as defiance, not merely of myself but of all teachers and all adults, an enormous sin *no child ever does in school.*

A child would tell me to get my nigger hands off him, and I couldn't see the pathos and self-mockery of the statement. A confused, unhappy boy would get up and storm out of the room, pleading that everyone hated him, and on his return I would lecture on discipline in the classroom. I would find a child not paying attention and pick on him vindictively.

It wasn't cruelty, though, or human stupidity. I have seen the most sensitive teachers doing the same thing time after time, and hating themselves for it. I remember days getting home from school angry at myself, confused by my behavior in the classroom, my wrangling and carping, my inability to let the children alone. I kept on saying, "That's not me, that's not me." For a while, as I learned to teach, the me in the classroom was an alien and hostile being.

But nevertheless it was me, terrified, showing my terror to everyone but myself. I remember one day in September Michael telling me, after a particularly long and bitter tirade: "Cool it, Mr. Kohl. Sam's upset, he didn't mean what he said."

I was afraid that if one child got out of my control the whole class would quickly follow, and I would be overwhelmed by chaos. It is the fear of all beginning teachers, and many never lose it. Instead they become rigid and brutal—everyone must always work or pretend to work. The pretense is fine so long as the semblance of control is maintained. Thus one finds the strange phenomena in ghetto schools of classes that seem well disciplined and at work all year long performing on tests as poorly as those that have made the fear and chaos overt.

This problem is particularly great if the children are strangers, that is if they couldn't possibly be your brothers, sisters, your own children or nieces or nephews. Then you don't know how their parents control them, and it is easy, in the grip of fear, to imagine that the children are never controlled—in fact uncontrollable. It is a short step from there to the belief that the children aren't really human at all but "animals," wild, undisciplined, formless, and chaotic. No animals are actually like that though—it is only human fear that is wild, undisciplined, formless, and chaotic. The myth of children as "animals," the fear that they may be uncontrollable, hangs over all the ghetto schools I have visited or taught in, and for a while it hung over my classroom.

The New York City school system has developed techniques to handle this problem, though so far as I can tell few teachers benefit and many children are permanently damaged by them. A child who cannot conform in a classroom, particularly in a ghetto school, is removed from the classroom, first to the principal's office to run errands, then to the "guidance" counselor, and finally to a special school for the "socially mal-adjusted," *i.e.*, a "600" school. To help the teacher maintain order the child is removed, yet it doesn't help. In a classroom and school governed by fear, the removal of one disorderly child merely creates another. Fortunately, there are few groups of children so resigned to adult tyranny that they will not generate and covertly encourage one defiant member. Be-cause of this, it was only with the greatest reluctance that I would resort to a class transfer for a child I was having diffi-culties with, and it was for the same reason I welcomed other teachers' "problems."

I have only known one successfully suppressive teacher. She taught down the hall from 6-1 and had a quiet, rigidly disciplined, clean and neat class. The first week she filtered out into other classes potential "problems," and by the second week, control was total. Her class marched in line, left the building in order, went regularly to the dental clinic, and drew nice pictures. When she retired at the end of twenty-five years, she truly felt she had done many children a great service by keeping them clean and quiet.

Fear is only overcome through risk and experimentation. As I became familiar with the children in 6-1 I became more willing to respond to the children individually and less de-pendent on the protection of the role of teacher. I let an insult pass and discovered that the rest of the class didn't take up the insult; I learned to say nothing when Ralph returned from pacing the halls, or when Alvin refused to do arithmetic. The children did not want to be defiant, insulting, idle; nor were they any less afraid of chaos than I was. They wanted more than anything to feel they were facing it with me and not against me. These discoveries were my greatest strength when I began to explore new things to teach the children. They were as impatient to learn something exciting as I was to find something that would excite them.

I have never solved the "discipline problem," but I no longer believe it needs solution. Children will disagree with each other and with the teacher; they will be irrational at times, and the teacher will be, too. An atmosphere must exist in the classroom where conflict, disagreement, and irrationality are accepted temporary occurrences. No child, because he defies, should thereby have to become "a defiant child," or because he refuses to work, "a lazy child." Such labeling makes the classroom a harsh, unforgiving place, a world not fit for children or adults.

Student Teacher Preferences for Elementary School Pupils Varying in Personality Characteristics[*]

NORMA D. FESHBACH

Educators and other social scientists have long been concerned with the measurement and identification of personality attributes and values characteristic of teachers as a group, attributes which distinguish teachers from other occupational groups, and attributes which differentially predict effective and successful teaching performance (Getzels & Jackson, 1963). However, little attention has been given to the values that teachers place on particular personality characteristics of the child. Research investigating teachers' and clinicians' attitudes toward childrens' behavior problems (Beilen, 1959) indicates that teachers have a more negative view than clinicians of behavior which disrupts the classroom. The focus of these studies, however, has been on symptoms and extreme behaviors. The present investigation proposes to assess student teachers' attitudes and evaluations of children manifesting different personality constellations which are all within the normal range. The aim

[*] Norma D. Feshbach, "Student Teacher Preferences for Elementary School Pupils Varying in Personality Characteristics," *Journal of Educational Psychology*, 60, 1969, 126–132. Copyright 1969 by the American Psychological Association, and reproduced by permission.

This research was supported in part by Contract No. 4–6–061646–1909 from the United States Office of Education, Department of Health, Education, and Welfare to the Research and Development Center, School of Education, University of California, Los Angeles.

of this study is to determine whether prospective teachers show a consistent preference for particular kinds of pupils, to identify these pupils' personality dimensions, and to consider the educational implications of such preferences.

There is an increasing amount of evidence indicating that teachers' perceptions, expectancies, and preferences may exert a considerable influence on the behavior and self-perceptions of their pupils. Several studies have related the degree of teacher "liking" for specific pupils to the child's self-perceptions (Davidson & Lang, 1960; Fox, Lippitt, & Schmuck, 1964), to the child's positive behavior toward the teacher (Bush, 1954; Sears, 1963) and to the child's level of isolation from the teacher (Fox, et al., 1964). A recent study by Rosenthal (1966) demonstrates that the impact of teacher attitude and expectancies can influence cognitive performances as well as more affective behaviors. Rosenthal gave teachers fictitious information regarding the intellectual competencies of some of their students. These students subsequently achieved higher intellectual quotients which were in the direction of the inflated false scores given the teachers.

The literature bearing upon the effects of the teacher as a role model (Bandura & Walters, 1964; Burnstein, Stotland, & Zander, 1961; Feshbach, 1967; Portuges & Feshbach, 1968; Rosenblith 1959, 1961; Ross, 1966) is especially relevant to this issue. These studies, carried out over a wide age range, indicate that children imitate teachers' behavior and values that are incidental to the curriculum objectives. The imitative tendencies of pupils may be viewed as one of the factors mediating the influence of teacher attitude upon the child. This influence may result from the child's identification with the teacher and, in addition, from the adoption of the teacher's attitudes by the classroom peer group which may then serve to reinforce the impact of the teacher.

Selection of Personality
Combinations

One factor guiding the selection of various personality attributes for evaluation by the teachers was the desire to include personality traits which were consistent with, and in contrast to, those of the group making the judgments. Studies by Byrne and his coworkers (Byrne, 1961; Byrne & Griffitt, 1966; Byrne, Griffitt, & Stefaniak, 1967), Feshbach, Singer, and Feshbach (1963), and Feshbach and Roe (1968) have indicated the importance of similarity between the perceiver and the stimulus object as a factor influencing the judgments and evaluations of individuals. Empirical data, and sociological analyses bearing upon teachers' personalities suggest that teachers as a group tend to be more conforming, restrained, controlled, cautious, and acquiescent than nonteachers (Lazarsfeld & Thielins, 1958; Reisman, 1959; Stern, 1963). Consequently, the following two triadic clusters of personality attributes with their polar counterparts were selected for evaluation by the teachers: flexible, nonconforming, untidy— rigid, conforming, orderly; active, independent, assertive— passive, dependent, acquiescent.

Another factor influencing the selection of the four personality combinations was the literature bearing upon the relationship between personality characteristics and intellectual competence in children. These studies indicate that the more independent and nonconforming child is also more intellectually competent (Maccoby, 1966). However, the same qualities of autonomy and challenge may interfere with classroom process as it is usually structured and may therefore elicit negative, critical responses from the teacher. It would be of interest to determine whether those behaviors associated with intellectual capability are less valued by prospective teachers.

Hypothesis

The data relating to teacher personality and values, as well as the findings regarding the effects of similarity on evaluation and judgments, suggest the following hypothesis: Student teachers prefer children whose behaviors reflect control, caution, and conformity as compared to children whose behaviors reflect independence, challenge, and flexibility. This difference should be reflected in their assigning more positive ratings of intellectual and social attributes to children manifesting more rigid, conforming, tidy, dependent, passive, acquiescent behaviors than to children manifesting flexible, nonconforming, untidy, independent, active, assertive behaviors.

Since some of these behaviors are sex typed, interactions

are expected between the sex of the child and the personality triad being assessed; for example, while it is hypothesized that assertiveness and independence will receive less favored ratings when displayed by boys or girls, it should be even less acceptable in girls since these traits are less compatible with the female role.

Method

Subjects

Two groups of graduate students enrolled in elementary school student teaching at the University of California, Los Angeles were included as Ss. Group 1 was composed of 151 female students beginning their first assignment in student teaching and Group 2 was composed of 89 female students beginning their second student-teaching assignment. The latter group had spent the prior quarter student teaching and had been trained for 10 weeks in an elementary school classroom.[1] The mean age of Group 1 and Group 2 was 23.6 years and 23.3 years, respectively, and the modal age of both groups was 22 years. The Ss in both groups were predominately from middle-class Caucasian backgrounds.

Instrument

The measure used to assess the influence of pupil personality was the Situation Test which was constructed specifically for this study.[2] This instrument consists of 16 story situations, depicting elementary school children engaged in relevant classroom activities. The child in each of the story situations manifests a behavioral sequence indicative of one of the four triadic clusters. Two situations featuring a boy and two situations featuring a girl were constructed for each trait cluster (flexible, nonconforming, untidy; rigid, conforming, orderly; active, independent, assertive; passive, dependent, acquiescent) making 16 situations in all. The stories for both sexes

[1] This sample represented all of the student teachers enrolled in elementary school student teaching for that quarter. The protocols of the 10 male teachers were not included in the statistical analysis.

[2] The author wishes to thank Astrid Beigel and Jean Becket for their assistance in the construction of the situations.

were matched as closely as possible. In addition, all the situations were matched for intensity of activity as well as number of words; each story varying between 85 and 95 words.

For each situation presented, Ss rated the child in the story on five behavioral dimensions. A 6-point scale ranging from "considerably below average" to "considerably above average" was used for ratings on each dimension. Judgments for each situation were made regarding (a) how intelligent (bright) the child is, (b) what grades the child usually receives, (c) how generous the child is, (d) how popular the child is, and (e) in comparison to other children, how much S would like to have the child in her class.

The judgments that Ss made on these five dimensions were primarily inferences and generalizations drawn from the classroom behavior of the child. While in a few situations there might have been minimal cues relating to intellectual ability, in no instance was there any information imparted regarding the child's popularity, generosity, or grades. The five ratings were always presented in the same order. The order of presentation of the situations was randomly determined and was the same for all Ss. The following are two examples of the male situations representing one of the triadic personality clusters of flexible, nonconforming, untidy; and rigid, conforming, orderly:

Flexible, Nonconforming, Untidy

Steve is working on a model for the space project. He decides to make a space capsule and works out a design for it. While he works he scatters glue, wood, and nails on the floor. When he can't find a piece of the wood the right shape, he re-designs part of his model. When he catches his shirt on a nail, he pulls it loose carelessly. Although there is always a 10-minute cleanup period after a work project, Steve continues working on his model until the final bell rings.

Rigid, Conforming, Orderly

The children are learning how to handle and feed hamsters. The teacher asks David to help take them out of the cages for their food. Although David thinks it will be messy, he agrees to help. After putting on a lab coat, he gets some newspaper and covers the floor with it. He lines up the food dishes in front of the cages and carefully pours the food. He closes the food container tightly and returns it to the shelf. David follows the teacher's directions precisely in feeding each hamster.

To ensure that the situations be representative of the personality-trait clusters they were intended to reflect, five psychologists, unfamiliar with the purpose of the study, were given a list of 20 adjectives, 12 of which were descriptive of the various personality-trait clusters depicted in the situations. The psychologists were asked to indicate which traits characterized the child in a story, for each of 50 stories, comprising the initial pool of situations constructed for this study. The situations which constitute the Situation Test were selected from among those in which all five raters selected at least two of the three adjectives constituting the trait cluster the situation is intended to depict.

Procedure

The Situation Test was group administered at three specially scheduled meetings. Those students who were unable to attend the regularly scheduled sessions were contacted individually and the test was administered at a later time. The project was introduced by the investigator as part of an ongoing research program in the area of teacher education. It was emphasized that the purpose of the project was to improve the student teacher program and that the focus was to study groups rather than individuals. To further encourage cooperation, Ss were assured that the data would remain confidential.

Before administering the situation stimuli, Ss were informed that the incidents to be presented described children who had been observed in third- and fourth-grade classrooms. They were requested to read the situation appearing at the top of each page and then to rate the children on each of the five dimensions. The Ss were instructed to complete all items even though some judgments might be difficult to make. The total time to complete the Situation Test was approximately 20 minutes.

Results

The data presented in this section are based upon the combined distributions of Group 1 (first placement students) and Group 2 (second placement students) since only one comparison out of 192 means and variances proved to be significant. Apparently, the 10 weeks the second placement students (Group 2) had spent in direct classroom contact with children had not affected their expectations and attitudes toward children.

The mean ratings made by the student teachers for the two situations representing a personality cluster for each sex were averaged, yielding eight means for each of the five behavioral dimensions. In addition, a mean total score, an average of the five behavioral ratings for each situation, was calculated. These means are presented in Table 1. Separate analyses of variance, using a complete factorial 4×2 design (Personality Cluster $\times$ Sex), were conducted for each of the five behavioral dimensions and for the total score. These results are summarized in Table 2.

The data provide strong support for the primary hypothesis of this study; prospective teachers rate more favorably students exhibiting behaviors associated with control, caution, and conformity. For the total score and three of the individual dimensions (popularity, generosity, and preferred child in the classroom), teachers rated the four clusters in the following order of preference: rigid, conforming, orderly; dependent, passive, acquiescent; flexible, nonconforming, untidy; independent, active, assertive. The majority of these differences were significant at less than the .01 level using the Tukey modified statistic for testing the difference between means following a significant overall F (Winer, 1962, p. 87).

The results for the two ratings associated with the more intellectual dimensions, intelligence and grades, differ somewhat from the trends for the more social dimensions. As Table 1 indicates, children reflecting the personality cluster of dependent, passive, acquiescent are viewed as least intelligent while the flexible boy and the assertive boy received the second and third highest mean ratings. However, when the clusters are compared with respect to anticipated grades (Table 1), the ratings appear to be a resultant of the judgments of social characteristics and the judgments of intelligence. Although the teachers predict that the flexible boy is highly intelligent, they also anticipate his grades to be below those of the children in the other three categories.

TABLE 1
Mean Judgments of Child's Attributes as a Function of Personality Cluster and Sex of Child

CLUSTER SITUATION	INDE-PENDENT, ACTIVE, ASSERTIVE	DEPEND-ENT, PASSIVE, SUBMISSIVE	FLEXIBLE, NONCON-FORMING, UNTIDY	RIGID, CONFORM-ING, ORDERLY
Total Score				
Boys	18.84	19.87	19.28	22.38
Girls	17.49	20.27	18.11	23.60
Popularity				
Boys	3.39	3.78	3.72	4.19
Girls	3.16	3.86	3.57	4.35
Generosity				
Boys	3.37	4.25	3.55	4.42
Girls	3.16	4.37	3.53	4.57
Prefer child in class				
Boys	3.59	4.07	3.70	4.67
Girls	3.28	4.17	3.61	4.96
Intelligence				
Boys	4.47	3.92	4.62	4.45
Girls	4.14	3.94	4.01	4.70
Grades				
Boys	4.05	3.85	3.74	4.65
Girls	3.76	3.95	3.41	5.03

Note.—The mean difference required for the .01 level of significance is .90 for total score, .22 for popularity, .22 for generosity, .25 for prefers child in class, .23 for IQ, and .22 for grades; for the .05 level of significance a mean difference of .77 is required for total score, .19 for popularity, .19 for generosity, .21 for prefers child in class, .19 for IQ, and .19 for grades.

With the exception of intelligence there were no main effects for sex. However, there was a significant interaction between sex and personality cluster for each judgment dimen-

TABLE 2
Analysis of Variance of Total Ratings and of Ratings for Each Behavior Dimension

SOURCE OF VARIATION	df	TOTAL		POPULARITY		GENEROSITY		PREFERS CHILD IN CLASS		INTELLIGENCE		GRADES	
		MS	F	MS	F	MS	F	MS	F	MS	F	MS	F
Cluster (A)	3	4474.17	299.43[b]	165.21	189.90[b]	337.97	388.47[b]	357.07	321.68[b]	69.36	74.58[b]	286.63	318.48[b]
Sex (B)	1	47.48	3.18	.25	.29	.13	.15	.00	.00	30.28	32.56[b]	1.39	1.54
A × B	3	369.11	24.71[b]	7.03	8.08[b]	6.41	7.37[b]	15.97	14.39[b]	36.83	39.60[b]	26.48	29.42[b]
Error	3,832[a]	14.94		.87		.87		1.11		.93		.90	

[a] The separate error estimates of S × Cluster, S × Sex, S × Cluster × Sex and between Ss may be regarded as homogeneous and are combined to yield a pooled S × Cluster—sex mean square with $df = 1,912$. An additional 1,920 degrees of freedom are added by the replication of situations.

[b] $p < .01$.

sion. In order to provide a clearer description of these interactions, an overview of the effects of personality clusters for each sex is presented in Table 3. For each judgment dimension, the eight means presented in Table 1 were ranked in order of size. The highest mean obtained for a dimension was assigned a rank of 1, the second a rank of 2 and so on, a rank of 8 being assigned to the lowest mean. This ranking procedure was carried out for each judgment dimension and for the total score.

TABLE 3
Rankings of Personality Cluster by Sex in Order of
Mean Scores Obtained on Each Judgment Dimension

CLUSTER SITUATION	INDEPENDENT, ACTIVE, ASSERTIVE		DEPENDENT, PASSIVE, SUBMISSIVE		FLEXIBLE, NONCONFORMING, UNTIDY		RIGID, CONFORMING, ORDERLY	
	Boy	Girl	Boy	Girl	Boy	Girl	Boy	Girl
Total	6	8	4	3	5	7	2	1
Popular	7	8	4	3	5	6	2	1
Generous	7	8	4	3	5	6	2	1
Prefer child in class	6	8	4	3	5	7	2	1
Intelligent	3	5	8	7	2	6	4	1
Grades	3	6	5	4	7	8	2	1

The order of the rankings indicate that, in general, the ratings of personality clusters follow a similar trend for each sex. However, within each personality cluster the ranks of the boys compared to the girls are sometimes reversed. For the rigid and dependent clusters, girls are rated more highly than boys. For the flexible and independent clusters, the boys obtain higher rankings than the girls. This pattern holds for all of the judgment dimensions. The expectation that sex-typed behaviors are more acceptable when displayed by the appropriate sex is supported by these findings. While flexibility and independence are least valued by the student teachers, they are even less acceptable when displayed by girls. Conversely, rigidity and dependence are more highly valued in girls than in boys.

The deviation of the ratings of intelligence and grades from the overall pattern vary somewhat with the sex of the child. The dependency cluster elicits low ratings of intelligence in both boys and girls while the flexibility cluster elicits low ratings in girls only. Also, the least negative ranking for the girls manifesting independent and assertive behavior is for the intelligence dimension.

Discussion

The results provide striking support for the hypothesis that student teachers prefer pupils whose behavior reflects rigidity, conformity, and orderliness or dependency, passivity, and acquiescence than pupils whose behavior is indicative of flexibility, nonconformity, and untidiness or independence, activity, and assertiveness. The higher value afforded certain personality clusters, in conjunction with the sex typing of the behavior, yielded a consistent ordering of judgments. In general, it appears that student teachers perceive most positively the rigid, conforming girl and secondly, the rigid, conforming boy. The third position in the preference order is occupied by the dependent, passive girl who is closely followed by her male counterpart. The flexible boy is fifth in the ordering while the flexible girl and the independent boy vie for sixth and seventh positions. The lowest ratings are given to the independent, assertive girl.

This pattern of ratings was obtained in response to the question, "In comparison to other children how much would you like to have this child in your class?," the item which most directly taps the teachers' attitudes toward the pupil depicted in the situation. It was also reflected in their judgments of traits such as popularity and generosity. The consistency of the ratings and the projective nature of the judgments suggest that the student teachers' judgments are primarily based on their attitudes and personal values rather than on the veridicality of contextual cues. The behaviors depicted in the situations evoked varying degrees of approval from the student teachers. Their attitude toward these behaviors apparently formed the basis for expectations concerning the child's ability, achievement, popularity, and generosity.

This study did not assess the teachers' behaviors in the classroom and there is undoubtedly a gap between the preferences they express and how they actually behave. Nevertheless, in view of the considerable amount of social-psychological evidence that attitudes and expectations exert a significant effect upon behavior, it seems reasonable to assume that the preferences of the student teachers would be manifested in their classroom behavior. Teachers reward the behaviors they prefer and their expectancies and attitudes, which are communicated to the children in direct and indirect ways, will influence the values and expectancies of the children they teach.

Even if teachers' expectancies affect their behavior, caution should be exercised in generalizing from the preferences of student teachers to those of experienced teachers. The teacher-training experience is a relatively stressful one for the trainee (Sorenson & Halpert, 1968). Under these conditions, the student teacher may be more preoccupied with problems of classroom management and control than the inservice teacher. It is possible, then, that with greater experience, the preferences of the student teachers may move in the direction of a less cautious and conforming child.

The question arises as to the educational implications of the preferences which this student-teacher group expresses for particular types of children. The picture that emerges of the type of child that they most prefer is one whose behavior will facilitate expedient classroom management perhaps at the cost of other educational objectives such as spontaneity and creative problem solving. In view of the observations indicating that teachers tend to be cautious and conforming (Stern, 1963), the pupil attributes which student teachers prefer appear to be consistent with the attributes which characterize teachers as a group. If subsequent research indicates that these preferences persist past the teacher-training stage, then modifications in existing training and selection procedures would appear to be necessary. Nevertheless, educators responsible for teacher training should attempt to increase student teachers' awareness of their particular preferences and the possible effects of these preferences upon their evaluation of, and behavior toward, varying kinds of pupils.

References

Bandura, A., & Walters, R. H. *Social learning and personality development*. New York: Holt, Rinehart and Winston, Inc., 1964.

Beilen, H. Teachers' and clinicians' attitudes toward the behavior problems of children: A reappraisal. *Child Development*, 1959, 30, 9–25.

Burnstein, E., Stotland, E., & Zander, A. Similarity to a model and self-evaluation. *Journal of Abnormal and Social Psychology*, 1961, 62, 257–264.

Bush, R. N. *The teacher-pupil relationship*. Englewood Cliffs, N.J.: Prentice-Hall, 1954.

Byrne, D. Interpersonal attraction and attitude similarity. *Journal of Abnormal and Social Psychology*, 1961, 62, 713–715.

Byrne, D., & Griffith, W. A developmental investigator of the law of attraction. *Journal of Personality and Social Psychology*, 1966, 4, 699–702.

Byrne, D., Griffitt, W., & Stefaniak, D. Attraction and similarity of personality characteristics. *Journal of Personality and Social Psychology*, 1967, 5, 82–90.

Davidson, H. H., & Lang, G. Children's perceptions of their teacher's feelings toward them related to self-perception, school achievement and behavior. *Journal of Experimental Education*, 1960, 29, 107–118.

Feshbach, N. Variations in teachers reinforcement styles and imitative behavior of children differing in personality characteristics and social background. CSEIP Technical Report No. 2, 1967, University of California, Los Angeles.

Feshbach, N., & Roe, K. Empathic behavior in six and seven year olds. *Child Development*, 1968, 39, 133–145.

Feshbach, S., Singer, R. D., & Feshbach, N. Effects of anger arousal and of hostility to pictorial stimuli. *Journal of Consulting Psychology*, 1963, 27, 248–252.

Fox, R. S., Lippitt, R. O., & Schmuck, R. A. Pupil-teacher adjustment and mutual adaptation in creating classroom learning environments. Washington, D.C.: United States Department of Health, Education, and Welfare, January, 1964.

Getzels, J. W., & Jackson, P. W. The teacher's personality and characteristics. In N. L. Gage (Ed.), *Handbook of research on teaching*. Chicago: Rand McNally, 1963.

Lazarsfeld, P. F., & Thielins, W., Jr. *The academic mind*. New York: Free Press, 1958.

Maccoby, E. E. *The development of sex differences*. Stanford, Calif.: Stanford University Press, 1966.

Portuges, S., & Feshbach, N. The effects of teacher's reinforcement style upon imitative behavior of children. Paper presented at the meeting of the American Educational Research Association, Chicago, February, 1968.

Reisman, D. The influence of student culture and faculty values in the American college. In G. Z. F. Bereday & J. A. Lauwerys (Eds.), *Higher education*. Yonkers, N.Y.: World Book, 1959.

Rosenblith, J. F. Learning by imitation in kindergarten children. *Child Development*, 1959, 30, 69–80.

Rosenblith, J. F. Imitative color choices in kindergarten children. *Child Development*, 1961, 32, 211–223.

Rosenthal, R. *Experimenter effects in behavioral research*. New York: Appleton, 1966.

Ross, D. Relationship between dependency, intentional learning and incidental learning in pre-school children. *Journal of Personality and Social Psychology*, 1966, 4, 374–381.

Sears, P. S. *The effects of classroom conditions on the strength of achievement motive and work output of elementary children*. Stanford, Calif.: Stanford University Press, 1963.

Sorenson, G., & Halpert, R. Stress in student teaching. *California Journal of Educational Research*, 1968, 19, 28–33.

Stern, G. Measuring noncognitive variables in research on teaching. In N. L. Gage (Ed.), *Handbook of research on teaching*. Chicago: Rand McNally, 1963.

Winer, B. J. *Statistical principles in experimental design*. New York: McGraw-Hill, 1962.

Teachers' Attitudes
and Actions
toward Their Students*

MELVIN L. SILBERMAN

Although much is known about the psychological effects of
teachers' perceptions and appraisals of their students, the specific behaviors through which these personal views are expressed remain unexamined. The present study responds, in
part, to this deficiency in our understanding by focusing on
how teachers' attitudes toward their students are revealed in
the teachers' classroom behavior.

Teachers' attitudes toward their students go beyond simply
liking or disliking them. In previous interviews with 32 teachers conducted by the author, four distinct attitudes emerged in
their descriptions of students. They have been labelled attachment, concern, indifference, and rejection.

"Attachment" is directed toward those students whom the
teacher experiences as sources of pleasure in her work. The
affectionate tie with such students is partially a result of the
teacher's appreciation for, and perhaps a dependence on, the
child's steadfast conformity to institutional and teacher
expectations.[1] For example, one teacher reports, "She's one
that I would be very happy to keep. She enjoys school and
certainly is never any trouble or difficulty to me." Another

[1] Philip W. Jackson, Melvin L. Silberman, and Bernice J. Wolfson,
"Signs of Personal Involvement in Teachers' Descriptions of Their Students," *Journal of Educational Psychology*, 1969, 60, 22–27.

* Adapted and Revised Version of "Behavioral Expression of Teachers'
Attitudes Toward Elementary School Students," *Journal of Educational
Psychology*, 1969, 60, 402–407.

teacher speaks of a girl on whom she is "rather dependent; she is kind of an interpreter of my wishes to the class because she responds to me in the way I want my whole class to." A candidate for the teacher's affection, then, fulfills personal needs and makes few demands on the teacher's energies.

"Concern" is directed toward those students whom the teacher believes make extensive but appropriate role demands of her. She is willing to serve such children not only because she is sympathetic to their needs but also because she derives personal satisfaction from helping children who are receptive and appreciative. One teacher describes such a child as, "my project of the year." Another teacher feels that such a child is "very gratifying to work with because she can see what you're trying to show her and really take off on it." Thus, a candidate for the teacher's concern is, in the teacher's eyes, a worthy recipient of her professional attention.

"Indifference" is directed toward those students who, although in the same setting as the teacher, lie outside the scope of the teacher's involvement. They do not excite or dismay the teacher. For example, one teacher admits, "I really tend to forget she's in the room. I don't really have feelings toward her one way or the other." Another teacher says, "She doesn't strike me as either a goody-goody or a baddy-baddy." Since such students are often in the periphery of the teacher's professional vision, whatever demands they make go unnoticed.

"Rejection" is directed toward those students who are not worthy, in the teacher's estimation, of her professional energies. Such students make as many demands as do students who concern teachers, but theirs are perceived as illegitimate or overwhelming. As one teacher testifies, "He has problems that are beyond the scope of the classroom teacher; I've given up." Another teacher claims, "His arrogance makes him impossible to deal with."

At first glance, it would seem obvious that these attitudes would prompt the teacher to treat certain students differently, depending on how she felt about them. But, when the constraints on attitude expression operating in classrooms are considered, the link between attitude and action is no longer so obvious. For example, students expect their teacher to avoid favoritism. As a result, the teacher may be reluctant to treat students she likes any better than students she dislikes. Also certain students whom the teacher might wish to ignore always seem underfoot. To deal with them often means postponing contact with those students in whose company the teacher might prefer to be.

Despite these constraints, it is contended that teachers act differently toward students who are objects of the attitudes under investigation. The rewards teachers gain from expression of their attitudes probably outweigh the costs they incur from doing so. By acting spontaneously, which involves acting on the basis of feeling, teachers are able to cope with their numerous daily encounters with students without having to stop to weigh all the options available to them. They are able to perpetuate the satisfaction they derive from working with certain students as well as defend themselves against threats to their professional self-image posed by other students. Teachers can ignore, to some extent, students' demands for fairness because their behavior typically is not witnessed by colleagues and superiors. Furthermore, their students have few channels by which they can seek redress for any abuse of their teacher's authority.

Method

Ten third-grade teachers from upper-middle-class suburban school systems participated in the study. All were women with at least three years of teaching experience. Each teacher was in charge of a class containing 24 to 30 students.

Every teacher was asked, in a taped interview, four questions, each designed to reveal the identity of one student toward whom she held each of the attitudes under investigation. The questions for each attitude category were:

1. Attachment. If you could keep one student another year for the sheer joy of it, whom would you pick?
2. Concern. If you could devote all your attention to a child who concerns you a great deal, whom would you pick?
3. Indifference. If a parent were to drop in, unannounced, for a conference, whose child would you be least prepared to talk about?
4. Rejection. If your class was to be reduced by one child, whom would you be relieved to have removed?

To determine if the teacher acts on the attitudes she holds, the teacher's behavior toward the students chosen in the interview was observed. The observation took place soon after the interview to reduce the possibility of change in the teacher's attitudes. Each class was visited for twenty hours. During this time, an observer kept a running tally of selected teacher actions toward the students who were targets of special attitudes. The reader is referred to a previous report of this study for these quantitative results (see asterisked footnote). Descriptive records were also kept and will serve as the basis for discussion here.

Results

Attachment

The intensity of teachers' feelings toward students to whom they were attached was not matched by their classroom expressions of attachment. In the initial interview, teachers described these children in such glowing terms as:

> "About as much as you could ask of any child if you had children who respond the way she does."
> "You couldn't ask for a nicer boy. I would take him home."
> "He is an absolutely delightful, freckled faced little boy."
> "He has the finest qualities of character and personality that we hope for in a leader."
> "He's really fantastic."

Yet, as attached as they were to these students, teachers bent over backward to avoid indicating, especially to other students, how they felt about them.

When the teacher was instructing the entire class, she often ignored the student to whom she was attached. She seldom selected him to answer questions because she feared that he always knew the correct answers. Likewise, it was usually to no avail for the attachment student to raise his hand to be called on. One of these students, a girl, persisted in raising her hand during many of the observer's visits. Occasionally, the teacher acknowledged the raised hand by saying, in a conceding tone, "Well, all right, Sue," as if conveying to the class, "I

don't really want to, but I have to give Sue a chance some-
time." Often, the temptation to call on an attachment student
was considerable. There were several instances, for example,
in which a teacher wanted a good contribution to a discussion
or an answer to a difficult question, but at such times, to avoid
any hint of favoritism or special regard, she usually chose to
call on another student whose contribution or answer could
not be expected to be as excellent.

It is doubtful, however, that the teacher's attempt to conceal her feelings of fondness for a child was completely successful. The avoidance of an attachment student was so obvious that the class probably understood that the student was
special enough to warrant such teacher restraint. One child,
who had interpreted the teacher's behavior in this way, told
the observer, "Brian's the teacher's favorite, but she tries not to
let us know it."

One way through which the teacher somewhat openly expressed her esteem for the child to whom she was attached
was a type of praise most of his classmates did not receive.
The teacher would often make a point of praising an attachment child not for his benefit alone but also for the entire
class. The teacher's attachment to a child seemed, to some
extent, based on this ability to utilize that student as a model
for the others to emulate. One boy was frequently complimented for having his work out for a new activity "ready to
go." This student was also asked several times to explain to the
class how a particular classroom procedure should operate and
was praised for each explanation. Other attachment students
were praised for their suggestions in different activity areas
and requested to share their ideas with the class. For example,
one teacher interrupted an art period and said, "Class, Robbie
(an attachment student) just told me an excellent idea for
making a three-dimensional poster. Robbie, would you tell the
class your idea?"

The conflict between her fondness toward one student and
her obligations to other students was reflected in the teacher's
inconsistent disciplining of the student to whom she was attached. For instance, when he violated a classroom norm, his
teacher appeared reluctant to admonish him but did so in
order to maintain equality in the enforcement of her rules.
One such student would often call out answers in a class

question-and-answer period and each time was reprimanded before the rest of the students. Yet, during freer moments of the day when he was not as visible to the other students, he would habitually violate other rules with impunity. Sometimes, the teacher exhibited her ambivalence by messages to the student which both accepted and rejected his behavior. For example, four students of the attachment group rather frequently reported the misbehavior of other students to their teacher. Usually, she would respond to their disclosures by saying, in effect, "Well, I appreciate your telling me that but you know that we don't tattle in this class."

In general, then, teachers went to great lengths to suppress expression of attachment. To some extent, they did not succeed. Thus, it is difficult to determine whether attachment students were aware of their teacher's fondness. They probably believed that their teacher was positively disposed toward them, but it is unlikely that they were aware of the considerable pleasure their teacher derived from their being in her class.

Concern

The source of greatest classroom attraction to teachers was the student they were concerned about rather than the student to whom they were attached. Perhaps, this attraction was due to the teacher's judgment that he merited her time and professional energies. Examples of this point of view from descriptions were:

> "What has impressed me so much about her, why I feel the need to help so much is that she is forcing herself to learn."
> "You can't help feeling sorry for her and wanting to help her all you can."
> "He tries hard; he works hard at it and his attitude is such a nice one that it makes you want to help him."
> "If I could spend more time with him individually, he might grow, because he doesn't resist it, really."
> "He is a good student to work with."

The desire to be involved with a concern student was clearly evident in the teacher's classroom behavior. She often initiated contact with him in order to check on his academic and personal welfare, something she rarely did with other students. Examples of such behavior are: "Dan, I haven't checked your workbook much this morning. Come up and show me" and "Kaye, how are you coming?" One particular episode observed by the writer captures this kind of concern for a student. Upon the return to class of three students who had been absent for a few days, the teacher uninhibitedly singled out one of the students and said: "Glad you're back, Suzanne. Are you feeling all right?" Throughout that morning, this teacher was quite anxious that Suzanne knew what work she had missed and how to do it. At one point, the teacher spent fifteen minutes giving her individual help.

The teacher placed few conditions on the concern student's freedom to seek her attention. Many of his appeals were catered to when similar requests of other children were refused. In particular, a concern student was commonly allowed to ask a question of his teacher when she was working with other students, even though such behavior by his classmates was not generally tolerated. Furthermore, he received help without hesitation, whereas assistance was often denied to others on the grounds that they had not "tried hard enough first on their own." The teacher even responded to his appeals when they outnumbered those of other students.

The teacher made a special effort to evaluate his work. She often praised his unsuccessful struggles (for example, "You really tried hard this time, but I realize it's tough") or expressed pleasure at unexpected accomplishments ("What a pleasant surprise. I didn't think you could do that"). When the teacher expressed negatively toned evaluations, they tended to communicate her anxiety concerning the student's slow progress rather than a personal criticism. For example, a concern student was observed working on a multiplication problem at the blackboard. When he finished, his teacher informed him that something was wrong with his answer. After three unsuccessful attempts by the student to correct the answer, the teacher said in an imploring tone, "I just don't know what to do with you next." This same teacher described her plight in the interview by saying, "I think he can do the work and he certainly tries hard but I've tried pushing so many buttons and I haven't found anything that works yet."

Usually, then, a teacher was open in her classroom expression of concern. She exhibited it in public and in private, regardless of her commitment to other students, and regardless of whether she had to relax classroom rules to do it.

Indifference

When the observer focused on the movements of a teacher, the student to whom she was indifferent rarely came into view. The teacher did not avoid him intentionally. She simply was unmindful of his presence in the room. He, in effect, was an empty seat.

The nonsalience of indifference students was not due to their attributes alone. When teachers describe them, they revealed a definite lack of enthusiasm for such students. Some examples taken from their descriptions are:

"She doesn't have the kind of personality that would excite me."
"To me, Judy's kind of colorless."
"I could very easily miss her in the group."
"I feel neither here nor there with her."
"She's nice and all but it isn't satisfying to teach her."

Classroom interaction between a teacher and the student to whom she felt indifference was very infrequent. When the teacher initiated the contact, it was rarely for any purpose other than to give the indifference student his turn in discussions and the teacher's questioning. The teacher's avoidance of the indifference student was especially noticeable when she moved around the room checking the work of each student. At these times, she seldom made comments of any nature to him as she passed his seat. When the indifference student initiated the contact, the teacher's response was usually brief, perfunctory, and merely adequate. Often, after such a child showed his work to the teacher, she simply responded "o.k." and walked away. The teacher also tended to ignore any concern expressed by him. For instance, an indifference student pointed out to his teacher that the class was late for physical education. The teacher shrugged off the information by saying, "oh, that's all right," yet immediately and quite anxiously organized the class's departure.

Beyond the infrequency and brevity of teacher contact, an indifference student was not treated any differently than were most other students in his class. Except for the response, "good," to a correct answer, his teacher uttered few comments of praise. Negative evaluations mainly consisted of simple prohibitory messages such as "That's enough talking. Let's get back to work." Nearly all the student's appeals were responded to favorably, as an indifference student, like most of his classmates, made only those requests to which he felt assured his teacher would consent.

Rejection

If concern students could do no wrong in the eyes of their teachers, then rejection students could do no right. The difference of view is perhaps explained by teachers' interpretation of their behavior. Teachers felt that concern students could not help themselves. But, teachers' descriptions of rejection students revealed that such students were viewed as capable of learning and controlling their behavior by themselves. Rather, their "attitude" was considered poor. The following examples illustrate these feelings:

> "Rick is a 'me first' type of child who wants more than his fair proportion of time from me."
> "He has become quite obnoxious for a number of reasons and could very easily be removed from the class."
> "He isn't willing to conform to room practices."
> "He's very bull-headed about things; he doesn't want to do the things that the rest of the group are doing."
> "He has a very belligerent attitude."

The rejected student was under continual surveillance. Thus, a large share of the contacts he received were attempts to control his behavior. He was subjected to numerous directions, prohibitions, and reprimands. It would be misleading, however, to give the impression that, apart from these acts of controlling, the teacher neglected a student whom she rejected. Actually, she frequently initiated conversations with him, perhaps intending to appease or win him over.

The teacher deliberately praised and criticized a student she rejected in front of the other students of the class. It was apparent that she believed her remarks would have a greater impact if the rejected student realized that his peers were witnesses to what the teacher said.

Whenever a rejected student surprised his teacher with model behavior, he was immediately and often elaborately praised. One particular incident will serve as an illustration of this general phenomenon. A student who the teacher complained was "messy and unkempt" started picking up his pencil sharpenings one day from the floor and disposing of them properly. The teacher made a great fuss over him. The next day, he began to pick up scraps of paper of other students. His teacher again praised him and furthermore, induced his classmates to approve his efforts. One girl even made a paper medal which he wore for several days until it was in tatters. Similar episodes were observed in other classrooms.

In their interviews, many teachers indicated that they felt compelled to give approval to students they rejected. One teacher commented, "Sometimes, you have to search for something he does that you can honestly praise him for." Another teacher remarked, "There really is so little to praise him for that I just grab onto anything I can think of."

Despite this compulsion to praise, the teacher seemed determined to demonstrate both to the student and the rest of the class the teacher's complete intolerance for his deviant behavior. By way of example, one teacher was observed shouting at her rejection student so that all could hear, "Nice, pleasant way to start off the morning, isn't it?" after the student failed to bring in his homework. Of course, there were times when a teacher, by her own initiative, had her wish for a student to be removed come true. Eight of the ten students in the rejection group were asked to leave the room, at least once, during the observer's visits.

In contrast to the concern student, the rejection student was often refused help when he approached the teacher while she was with other children and when he had not, in the teacher's estimation, worked sufficiently long on a problem by himself. Many of his appeals were not only refused but also criticized. One student asked during creative writing, "What can I write about?" and received the reply, "Well, you'll have to think of something or maybe that's asking too much." Another student requested during a library visit, "Can I take this book out?" His teacher shouted back, "Haven't you ever heard of waiting your turn in line?"

Although the teacher had little personal regard for the student she rejected, she still had to live with him in the classroom. She consequently felt that she had to appease him through attention and praise. Nevertheless, the teacher could not cope with his behavior and hence punished him by denial, criticism, and even expulsion from the room.

Discussion

The evidence suggests that the teacher's expression of attitudes is not completely unbridled. Constraints on attitude expression are partially effective in the case of attachment and rejection. Attitudes of concern and indifference, however, create little conflict in teachers. Teachers, nonetheless, affect the lives of children whether they act directly on the attitudes they hold or not. As we have observed, the teacher's attempts to counteract her attitude toward a student has just as significant an impact as her efforts to express it openly. Students in the same classroom do not share a common experience simply because the teacher does not feel the same way about them.

It is unlikely that any in-service program could train teachers to hold their feelings in abeyance in front of the class. Nor is it clear that teachers should. It may be desirable, however, for teachers to create classroom conditions which enable them to be as open as possible to children rather than predisposed to reacting to them in a certain manner. One way to achieve this end involves broadening interaction in the classroom so that the teacher is not always directly involved in every event. Defusing her role in this way might free the teacher to listen before jumping to conclusions.

The Acculturation
of the School Teacher*

GEORGE D. SPINDLER

EDITOR'S NOTE: *George D. Spindler has done extensive
work relating anthropology to the study of education.
His thesis in* The Transmission of American Culture *is
that the goals which are actually transmitted in schools
are at variance with those they intend to transmit. In
the excerpt presented here, Spindler focuses on the
unresolved value conflicts which cause many teachers
to behave differently from the way they profess to act
in the classroom.*

What has been established so far is that our culture is one in
which conflicts in values, and between goals and the means to
them, are present and patterned. And that teachers, as cultural
transmitters, convey these patterned conflicts to children in
their classrooms, with the consequence that many professed
goals are defeated, or at least obscured. It should also be clear
that I have not been castigating teachers. They are the agents
of their culture.

A further step must be taken if we are to see the full
meaning and scope of the problem. Teachers are a special
group. They are not selected at random as official culture
transmitters; they are trained and accredited to that status and
role. They must take courses in educational psychology, the
social foundations of education, curriculum design, philosophy
and history of education, the methods of education, and must

* Reprinted by permission of the publishers from George D. Spindler,
The Transmission of American Culture, Cambridge, Mass., Harvard University Press, Copyright, 1959, by the President and Fellows of Harvard
College.

do supervised practice teaching. In short, they must attend teacher-training institutions and graduate with the stamp of approval from the established professional cadre. But professional educational instruction and training consist not only of courses and training in techniques. Every institution with a history and internal organization and a specialized personnel has a culture or, more properly, a subculture. Certain values, symbols, beliefs, and certain basic premises are patterned into the structure and process of the institution. The institutions of professional education—the teacher-training schools and the literature of education—are no exception.

At this point it is necessary to refer back to the traditional and emergent value patterns. The traditional pattern includes emphasis on thrift, self-denial, faith in the future, a strong emphasis on success and a belief that hard work was the means to it, absolute moral norms, and a strong value placed upon the individual. The emergent pattern includes value placed upon sociability, sensitivity to the feelings of others, a relativistic attitude, a present-time orientation, and high value placed upon the group.

The dynamic process of greatest relevance to us at the moment is the relationship between the culture that the school teacher brings to the professional teacher-training institution subculture and the patterning of that subculture, the adaptation that the teacher-in-training makes to this patterning and the consequences in selective culture transmission in the classroom.

This is a complex relationship with many subtle ramifications. I have outlined it in the preceding chapter. Since an understanding of it is essential to the logic of the analysis to follow, I will restate and expand the argument. It is well established that the majority of public school teachers originate from a middle and lower-middle social class culture. The value pattern that I have termed "traditional" is probably found in this cultural context in its most pure form. To the extent this is so, it means that whatever selective processes are operating tend to bring many people of traditionalistic value orientation into teacher-training.

The question that the anthropologist raises is—what are the characteristics of the subculture of the teacher-training institution to which these students bring their traditionalist orientations? Analysis of a sample of some of the influential literature of curriculum design for elementary education reveals that there is present a strong values bias that fits in general terms the "emergent" pattern. The literature of child development and educational psychology reveals some of the same trends. Interpretations of the social behavior of boys and girls, intended for educational consumption, provide both implicit and explicit value judgments in the same pattern. The popularity of sociometric techniques is diagnostic of this orientation. The topical content of many of our teacher-training courses suggests it as well.

The basic premise underlying the specific emergent values is that what is most important is the social adjustment of the child. His place in the group, the responses of his peers to him, his ability to get along well, to work and play with others are penultimate concerns. This is not all bad by any means. The emphasis on social adjustment is the educator's attempt to meet the demands of a new kind of society, where this kind of adjustment is of vital importance. When balanced by a concern for individual differences, by support for the deviating child, the creative student, intellectual development, and the acquisition of cognitive skills, and when it does not become a form of "groupism," this emphasis on social adjustment is a possible compensatory process for some of the more harshly competitive anxiety-arousing patterns of our culture.

But the point is that however understandable and useful the emphasis may be, this pattern of values incorporated in the ethos of professional education is frequently at variance with what the new teacher-in-training brings into the situation. The neophyte in training must reorient his value system wherever the conflict in values is encountered.

When neophyte teachers in training or people in any other acculturating group adapt to sharply disjunctive value systems, their adaptations assume predictable forms. The individual meets the new value system and feels threatened because it challenges his established, familiar, and comfortable values. He does not, of course, necessarily interpret the experience in these terms. He is more likely to see it as a personal conflict, which heightens the intensity of the threat. After some exploration in the new dimensions of feeling and belief offered to him by the opposing system, his feeling of threat overcomes him and he seeks refuge in the comforting shelter of his established values. But something has changed. He has been driven back to his "native state" by threat. Therefore he overcompensates, and rigidifies the original system in what may be psychologically termed a reaction formation, or culturally termed a "nativistic reaffirmation." I will term him a "reaffirmative traditionalist" in the framework of this analysis. The teacher of this type will tend to be rigid in his uncompromising projection of traditional values in his classroom behavior.

An alternative adaptive response is represented by the person who encounters the new value system which is sharply disjunctive with his own, likewise feels threatened by the conflict in personal terms, but adapts by overcompensating in the direction of the new system. Perhaps he is more threatened by the possibility of being out of step than he is by the demand to change. He uncritically appropriates the new values in their entirety and frequently becomes a strident proselytizer for them. This kind of teacher I term a "compensatory emergentist." His channels of communication with children, and his criteria for their behavior, become narrowed to individual-in-harmony-with-the-group. "Groupism" reigns in his classroom. Individualistic differences and deviations become smothered by group conformity.

A third alternative adaptive response is exhibited by the person who encounters the conflict of value systems and superficially internalizes segments of both but does not rework them into any coherent synthesis. He is a mixed type but quite different from a type that I shall describe shortly. He is usually not particularly thoughtful about the conflicts he encounters and leaves them unresolved, but still a part of his acquired culture. This person as a teacher is likely to vacillate between different modes of group leadership and different modes of interaction with individual children. Obvious discontinuities in his classroom management cause trouble for both him and his students. We can call him the "vacillator."

The fourth alternative is a happier one than any of the others. This person comes into the acculturative situation with a capacity for adjustment to differences in values and conflicts between them. Usually he is thoughtful or philosophic-minded and has the ability to combine useful features from more than one system of belief on a rational basis. He does not need to overcompensate as a defense against conflict because he is not threatened by it. He is a mixed type but does not internalize the mixture segmentally. He recombines the aspects from both systems into a creatively coherent synthesis. I have labeled this an "adjusted" type.

As a matter of fact I believe that increasing numbers of students are of this latter type. They exhibit workable combinations of what seem to be the best of both the emergent and traditional values. For instance, they accept the need of the individual to be a member of the group but believe that the individual should also be self-possessed and self-actualized. They believe that hard work is necessary for success but that there is no point in being unpleasantly puritanic about it. They take a relativistic, tolerant view of differences between individuals and between groups, but they have a personal moral code that governs their own behaviors within broad but definite limits. Whether they represent a shift in the kind of training they receive or whether they represent a change in the culture of generations, or both, is not clear. In any event, I am happy to see them and hope their numbers increase, for I am convinced that large numbers of teachers, at least new ones, are reaffirmative traditionalists, compensatory emergentists, or vacillators.

A value judgment is made here because it seems clear that teachers falling into the first two adaptive categories tend to exhibit highly selective biases as culture transmitters. They transmit in narrow channels with few alternatives due to their rigidity. Without intending to do so, they open some doors to self-cultivating developments for some children but close them for many others. And the vacillator, though he is not rigid and transmits along many channels, issues only weak signals and produces little but static as a result.

A Case Study Illustration

To illustrate further what is meant, another case study that is representative of others we have made of elementary school teachers and their classrooms will be presented.[1] The salient

---

[1] The case study was done when the author was a member of a research team operating out of the School of Education at Stanford University.

features of this case classify him as a reaffirmative traditionalist. This type may be encountered more frequently in other
parts of the country than it is on the West Coast where my
observations were made, and the analysis should, therefore,
have wide applicability.

This fifth-grade teacher is a young man of twenty-five. He
originates from a clearly traditionalistic middle-class family.
His father is an executive of middle rank in a wholesale business organization and belongs to the usual service and frater-
nal organizations. His mother is college educated and active in
the League of Women Voters. His father is not college educated and achieved his position by hard work. Both parents
like to play bridge. They belong to the country club and own a
summer cottage where the subject spent many happy hours as
a boy. Twice during the subject's lifetime the family moved to
more expensive homes in better neighborhoods.

The subject likes to play golf, drinks socially but moderately, attends the Methodist church, and reads the local newspaper, *Reader's Digest*, and the *Saturday Evening Post*. He
aspires to be a school administrator and regards his teaching
experience as preparation for that role. He is a pleasant,
good-looking young man who appears somewhat constrained
but not visibly anxious. He is well liked by his colleagues and
is rated as one of the outstanding young teachers in the school
system.

His professed aims in teaching, beyond the management of
instruction so that his students acquire the requisite knowledge, are to bring out creativity to the maximum ability of
each child, help children to express themselves clearly and
help children to learn how to get along with each other. He
states that he tries to give every student in his class a chance
to participate. He prides himself particularly on being fair and
just with all the children. He says explicitly that every student
gets a "fair break" in his classroom. He feels that he is very
concerned about the problems of his students and always tries
to understand them. His statements about his aims and his
relations with his students are consistent with what his principal, his supervisor, and the members of the central staff of the
school system say about him.

He told me that many of his teacher-training courses were
"a waste of time." In probing this blanket indictment of profes-

sional educational preparation as he experienced it I discovered that he was dismayed and upset by certain points of view that he perceived as consistently appearing in his course work. He felt that his preceptors were trying "to give the school to the children," that they were more concerned with how children adjusted than what they learned, and that his instructors stressed cooperation, or at least group harmony, at the expense of competition. All of this he lumps together under the label "progressive education," which he rejects with feeling, but which he is content to leave as an unanalyzed abstraction.

He fits the criteria for the reaffirmative-traditionalist teacher type. He originated from a family culture where the traditional values previously described apparently existed in virtually pure form. He encountered the emergent-oriented values of the professional teaching subculture. He sensed the conflict, felt the threat, rejected the threatening alternatives, and sought refuge in the shelter of his original values.

The further presentation of data on this teacher and his classroom will inclue a few items selected from a considerable mass of information. We worked together for many months, and his file is extensive. But these few items will establish the pattern that permeated many of the interrelationships between him and his students.

One of our standard practices in case studies is to ask the teacher to fill out a form titled "Information Concerning the Student." It includes items on academic and social adjustment in the child's previous school, his home situation, approximate I.Q. test performance, special interests, hobbies, health history, his ambitions and plans for the future. The teacher is requested to fill out this form for each student without recourse to written records. He is scored on the number of items of information. A perfect score, indicating highest knowledge, would be ten.

This teacher averaged 3.2 for the forms filled out on all of his thirty-three students, which is lower, on the average, than the score attained by other teachers in our sample. The mean of his knowledge concerning children in his group originating from families of highest socio-economic status was 4.9. His mean score for those of lowest status was 2.8. It is apparent that some bias is operating that tends to contradict his professed aims.

He was asked to list the names of those students in his class that he considered to be the best adjusted—emotionally and socially. Of the seven children he listed as best adjusted only one child was included who originated from a family of less than middle-class status, and this child exhibited strong status-achievement drives. He was also asked to list the names of those students whom he considered least well adjusted. Of these seven children, only one came from a middle-class setting. The other six were from families of lower-class or special ethnic status. It is possible, of course, that he was correct in his appraisal, even from a psychiatric point of view. Other evidence concerning the behavior of these children indicates that he was not accurate in a number of instances. For our purposes at the moment what is significant is that the same bias in perception is revealed in this as was exhibited in his knowledge about students.

He was asked to list the 25 percent of his class group with whom he thought he had the most effective relationship. He listed eight children, and of these eight, five were from families of middle-class social status. He was also asked to list the 25 percent of his group with whom he felt he had the least effective relationship. All but one of these children were from families of lower-class status. Other evidence indicates that in this instance he appraised the situation more or less accurately. The pattern of selective perception, of differential bias in his interrelationships with children in his class group is, however, strengthened.

He was requested to name those children who were the most popular with or most accepted by their classmates. He listed eight, only one of whom represented a lower-class position. In only three instances did he name the same children that the students themselves did, according to sociometric information collected from the class. He was also asked to name those children to whom nobody in the class paid much attention. He listed six children, two of whom were middle-class in origin. The other four were from families of lower-class status. In four instances his perceptions matched those of the classroom group, but there were ten comparatively isolated children in that group, according to the sociometric data collected from the class. Of these ten, five were children originating from middle-class backgrounds, four of whom he missed in his appraisal. Again, there is a clear pattern of selective bias in his perception of the children in his classroom. It is difficult for him to implement his professed aims in the context of this pattern.

A few excerpts from anecdotal and verbatim records will strengthen the interpretation. One boy, who was quite isolated in the interaction among the boys in the class and who chose only girls in his own responses to a sociometric questionnaire was described by the teacher as a "real go-getter, one of the most magnetic personalities of any young child I have ever known. He has a very warm personality—truthful, sincere, with a good sense of humor. Tom gets along well with anyone, anywhere." This boy sometimes brought sample bottles of hair tonic, shoe polish, simple toys and gadgets to class in a small suitcase and tried to sell them to the other children. One day when I was observing, he was allowed to "make his pitch" before the class. He was, indeed, a motivated, magnetic, sales-man, and probably will go far. The teacher apparently per-ceived only this attribute—one that is congruent with some of his own achievement drives and their precedents in his family models. There is much else about this child that he needed to know in order to guide his development effectively.

In another instance of the same type the teacher described one girl as having a "horrible personality . . . egoistic, insin-cere, false. She never has a nice word to say about anyone but herself. I don't particularly care for Charlotte." She was the friendship choice of the "star-of-attraction"—the girl most fre-quently chosen as a friend by the other girls in their socio-metric responses. She was observed to interact effectively with most of the other girls. She had a high rating in status-reputa-tion data collected from the class. She came from a broken home in a lower-class setting.

In his response to oral reports by the children about what they were reading in their spare time, his gestures, facial expression, bodily postures, comments and silences were all patterned in the framework of the same selective bias. He com-municated approval of most of what the children of middle-class origins said, and of what they were reading. He commu-nicated lack of interest, or suppressed distaste for what the children of lower-class origins said, how they said it, and of what they were reading.

I have almost too much data on this teacher and his classroom, and have had to struggle against the inclination to continue with examples that all substantiate the same pattern of bias and selective perception in his relaionships with his students. He interacted effectively with only a minority segment of his classroom group—that segment which matched his own aspirations and values, derived from his own cultural setting. He opened doors for this selected group to channels of development they were already heading toward, and he sped them on their way. But for the larger number of his students, those who did not match his values and aspirations, he closed doors and left them waiting in the foyer of our culture.

Analysis of all of the data collected about this teacher and his operations in the classroom leads to the conclusion that his consistent selective bias was in part due to his own cultural background. But this pattern was accentuated by his reactive adjustment to the conflict between the culture he brought with him when he entered professional training to become a teacher and the special subculture he encountered there.

His exercise of the role of cultural transmitter was in contradiction to his own professed aims, and even to his own beliefs about what he actually did in the classroom. He was giving all children an opportunity to participate; he did not understand their problems; he was not being fair and just to all his students; they were not all getting a "fair break." All these aims and beliefs were contradicted by his highly selective positive interaction with a small segment of his class. He was wearing cultural blinders that limited his perceptions to a single channel. His transmitting apparatus was sending out positive signals only to that segment responding within the frequency of that single channel.

Pygmalion in the Classroom—
An Excerpt*

ROBERT ROSENTHAL
LENORE JACOBSON

EDITOR'S NOTE: *This excerpt from* Pygmalion in the Classroom *summarizes the results of a widely publicized study about the effects of teacher expectations on students. While the research was focused on whether teacher expectations concerning students' intellectual potentiality influenced intellectual functioning, it also examined their influence on social variables.*

The central idea of this book has been that one person's expectation for another's behavior could come to serve as a self-fulfilling prophecy. This is not a new idea, and anecdotes and theories can be found that support its tenability. Much of the experimental evidence for the operation of interpersonal self-fulfilling prophecies comes from a research program in which prophecies or expectancies were experimentally generated in psychological experimenters in order to learn whether these prophecies would become self-fulfilling.

The general plan of past studies has been to establish two groups of "data collectors" and give to the experimenters of each group a different hypothesis as to the data their research subjects would give them. In many such experiments, though not in all, experimenters obtained data from their subjects in accordance with the expectancy they held regarding their subjects' responses. Quite naturally, some of the experiments involved expectations held by the experimenters of the intellectual performance of their subjects.

In addition to those experiments in which the subjects were humans, there were studies in which the subjects were animals. When experimenters were led to believe that their animal subjects were genetically inferior, these animals performed more poorly. When experimenters were led to believe that their animal subjects were more favorably endowed genetically, their animals' performance was superior. In reality, of course, there were no genetic differences between the animals that had been alleged to be dull or bright.

If animal subjects believed to be brighter by their trainers actually became brighter because of their trainers' beliefs, then it might also be true that school children believed by their teachers to be brighter would become brighter because of their teachers' beliefs. Oak School became the laboratory in which an experimental test of that proposition was carried out.

Oak School is a public elementary school in a lower-class community of a medium-size city. The school has a minority group of Mexican children who comprise about one-sixth of the school's population. Every year about 200 of its 650 children leave Oak School, and every year about 200 new children are enrolled.

Oak School follows an ability-tracking plan whereby each of the six grades is divided into one fast, one medium, and one slow classroom. Reading ability is the primary basis for assignment to track. The Mexican children are heavily over-represented in the slow track.

On theoretical grounds it would have been desirable to learn whether teachers' favorable or unfavorable expectations could result in a corresponding increase or decrease in pupils' intellectual competence. On ethical grounds, however, it was decided to test only the proposition that favorable expectations by teachers could lead to an increase in intellectual competence.

All of the children of Oak School were pretested with a standard nonverbal test of intelligence. This test was represented to the teachers as one that would predict intellectual "blooming" or "spurting." The IQ test employed yielded three IQ scores: total IQ, verbal IQ, and reasoning IQ. The "verbal" items required the child to match pictured items with verbal descriptions given by the teacher. The reasoning items required the child to indicate which of five designs differed from the remaining four. Total IQ was based on the sum of verbal and reasoning items.

At the very beginning of the school year following the schoolwide pretesting, each of the eighteen teachers of grades one through six was given the names of those children in her classroom who, in the academic year ahead, would show dramatic intellectual growth. These predictions were allegedly made on the basis of these special children's scores on the test of academic blooming. About 20 percent of Oak School's children were alleged to be potential spurters. For each classroom the names of the special children had actually been chosen by means of a table of random numbers. The difference between the special children and the ordinary children, then, was only in the mind of the teacher.

All the children of Oak School were retested with the same IQ test after one semester, after a full academic year, and after two full academic years. For the first two retests, children were in the classroom of the teacher who had been given favorable expectations for the intellectual growth of some of her pupils. For the final retesting all children had been promoted to the classes of teachers who had not been given any special expectations for the intellectual growth of any of the children. That follow-up testing had been included so that we could learn whether any expectancy advantages that might be found would be dependent on a continuing contact with the teacher who held the especially favorable expectation.

For the children of the experimental group and for the children of the control group, gains in IQ from pretest to retest were computed. Expectancy advantage was defined by the degree to which IQ gains by the "special" children exceeded gains by the control-group children. After the first year of the experiment a significant expectancy advantage was found, and it was expecially great among children of the first and second grades. The advantage of having been expected to bloom was evident for these younger children in total IQ, verbal IQ, and reasoning IQ. The control-group children of these grades gained well in IQ, 19 percent of them gaining twenty or more total IQ points. The "special" children, however, showed 47 percent of their number gaining twenty or more total IQ points.

During the subsequent follow-up year the younger children of the first two years lost their expectancy advantage. The children of the upper grades, however, showed an increasing expectancy advantage during the follow-up year. The younger children who seemed easier to influence may have required more continued contact with their influencer in order to maintain their behavior change. The older children, who were harder to influence initially, may have been better able to maintain their behavior change autonomously once it had occurred.

Differences between boys and girls in the extent to which they were helped by favorable expectations were not dramatic when gains in total IQ were considered. After one year, and after two years as well, boys who were expected to bloom intellectually bloomed more in verbal IQ; girls who were expected to bloom intellectually bloomed more in reasoning IQ. Favorable teacher expectations seemed to help each sex more in that sphere of intellectual functioning in which they had excelled on the pretest. At Oak School boys normally show the higher verbal IQ while girls show the higher reasoning IQ.

It will be recalled that Oak School was organized into a fast, a medium, and a slow track system. We had thought that favorable expectations on the part of teachers would be of greatest benefit to the children of the slow track. That was not the case. After one year, it was the children of the medium track who showed the greatest expectancy advantage, though children of the other tracks were close behind. After two years, however, the children of the medium track very clearly showed the greatest benefits from having had favorable expectations held of their intellectual performance. It seems surprising that it should be the more average child of a lower-class school who stands to benefit more from his teacher's improved expectation.

After the first year of the experiment and also after the second year, the Mexican children showed greater expectancy advantages than did the non-Mexican children, though the difference was not significant statistically. One interesting minority-group effect did reach significance, however, even with just a small sample size. For each of the Mexican children, magnitude of expectancy advantage was computed by subtracting from his or her gain in IQ from pretest to retest, the IQ gain made by the children of the control group is his or her classroom. These magnitudes of expectancy advantage were then correlated with the "Mexican-ness" of the children's faces. After one year, and after two years, those boys who looked more Mexican benefited more from their teachers' positive prophecies. Teachers' pre-experimental expectancies for these boys' intellectual performance were probably lowest of all. Their turning up on a list of probable bloomers must have surprised their teachers. Interest may have followed surprise and, in some way, increased watching for signs of increased brightness may have led to increased brightness.

In addition to the comparison of the "special" and the ordinary children on their gains in IQ it was possible to compare their gains after the first year of the experiment on school achievement as defined by report-card grades. Only for the school subject of reading was there a significant difference in gains in report-card grades. The children expected to bloom intellectually were judged by their teachers to show greater advances in their reading ability. Just as in the case of IQ gains, it was the younger children who showed the greater expectancy advantage in reading scores. The more a given grade level had benefited in over-all IQ gains, the more that same grade level benefited in reading scores.

It was the children of the medium track who showed the greatest expectancy advantage in terms of reading ability just as they had been the children to benefit most in terms of IQ from their teachers' favorable expectations.

Report-card reading grades were assigned by teachers, and teachers' judgments of reading performance may have been affected by their expectations. It is possible, therefore, that there was no real benefit to the earmarked children of having been expected to bloom. The effect could very well have been in the mind of the teacher rather than in the reading performance of the child. Some evidence was available to suggest that such halo effects did not occur. For a number of grade levels, objective achievement tests had been administered. Greater expectancy advantages were found when the assessment was by these objective tests than when it was by the more subjective evaluation made by the teacher. If anything, teachers' grading seemed to show a negative halo effect. It seemed that the special children were graded more severely by the teachers than were the ordinary children. It is even possible that it is just this sort of standard-setting behavior that is responsible in part for the effects of favorable expectations.

The fear has often been expressed that the disadvantaged child is further disadvantaged by his teacher's setting standards that are inappropriately low (Hillson and Myers, 1963; Rivlin, undated). Wilson (1963) has presented compelling evidence that teachers do, in fact, hold up lower standards of achievement for children of more deprived areas. It is a possibility to be further investigated that when a teacher's expectation for a pupil's intellectual performance is raised, she may set higher standards for him to meet (that is, grade him tougher). There may be here the makings of a benign cycle. Teachers may not only get more when they expect more; they may also come to expect more when they get more.

All teachers had been asked to rate each of their pupils on variables related to intellectual curiosity, personal and social adjustment, and need for social approval. In general, children who had been expected to bloom intellectually were rated as more intellectually curious, as happier, and, especially in the lower grades, as less in need of social approval. Just as had been the case with IQ and reading ability, it was the younger children who showed the greater expectancy advantage in terms of their teachers' perceptions of their classroom behavior. Once again, children of the medium track were most advantaged by having been expected to bloom, this time in terms of their perceived greater intellectual curiosity and lessened need for social approval.

When we consider expectancy advantages in terms of perceived intellectual curiosity, we find that the Mexican children did not share in the advantages of having been expected to bloom. Teachers did not see the Mexican children as more intellectually curious when they had been expected to bloom. There was even a slight tendency, stronger for Mexican boys, to see the special Mexican children as less curious intellectually. That seems surprising, particularly since the Mexican children showed the greatest expectancy advantages in IQ, in reading scores and for Mexican boys, in over-all school achievement. It seemed almost as though, for these minority-group children, intellectual competence may have been easier for teachers to bring about than to believe.

Children's gains in IQ during the basic year of the experiment were correlated with teachers' perceptions of their classroom behavior. This was done separately for the upper- and lower-track children of the experimental and control groups. The more the upper-track children of the experimental group gained in IQ, the more favorably they were rated by their teachers. The more the lower-track children of the control group gained in IQ, the more unfavorably they were viewed by their teachers. No special expectation had been created about these children, and their slow-track status made it unlikely in their teachers' eyes that they would behave in an intellectually competent manner. The more intellectually competent these children became, the more negatively they were viewed by their teachers. Future research should address itself to the possibility that there may be hazards to "unwarranted," unpredicted intellectual growth. Teachers may require a certain amount of preparation to be able to accept the unexpected classroom behavior of the intellectually upwardly mobile child.

There are a number of alternative "theories" available to account for our general findings. One such class of theories, the "accident" theories, maintain that artifacts are responsible for the results obtained, that there is really nothing to explain. The problems of test unreliability and of pretest IQ differences were discussed and found wanting as explanations of our results. The possibility that teachers treated the special children differently only during the retesting process itself was considered. The patterning of results, the fact that a "blind" examiner obtained even more dramatic expectancy effects than did the teachers, teachers' poor recall of the names of their "special" children, and the fact that the results did not disappear one year after the children left the teachers who had been given the expectations, all weaken the plausibility of that argument. Most important to the tenability of the hypothesis that teachers' expectations can significantly affect their pupils' performance are the preliminary results of three replications all of which show significant effects of teacher expectations. These replications also suggest, however, that the effects of teacher expectations may be quite complicated and affected both as to magnitude and direction by a variety of pupil characteristics and by situational variables in the life of the child.[1]

It might reasonably be thought that the improved intellectual competence of the special children was bought at the expense of the ordinary children. Perhaps teachers gave more time to those who were expected to bloom. But teachers appeared to give slightly less time to their special children. Furthermore, those classrooms in which the special children showed the greatest gains in IQ were also the classrooms in which the ordinary children gained the most IQ. The robbing-Peter theory would predict that ordinary children gain less IQ where special children gain more IQ.

On the basis of other experiments on interpersonal self-fulfilling prophecies, we can only speculate as to how teachers brought about intellectual competence simply by expecting it. Teachers may have treated their children in a more pleasant, friendly, and encouraging fashion when they expected greater

[1] As this book went to press we learned of an additional experiment showing the effects on pupil performance of teacher expectation (Beez, 1967). This time the pupils were sixty preschoolers from a summer Headstart program. Each child was taught the meaning of a series of symbols by one teacher. Half the sixty teachers had been led to expect good symbol learning and half had been led to expect poor symbol learning. Most (77 percent) of the children alleged to have better intellectual prospects learned five or more symbols but only 13 percent of the children alleged to have poorer intellectual prospects learned five or more symbols ($p < 2$ in one million). In this study the children's actual performance was assessed by an experimenter who did not know what the child's teacher had been told about the child's intellectual prospects. Teachers who had been given favorable expectations about their pupil tried to teach more symbols to their pupil than did the teachers given unfavorable expectations about their pupil. The difference in teaching effort was dramatic. Eight or more symbols were taught by 87 percent of the teachers expecting better performance, but only 13 percent of the teachers expecting poorer performance tried to teach that many symbols to their pupil ($p < 1$ in ten million). Surprisingly, however, even when these differences in teaching benefit were controlled, the children expected to be superior showed superior performance ($p < .005$, one-tail), though the magnitude of the effect was diminished by nearly half. We are very grateful to W. Victor Beez for making his data available to us.

intellectual gains of them. Such behavior has been shown to improve intellectual performance, probably by its favorable effect on pupil motivation.

Teachers probably watched their special children more closely, and this greater attentiveness may have led to more rapid reinforcement of correct responses with a consequent increase in pupils' learning. Teachers may also have become more reflective in their evaluation of the special children's intellectual performance. Such an increase in teachers' reflectiveness may have led to an increase in their special pupils' reflectiveness, and such a change in cognitive style would be helpful to the performance of the nonverbal skills required by the IQ test employed.

To summarize our speculations, we may say that by what she said, by how and when she said it, by her facial expressions, postures, and perhaps by her touch, the teacher may have communicated to the children of the experimental group that she expected improved intellectual performance. Such communications together with possible changes in teaching techniques may have helped the child learn by changing his self concept, his expectations of his own behavior, and his motivation, as well as his cognitive style and skills.

It is self-evident that further research is needed to narrow down the range of possible mechanisms whereby a teacher's expectations become translated into a pupil's intellectual growth. It would be valuable, for example, to have sound films of teachers interacting with their pupils. We might then look for differences in the way teachers interact with those children from whom they expect intellectual growth compared to those from whom they expect less. On the basis of films of psychological experimenters interacting with subjects from whom different responses are expected, we know that even in such highly standardized situations, unintentional communications can be incredibly subtle and complex (Rosenthal, 1966). Much more subtle and much more complex may be the communications between children and their teachers, teachers not constrained by the demands of the experimental laboratory to treat everyone equally to the extent that it is possible to do so.

The implications of the research described herein are of several kinds. There are methodological implications for the conduct of educational research, and these were discussed in the last chapter. There are implications for the further investigation of unintentional influence processes especially when these processes result in interpersonally self-fulfilling prophecies, and some of these have been discussed. Finally, there are some possible implications for the educational enterprise, and some of these will be suggested briefly.

Over time, our educational policy question has changed from "who ought to be educated?" to "who is capable of being educated?" The ethical question has been traded in for the scientific question. For those children whose educability is in doubt there is a label. They are the educationally, or culturally, or socioeconomically, deprived children and, as things stand now, they appear not be be able to learn as do those who are more advantaged. The advantaged and the disadvantaged differ in parental income, in parental values, in scores on various tests of achievement and ability, and often in skin color and other phenotypic expressions of genetic heritage. Quite inseparable from these differences between the advantaged and the disadvantaged are the differences in their teachers' expectations for what they can achieve in school. There are no experiments to show that a change in pupils' skin color will lead to improved intellectual performance. There is, however, the experiment described in this book to show that change in teacher expectation can lead to improved intellectual performance.

Nothing was done directly for the disadvantaged child at Oak School. There was no crash program to improve his reading ability, no special lesson plan, no extra time for tutoring, no trips to museums or art galleries. There was only the belief that the children bore watching, that they had intellectual competencies that would in due course be revealed. What was done in our program of educational change was done directly for the teacher, only indirectly for her pupils. Perhaps, then, it is the teacher to whom we should direct more of our research attention. If we could learn how she is able to effect dramatic improvement in her pupils' competence without formal changes in her teaching methods, then we could teach other teachers to do the same. If further research shows that it is possible to select teachers whose untrained interactional style does for most of her pupils what our teachers did for the special children, it may be possible to combine sophisticated teacher selection and placement with teacher training to optimize the learning of all pupils.

As teacher-training institutions begin to teach the possibility that teachers' expectations of their pupils' performance may serve as self-fulfilling prophecies, there may be a new expectancy created. The new expectancy may be that children can learn more than had been believed possible, an expectation held by many educational theorists, though for quite different reasons (for example, Bruner, 1960). The new expectancy, at the very least, will make it more difficult when they encounter the educationally disadvantaged for teachers to think, "Well, after all, what can you expect?" The man on the street may be permitted his opinions and prophecies of the unkempt children loitering in a dreary schoolyard. The teacher in the schoolroom may need to learn that those same prophecies within her may be fulfilled; she is no casual passer-by. Perhaps Pygmalion in the classroom is more her role.

Shaw's Summary

. . . You see, really and truly, apart from the things anyone can pick up (the dressing and the proper way of speaking, and so on), the difference between a lady and a flower girl is not how she behaves, but how she's treated. I shall always be a flower girl to Professor Higgins, because he always treats me as a flower girl, and always will; but I know I can be a lady to you, because you always treat me as a lady, and always will.

G. B. Shaw, *Pygmalion*

References

Bruner, J. S. *The process of education.* Cambridge, Mass.: Harvard University Press, 1960.

Hillson, H. T., and Florence C. Myers. *The demonstration guidance project: 1957–1962.* New York: New York City Board of Education, 1963.

Rivlin, H. N. *Teachers for our big city schools.* New York: Anti-Defamation League of B'Nai B'Rith, undated.

Rosenthal, R. *Experimenter effects in behavioral research.* New York: Appleton, 1966.

Wilson, A. B. Social stratification and academic achievement. In A. H. Passow (Ed.) *Education in depressed areas.* New York: Bureau of Publications, Teachers College, Columbia University, 1963. Pp. 217–235.

Discussion

A major part of a student's school experience is his relationship with teachers. As every student knows, how the teacher feels about you affects how pleasant or miserable school will be. While a child can count on his parents' admiration and affection much of the time, he may not receive the teacher's acceptance as readily. Teachers after all, have about thirty students in their charge. There are bound to be some children who lie in the periphery of their concern and others for whom teachers have little patience.

A teacher's feelings about a particular student are necessarily shaped by how the teacher perceives that student. Moreover, whether a teacher's perceptions will be positive or negative depends, in part, on how the student affects the teacher's work. If a student actively supports the teacher's efforts, his teacher will most likely view him in a positive light. Conversely, if a student opposes the teacher's objectives, his teacher will be inclined to ascribe negative qualities to him.

Kohl's reflections on his first days teaching in a Harlem classroom exemplify what I mean. He was concerned, as many beginning teachers are, that things go well and especially that the students like him. He did not recognize at first that his concern over gaining the students' acceptance was a response to fears of losing control. Students who did not want to work at all or conform in other ways to the norms of the classroom were especially threatening. By labeling them as defiant, unmanageable, or disturbed, Kohl could reject these students' claim on his attention and still preserve his self-image as a responsive teacher.

What characteristics teachers prefer in students are also influenced by teachers' expectations of what supports or obstructs their work. Feshbach's findings suggest that student teachers expect that independent, active, but nonconforming students will disrupt the classroom process and therefore, they prefer instead to have rigid, conforming, and orderly students. To support their preference, student teachers believe that assertive students will be less popular, generous, intelligent, and lower achieving than their conforming counterparts.

Of course, teachers can rarely request to have a student

removed from their class or to keep a student for another year. These wishes, nonetheless, might influence how teachers treat these students. Social psychologists have long held that how we perceive people affects how we behave toward them, but, as Feshbach wonders, perhaps a gap exists between the expressed feelings of teachers and their actual behavior. My study demonstrates, however, that experienced teachers express their attitudes toward students more often than not, despite strong pressures to hold back their feelings. They reveal them because they have little time to think before reacting in front of a class. The study also suggests that teachers do not dislike students simply because they place numerous demands on their time and energy. Much depends on the personal gratification they derive from their relationship with a student. For example, students who were of concern to teachers requested their attention as frequently as did students whom they rejected, but the demands of the former were considered more meaningful to teachers. This difference in perception led to vastly different classroom experiences for these two groups of students.

Teachers' views as to which students are gratifying to teach are influenced not only by the needs which arise for teachers in the classroom but also by the values they bring to it. Spindler's case study illustrates this point. The teacher he discusses developed favorable attitudes toward students who reinforced his own social-class values and aspirations and unfavorable attitudes toward those who threatened them. These attitudes, in turn, affected how he related to students. He actively facilitated the growth and development of those students to whom he was positively predisposed, but he was unfair and insensitive to students to whom he was negatively predisposed.

When teachers are differentially predisposed toward their students, they are apt to expect them to behave in ways which justify their predispositions. In a number of studies, Rosenthal has gathered evidence that expectations create self-fulfilling prophecies; that is, if a person is treated in a manner consistent with our expectations for him, he will act in such a way as to support our initial perceptions. The interesting thing about the study presented here by Rosenthal and Jacobson is that the specific expectation of intellectual gain altered not only students' intellectual performance but also, at least in the teacher's eyes, their intellectual curiosity, happiness, and need for social approval. In other words, a single teacher expectation can have widespread effects. One of the reasons, perhaps, that teacher expectations are so effective is their functional value to teachers. Holding differential expectations for students enables teachers to know where to place their efforts when their energies are at a premium. To believe, to use Kohl's example, that a student is unreachable, allows a teacher to give up trying to reach him.

Putting together the evidence, we find that students' psychological well-being in school is greatly affected by how teachers perceive them. Given the demands of their job, teachers protect themselves from being all things to all students by utilizing their values and attitudes to simplify the task of relating to many children. Some students, in the process, are lucky enough to have teachers who believe in them, care for them, and help them learn. The students who are the victims of teachers' biased vision, however, often receive less attention and concern. They, in turn, react to this neglect in ways which confirm and perpetuate their teachers' selective perception.

The problem of changing how teachers perceive their students is exacerbated by the categories used in schools to describe children. When students are viewed in terms of their IQ, achievement-test scores, social-class background, and conformity to classroom rules and procedures, the possibility that they will be stereotyped rather than seen as individuals is increased. All too frequently, these categories are merely used by teachers to make quick predictions about a child. If the predictions are negative, the temptation to ignore or reject him is great. Occasionally, teachers reveal instances in which they regretted the fast impression they formed of a child. After getting to know him, they had a richer view of the student as a person and were able to respond more warmly to him. Unfortunately, some children do not get a "second look" and even if they did, they may already have begun to act in ways which fulfill the teacher's initial expectations. What we need are conceptions of the teaching-learning process in which teachers would not have to depend so greatly on tight categories of perceiving children. If we had them, then teachers might be less influenced by these traditional indexes of what to expect from students and thus, more open to who they really are.

Part III

CROWDED CLASSROOMS

Inequalities
of Teacher-Pupil Contacts*

PHILIP W. JACKSON
HENRIETTE M. LAHADERNE

Elementary school classrooms are busy places, as every teacher who works in one knows. Activities stop and start, conversations wax and wane, minor crises come and go. The teacher moves about the room, from blackboard to desk, to supply closet, now talking to a group in front of the map, now pausing to quell a disturbance at the science table, now examining the work of a girl in the corner, now shaking his head at a boy on his way to the pencil sharpener. Bells ring, chalk breaks, books drop, and a small boy enters with an announcement that today there will be an indoor recess. Anyone witnessing such events for a considerable length of time is inevitably impressed, if not overwhelmed, by the variety of things going on in these densely populated hives of educational activity.

The purpose of this report is to describe and discuss one aspect of this business as it was observed in four sixth-grade classrooms. The observations focussed on the flow of communication between the teacher and individual students. Certain features of that flow are evident to even the most casual observer. For example, the teacher's communicative energies are spread about and, sooner or later, they touch all of his students. For a time he talks to Billy, then he turns to Sam, then to Sarah, then back to Billy, then on to Elaine, and so forth. Only slightly less obvious is the uneven distribution of these

* *Psychology in the Schools*, 4, 1967, 204–208. Reprinted by permission of the publisher and authors.

Expanded version of a paper read as part of a symposium entitled, "Observing in Schools: Studies of Classroom Life" at the American Psychological Association meetings in New York City, September 3, 1966.

energies throughout the class. Over a long period of time Billy may get more than his share of personal attention from the teacher, and Sarah less than her share. Another salient feature of these communications is that either the teacher or the student may initiate them. Moreover, some students speak to the teacher only when called on; others are incessant hand-wavers. Finally the careful observer may note that students differ not only in the total amount of attention, or communicative "bits," they receive from their teacher but also in the overall content of these interchanges. Some students talk about instructional matters more than do others; some receive more disciplinary messages than do most of their classmates. The aim of this study was to describe these apparent inequalities with greater precision than is possible through casual observation.

Method

The data were collected in four sixth-grade classrooms located in a predominantly white, working-class suburb. Two of the classrooms, each containing 34 pupils, were in one school; the other two, each containing 29 pupils, were in another school. Two of the four teachers were men and two were women. Pupil placement in the two schools was based solely on the student's place of residence. So far as could be determined by test results and observation, the pupil composition of each room was heterogeneous.

Visits to the classrooms began in late September and continued for two months. The length of the visits ranged from a half hour to a full day. During each visit periodic tallies of teacher-pupil communications were made along with other observations whose content is not relevant to this paper. When the visit lasted for an hour or longer, the communication tallies were spaced throughout that time in units of approximately twenty minutes each.

Cumulatively, the periods during which communication counts were taken averaged about nine-and-a-half hours in each room. The exact totals for the four classrooms were 9.0, 9.4, 9.7, and 10.2 hours. These totals comprised approximately 36 periods of tallying in each room. The observations were distributed over the entire school week and sampled all the activities of each room.

The observation schedule required an entry to be made on a tally sheet each time there was an intentional transmission of information between the teacher and an individual student. Messages directed to more than one student were ignored. The tally sheet was designed so that each entry designated (a) which student was involved in the communication; (b) whether the initiator of the message was the teacher or the student; and (c) whether the content of the message was primarily instructional, managerial, or prohibitory. Instructional messages were defined as those in which some reference was made to curriculum content or to the attainment of educational objectives. Managerial messages dealt with the interpretation of classroom rules and the definition of permissible behavior. Prohibitory messages dealt with keeping order and punishing misbehavior.

A major advantage of the observational technique, from the standpoint of the person using it, is its simplicity. The number of content categories are relatively few and fairly clear-cut. A second advantage is that it can be employed even when the precise content of the teacher's or student's remarks cannot be heard or when the communication is non-verbal. When a student approaches the teacher with an open workbook in his hand or when the teacher leans over the desk of a student to examine his seatwork, the observer is usually safe in classifying the interchange as instructional, even though the remarks are inaudible. Similarly, when a teacher snaps his fingers and points to a student across the room, the observer can be fairly certain that he is witnessing a prohibitory message even though no words are spoken. The ability to categorize messages that are only partially overheard or that do not entail words is particularly important in elementary classrooms where teachers and students are very mobile and where the occasion for certain messages recurs so frequently that their transmission becomes highly stylized and abbreviated.

Although the simplicity of the observational scheme is one of its chief advantages, it is also its major weakness. When the buzz of classroom talk is reduced to a set of hash marks clustered under three broad headings, the resultant picture reveals only the palest outline of the complex reality from which it was extracted. Instructional talk can be clear or confused, managerial messages can be consistent or inconsistent, disciplinary commands can be shouted or whispered. Under the present scheme all of this richness, which includes much of the information on which teacher evaluations are commonly based, is lost. It is true that all observational procedures succeed in capturing only a small fraction of the events to which they are applied, but the device employed here is perhaps a more ruthless filter than most.

Results

The choice of four classrooms at the same grade level and in the same community was designed to reduce the effect of grade level and social class variation. An eleven-year-old child in this community might have been assigned, by chance, to any one of the four rooms. What difference would the assignment make to the individual teacher-pupil contacts he would witness and participate in? A partial answer to that question is provided by the data in Table 1.

TABLE 1
Hourly Rates of Teacher-Pupil Interaction

CONTENT OF INTERACTION	CLASSROOM			
	A	B	C	D
Instructional	73	76	82	88
Managerial	24	9	8	12
Prohibitory	24	8	13	10
Total	121	93	103	110

The most obvious conclusion to be derived from Table 1 is that no matter in which room a student found himself he would discover his teacher to be busy talking to individual students. The number of hourly interchanges described in that table becomes even more impressive when it is recalled that communications with groups of students or with the entire class are not included in this summary. Here, incidentally, is one more scrap of evidence, if any more is needed, to explain why teachers are fatigued at the end of a working day.

Only slightly less obvious than the rapid rate of interaction is the fact that most of the four teachers' time is taken up in instructional interchanges. In other words, the teachers spend much energy communicating with individual students and most of that energy is spent talking about or listening to academic matters. Moreover, so far as the sheer frequency of instructional interchanges is concerned, it still does not seem to matter too much in which of the four classrooms an eleven-year-old lands. No matter where he goes he is apt to see his teacher talking with an individual student about an instructional matter slightly more often than once a minute.

The four rooms, however, no longer look alike when compared on hourly rates of managerial and prohibitory interchanges. Classroom A is noticeably different from the other three. Presumably a student in that room would witness or be involved in almost three times as many managerial interchanges as would, say, a student in Classroom C. He might also perceive three times as many disciplinary commands as might a student in Classroom B—the room directly across the hall.

Although they usually can be clearly differentiated by the observer, managerial and prohibitory messages have something in common. They both deal with the institutional workings of the classroom. They entail the expectations defining the rights and privileges of students and governing the flow of people and material in the room. In these terms, the teacher in Classroom A seemed to be much more involved in institutional matters than were his colleagues. This is not to say that such a difference in involvement is good or bad, only that it exists and seems pronounced enough to be noticed by a student moving from Classroom A to one of the other rooms.

Finally, in order to appreciate the size of the differences revealed in Table 1 it is necessary to recall that the numbers depicted there are hourly rates based on observations spanning a period of two months. If each of those rates were multiplied by the number of hours in a school year (approximately 1000), the absolute differences among the four classrooms would become quite striking. Thus, over the year a student in Classroom

A might witness as many as 16,000 more disciplinary messages than might a student in Classroom B. In Room A, when the teacher turns to a misbehaving student and says, "If I've told you once, I've told you a thousand times . . ." he probably means it. Admittedly, this kind of comparison is questionable because it assumes that the hourly rates hold throughout the year. Nonetheless, the projected yearly totals call attention to the cumulative significance of events that otherwise might pass unnoticed during a brief observation.

The data in Table 2 reveal who initiates the interchanges. The line showing the totals reveals that the flow of communication in these four classrooms is much more under the control of the teacher than of the students. Moreover, the hourly rate of initiated messages is fairly uniform for the four teachers. In each room the teacher sets into motion about 80 individual interchanges every hour.

TABLE 2
Hourly Interactions Initiated by Teachers and Pupils

| CONTENT OF INTERACTION | CLASSROOM | | | | | | | |
| | A | | B | | C | | D | |
	Teacher	Pupil	Teacher	Pupil	Teacher	Pupil	Teacher	Pupil
Instruction	49.0	24.0	67.0	8.0	67.0	15.0	56.0	32.0
Managerial	9.0	15.0	3.0	6.0	6.0	2.0	6.0	6.0
Prohibitory	23.7	0.3[a]	7.9	0.1	13.0	0.0	9.5	0.5
Total	81.7	39.3	77.9	14.1	86.0	17.0	71.5	38.5

[a] A pupil occasionally requested a teacher to discipline one of his classmates. This was the only way in which a pupil could initiate a prohibitory message.

Although the initiation rates are roughly equal for the four teachers, the rates for the students are not. In two of the classrooms, A and D, students are much more active in initiating messages than they are in the other two. Also, in Classrooms A and D the students directed unsolicited communications to their teacher two or three times as often as they did in Classrooms B and C. One gets the feeling that the teachers in rooms with high student initiation are kept more on the go, in the sense of being called on to respond to students' queries.

The subdivision of the interactions into the three categories

—instructional, managerial, and prohibitory—reveals further differences in the patterns of initiating messages. The rooms having high student initiation rates differ in the way students divide their energies between instructional and managerial matters. When students initiate contacts with the teacher in Classroom D they are more likely to deal with instructional affairs than is true in Classroom A. In the latter classroom, student queries more frequently have an institutional focus. Thus, although the teachers in both rooms seemingly deal with about the same number of students' requests every hour, the professional demands represented by those requests are noticeably different in the two settings.

The classroom differences revealed by this crude analysis are blurry, to be sure, but they are sufficiently clear to confirm what every school boy knows: the quality of school life depends partially on the particular room in which fate deposits him. In addition, the differences call attention to the institutional character of school life, a feature so pervasive that it is often overlooked. Classrooms may be designed for instructional ends, but much that goes on there has little to do with instruction per se. Furthermore, there seem to be real differences from room to room in the extent to which the institutional aspects of school are salient. In some rooms, if our data are to be believed, students seem to bang against the bars more than in others.

So far as total classroom experience is concerned it matters not only in which room a pupil is but also whether the pupil is a boy or a girl. Even with observational categories as broad as those employed in this study, there emerges a marked sex difference in teacher-pupil interaction. This difference is summarized in Table 3.

The percentages in Table 3 almost speak for themselves. They show, first, that though sex makes a difference in every classroom it does not always make the same difference. Second, they dramatically confirm the popular notion that boys are the major source of classroom misbehavior. Each of these findings deserves comment.

The least clear pattern of sex differences is seen in the findings on instructional messages. In Classrooms A and D, boys receive more than their share of such messages and in Classroom C, they receive less than their share. The boys in

Classroom B participate in a proportion of instructional interchanges commensurate with the size of their sub-group. Thus, at least with respect to this observational category there seems to be no sex difference that holds across all four classes. Yet the fact that three of the four percentages differ significantly from what might be expected by chance suggests that the sex of students is an important variable even though it may function differently from room to room.

TABLE 3
Percentages of Teacher-Pupil Interactions Involving Boys

CLASSROOM	PERCENTAGE OF MALE PUPILS	PERCENTAGE OF INTERACTIONS		
		Instructional	*Managerial*	*Prohibitory*
A	50.0	60.9[a]	61.6[a]	89.6[a]
B	58.8	61.2	75.0[b]	85.5[a]
C	44.8	36.4[a]	42.0	69.6[a]
D	44.8	61.0[a]	58.9[a]	90.1[a]

[a] $p < .01$.
[b] $p < .02$.

The percentages of managerial interchanges involving boys are somewhat more consistent than are those dealing with instructional matters. In three of the four classrooms boys are involved in noticeably more than their share of these interactions. Even in Classroom C, where they received proportionately fewer instructional interchanges than did girls, boys seem to hold their own when it comes to talking with the teacher about managerial affairs. Remembering what was said earlier about the institutional character of managerial communications, we might consider these percentages to mean that boys, more often than girls, are actively engaged in coping with the network of rules, regulations, and routines in which they are embedded as students.

The final set of differences in Table 3, involving the percentages of prohibitory messages, is clearest of all and leaves no doubt about this one aspect of classroom life. When these four teachers responded to instances of classroom misbehavior they were almost always reacting to a boy. This fact comes as no surprise but although the direction of the difference might have been easily predicted, the actual percentages are impressively large. The psychological significance of these differences becomes more evident when the percentages are transformed into the absolute number of prohibitory messages observed in the various rooms. In Classroom A, for example, the teacher delivers approximately 24 prohibitory messages every hour, or roughly 120 messages each day. About 108 of those daily messages are received by one or another of the 17 boys in that room.

Another aspect of the sex differences in teacher-pupil interaction is revealed in relationships observed among the three different message categories. These relationships are summarized in the form of correlation coefficients in Table 4. The correlations in that table show the communicative behavior of boys to be more of a piece, as it were, than is true for girls. Boys who are active in instructional interchanges tend also to be active in managerial interchanges and those same boys, it would seem, tend to have more than their share of disciplinary messages from the teacher. A similar phenomenon is not apparent for girls, and though it does seem to appear in the relationship between managerial and control messages, it is much less pronounced than is true for boys.

TABLE 4
Intercorrelations among Three Types of Teacher-Pupil Interactions

	INSTRUCTIONAL	MANAGERIAL	PROHIBITORY
Instructional		.41[a]	.43[a]
Managerial	.20		.66[a]
Prohibitory	.18	.29[b]	

	Correlations for girls below the diagonal	Correlations for boys above the diagonal	

[a] $p < .01$.
[b] $p < .05$.

The greater cohesiveness of the three types of interaction for boys was not predicted and, therefore, the reaction to it can only be speculative. If boys have as many brushes with teachers as the data indicate, the teachers may find it advantageous to sidestep as many open clashes as possible. Thus, they some-times might use instructional or managerial messages as pre-ventive measures for averting harsher and more disruptive in-terchanges. When a teacher calls on a boy whom he suspects of daydreaming or when he refuses to give a pupil permission to go to the pencil sharpener because of what he believes will happen on the way, he is using nonprohibitory messages for control puposes. Anyone who has ever watched teachers at work can doubtlessly offer many more examples of these some-what devious strategies. If these techniques were used fre-quently enough they would result in heightened correlations among the three interaction categories such as those appearing for the boys in Table 4.

In the final analysis, the quality of school life is determined not only by a pupil's sex or by what room he is in but also by what he is like as a person. Within each room and within each sex group there remain wide differences in the pattern of teacher-pupil interactions. Such differences only become dis-cernible when the descriptive unit is the individual student and his experience.

In each of the four classrooms one or two students have fewer than one interchange per hour with their teacher. At the other extreme a few students in each room have so many communications that, if the interactions were distributed equally throughout the day, these students would be in contact with their teacher every five or ten minutes. Unexpectedly, the totals for the least active students are strikingly similar for the four classrooms, whereas the totals for the most active students are markedly different from room to room. A plausible explana-tion for the differences between these two extremes is that some minimal level of interaction with the teacher is de-manded by the mere fact of membership in the class whereas the maximal number possible is more a function of the idiosyn-cratic matching of teachers and students.

The educational significance of these differences emerges when we imagine a classroom composed exclusively of either low-interacting or high-interacting students. If it were neces-sary for a teacher to interact with each student only once an hour, and if he maintained a "moderate" rate of interaction, that is, engaging in a hundred or so individual interactions each hour, he possibly could manage a class of a hundred or so students. Conversely, if a teacher had to interact with each student ten or twelve times an hour and he maintained the same rate of interaction, he could barely accommodate a dozen students in his class.

These extreme situations are no more than fanciful speculations, but they do lead to further thoughts about what life must be like in a regular classroom. For at least a few students, individual contact with the teacher is as rare as if they were seated in a class of a hundred or more pupils, even though there are actually only 30 or so classmates present. For others, the teacher's presence is the same as it might be if there were but a handful of classmates in the room. What does it mean, therefore, when we describe a child as being in a classroom of thirty pupils? Such a description does tell us how many people are present, but it tells very little about the social density of the child's psychological world and the relative saliency of his teacher in that world.

Discussion

The view of classroom activity provided by the observations is exceedingly narrow, but it was sufficient to direct attention to several important educational issues. These issues have been discussed partly in the presentation of results and now are briefly reviewed to bring them into sharper focus.

First, the data have shown how classrooms can be very different from one another even when described in ways that were not meant to underscore the differences. Moreover, the differences revealed by the findings are not easily placed on a continuum whose poles represent pedagogical vice and virtue. It is difficult to say, for example, whether a great number of managerial interchanges is a good or a bad thing, or whether it is better to have students or teachers initiate instructional interchanges. This ambiguity is tolerable so long as the differences described hold the promise of being related to the total quality of the student's experience in school—so long, in other words, as the differences cannot be brushed aside as psychologically trivial.

Second, the data have called attention to the institutional character of classroom life. Schools are places where large groups of people congregate and work together. Inevitably, a significant portion of the total energy required to operate a classroom is spent in the mundane business of managing the movement of social traffic and of responding to violations of institutional expectations. Perhaps these matters are incidental to the main business of teaching and learning, but psychologists in particular need no reminder that school has a greater impact on a student's total personality than an examination of textbooks and curriculum guides would have us believe. In addition to learning their ABC's children must learn to make their way in the social labyrinth of the school. The high frequency of managerial and control messages in the observations suggests how important, and possibly how tough, that learning can be.

Third, the findings support the commonly held belief that boys have a more difficult time in school than do girls. If control messages are treated as crude measures of that difficulty, these sixth-grade boys, as a group, have eight or ten times more trouble than do their female classmates. Although it is wrong to leap to the conclusion that the boys are miserable in school and girls wild about it, the experience of going to school is clearly very different for boys than for girls. Perhaps this fact is too well known to require further scrutiny, but the frequency with which sex is ignored in educational research would lead one to suspect otherwise.

Fourth, and finally, the findings reveal a range of individual differences in each classroom broad enough to weaken any hopes of making facile generalizations about what goes on there. In each classroom there are a few students who are almost out of the teacher's range of vision, so to speak, and a few others who are almost always underfoot. What this difference means and how it comes about is anybody's guess, but it is fair to conclude that by the end of the year some students likely will be more familiar to the teacher than will others, even though they have all lived together in the same room for about the same number of days. This observation calls into question the conventional view of looking upon each classroom as a unit whose participants have shared a common educational experience. In a sense, each classroom contains as many environments as it does pairs of eyes through which to view them.

Discipline and Group Management in Classrooms— An Excerpt*

JACOB S. KOUNIN

EDITOR'S NOTE: *This excerpt from Kounin's recent work summarizes the results of several years of research on classroom management. Kounin's findings reveal that "discipline problems" are often a result of the difficulties teachers face in managing crowded classrooms. He suggests that classroom involvement is influenced more by how a teacher organizes students for work than by how students are disciplined.*

The preceding researches were attempts to secure answers to a practical problem of classroom teachers—that of classroom discipline. How should a teacher handle a child who misbehaves? Since a classroom teacher must deal with a group, the question was rephrased to include the group effects of disciplinary actions. This was called the *ripple effect*. In what ways does a teacher's technique of handling a misbehaving pupil influence *other* pupils in the classroom?

The author would like to summarize what he has learned as a result of his efforts and of those of the many persons working with him. These learnings relate to research methodology as well as to the management of behavior in classrooms.

The first question raised was whether or not there is a ripple effect. Are students who are not targets of a disciplinary event affected by it? And if they are affected, in what ways are

* From *Discipline and Group Management in Classrooms* by Jacob Kounin. Copyright © 1970 by Holt, Rinehart and Winston, Inc. Reprinted by permission of Holt, Rinehart and Winston, Inc.

they affected? The second question is whether different qualities of teachers' desists produce different kinds of effects. For example, does a desist with anger have different ripple effects than a desist without anger? Preliminary studies gave affirmative answers to both of the above questions. Systematic observations conducted during the first week of kindergarten, and experiments with college, high school, and elementary school students *all* showed a ripple effect and *all* showed that variations in desist qualities produced different kinds of ripple effects. For example, in the Kindergarten Study, ripple effects were evidenced and were also influenced by the clarity, firmness, and anger of the teachers' desists. Desists with clarity produced more appropriate behavior and less deviancy on the part of audience children than desists without clarity. Desists with firmness produced the same ripple effects as did those with clarity but only for audience children who were themselves deviant or interested in deviancy at the time. Desists with anger and/or punitiveness produced work disruption and signs of emotional upset, but didn't change the conformity or deviancy of the audience children. We thus also learned that anger is not an intensification of firmness but that it is a different quality with different effects.

The results from the Kindergarten Study were not supported by a similar study conducted in a camp. There were no discernible ripple effects in camp—nor did variations in counselors' desist techniques make any difference in how audience campers reacted. (The only quality of a desist that made a difference was high attraction with novelty. If a counselor desisting Jim talked about a watermelon party, then John paid a little more attention to the desist event than he otherwise would. But John did not change his conformity or deviancy.)

The differences between the Kindergarten and Camp Studies were partly explained by the fact that these are different milieus. Interviews revealed that children have different concepts and concerns about misbehavior in camp, home, and school milieus. The kinds of misconducts they talk about for home, camp, and school are quite different. They also see different kinds of consequences for misconduct in camp, home, and school. Examples of some of the differences: Children are more preoccupied with breaking things at home than at school and are more concerned with rule violations at school than at home; there was more aggressivity in the camp misconducts than in the school misconducts. What is more, children perceive the roles of parents, teachers, and camp counselors in issues of misbehavior as quite different. Some of the differences are: Parents suffer (worry, have to pay repair bills) while teachers do not; parents are seen as punishing more severely and with more corporal punishment while teachers are seen as more inclined to explain realistic consequences.

Milieu differences are further apparent in the way children describe camp counselors and teachers. What they see as salient for one role is different from what they see as important for another. Camp counselors, for example, are perceived predominantly in terms of "gratuitous giver" (brings us candy) while teachers are rarely described in this dimension.

These findings taught us that studies of adult-child relationships, of which discipline is one facet, cannot be separated from the milieus in which they occur and the major roles of central adults in these milieus. An understanding of teacher-child relationships must be based upon research conducted with teachers in classroom settings. We are not justified in arriving at conclusions about teacher-child relationships in classrooms from studies conducted with parents in homes, counselors in offices, psychotherapists in clinics, or recreation leaders in recreation settings.

There were also differences between findings obtained from experiments in simulated classrooms and findings obtained from interviews and questionnaires conducted about real classrooms. In simulated classroom groups, or in actual classroom groups with an experimental teacher conducting the classroom for the first time, different desist techniques *did* produce different ripple effects. For example, task-focused desists ("You can't learn if you play with paper clips") produced more favorable ripple effects than approval-focused techniques ("I don't like children who play with paper clips").

In contrast, interviews conducted with high school students about their actual classrooms showed that qualities of desist techniques did *not* relate to ripple effects. Ripple effects *were* related to students' degree of motivation to learn the subject being taught and to their liking for the teacher. The prevailing variable of motivation was related to task-connected ripple effects such as inclination to behave better after a desist directed at another. The prevailing variable of liking for the teacher predicted to ripple effects related to evaluative judgments of the teacher, such as fairness. These prevailing variables or commitments did *not* correlate with ripple effects in experiments.

The contrast between the results obtained from the interviews and those obtained from the experiments provided another learning. We learned that the commitments of a subject in an experiment are different from the kinds of commitments that develop in real life situations. We also learned that simulated conditions may teach us something about the psychology of first impressions. These initial perceptions and reactions may be quite different from the perceptions and reactions to similar events in ongoing real situations.

These learnings about the qualities and determinants of ripple effects led us to utilize a more ecologically oriented approach to the study of classroom management. We decided to accumulate video-tapes of naturally occurring classrooms. This was done more in a spirit of inquiry to see what we could learn than in a spirit of debate to see what hypothesis we could test. Videotapes would enable us to study what was occurring and not merely what was perceptually outstanding, interesting, or in line with some existing hypotheses. Moreover, they could be replayed over and over and thus enable the measurement of many different coexisting variables as well as variables not thought of at the time of data gathering.

An analysis of the desist events observed in the videotaped classrooms showed that the qualities of desists bore *no* relationship to children's reactions. The finding of no relationship between teachers' desist techniques and the behavior of children held for the immediate reaction of children to specific desists, as well as for the overall amount of deviancy and deviancy-contagion present in a classroom.

This latter learning involved unlearning on my part, in the sense of having to replace the original question by other questions. Questions about disciplinary techniques were eliminated and replaced by questions about classroom management in general. The variable of work involvement was added to the variable of deviancy. And preventing misbehavior was given higher investigative priority than handling misbehavior.

Accordingly, all classrooms were scored for work involvement and deviancy. Classroom management was defined as dealing with the surface behavior of children as measured by overt signs of work involvement and by deviancy. What is it that teachers do that correlates with these behaviors?

Some dimensions of teacher style were measured that correlated significantly with children's behavior in learning settings. These were:

1. *Withitness* and *overlapping*. These dimensions deal with a teacher's communicating that she knows what is going on regarding children's behavior and with her attending to two issues simultaneously when two different issues are present.

2. *Smoothness* and *momentum*. These parameters measure how the teacher manages movement during recitations and at transition periods.

3. *Group alerting* and *accountability*. These aspects of a teacher's technique deal with the extent to which she maintains a group focus during recitations in contrast to becoming immersed in a single child.

4. *Valence* and *challenge arousal*.

5. *Seatwork variety* and *challenge*. This dimension deals with the teacher's programming learning activities with variety and intellectual challenge, especially in seatwork settings.

The magnitude of the correlations between the above dimensions of teacher style and children's behavior depends upon whether one is dealing with the deviancy or work involvement of the children, or with recitation or seatwork as learning settings within the classroom.

It is possible, then, to delineate concrete aspects of teacher behavior that lead to managerial success in a classroom. These techniques of classroom management apply to emotionally disturbed children in regular classrooms as well as to nondisturbed children. They apply to boys as well as to girls. (We found no consistent differences between boys and girls in behavior scores, nor did we find that scores for managerial success correlated with the boy-girl ratios of the classrooms studied.) These techniques of classroom management apply to the group and not merely to individual children. They are techniques of creating an effective classroom ecology and learning milieu. One might note that none of them necessitate punitiveness or restrictiveness.

This focus upon group managerial techniques in classrooms is intended to go beyond simplified slogans such as "create rapport" or "make it interesting." Neither does this focus entail a preoccupation with such characteristics as "friendly," "warm," "patient," "understanding," "love for children," and similar attributes of people in general. These desirable attributes will not manage a classroom. Rather, the business of running a classroom is a complicated technology having to do with developing a nonsatiating learning program; programming for progress, challenge, and variety in learning activities; initiating and maintaining movement in classroom tasks with smoothness and momentum; coping with more than one event simultaneously; observing and emitting feedback for many different events; directing actions at appropriate targets; maintaining a focus upon a group; and doubtless other techniques not measured in these researches.

The mastery of classroom management skills should not be regarded as an end in itself. These techniques are, however, necessary tools. Techniques are enabling. The mastery of techniques enables one to do many different things. It makes choices possible. The possession of group management skills allows the teacher to accomplish her teaching goals—the absence of managerial skills acts as a barrier.

The focus upon group management skills is not opposed to a concern for individual children. The mastery of group management actually enables the teacher to program for individual differences and to help individual children. If there is a climate of work involvement and freedom from deviancy, different groups of children may be doing different things, and the teacher is free to help individual children if she so chooses.

One might say that a mastery of group management techniques enables a teacher to be free from concern about management.

Realities of Teaching—
An Excerpt[*]

RAYMOND S. ADAMS
BRUCE J. BIDDLE

EDITOR'S NOTE: *This excerpt from* Realities of Teaching *by Adams and Biddle discusses the implications of a study in which thirty-two videotaped lessons were analyzed. Sixteen classrooms in highly rated schools were used. Grades I, VI, and XI were represented in the sample. Among the important findings of the study were: Whole class activities took place 85 percent of the time; the teacher was the principal actor in 84 percent of the communication episodes taped; and less than one-half of 1 percent of the time was spent on matters dealing with feelings and interpersonal relationships.*

These last paragraphs have been concerned with some of the specifics of everyday interaction—the regular patterns of behavior that exist in the classroom. Sociologists use the term "norm" to account for patterns of behavior that persist over time. Some of the behaviors we discovered could be explained in this way. For instance, there is apparently one "norm" operating to keep the front of the room sacred to teachers. There is another that serves to limit, if not prohibit, private exchanges in the classroom, and so on. Sociologists use the term "norm" to account for patterns of behavior that persist over time. Some of the behaviors we discovered could be explained in this way. For instance, there is apparently one "norm" operating to keep the front of the room sacred to teachers. There is another that serves to limit, if not prohibit, private exchanges in the classroom, and so on. Sociologists also use the term "value" to indicate that lying behind the norm there is a belief that behaving in this particular way is "good" (or "bad"). Up to this point in the discussion we have not been particularly concerned with the values that lie behind and buttress the behavior of teachers and their pupils, but we would be remiss if we neglected them completely.

There are in fact two ways to look at values. First they can be seen as *stated values*: things people tell you they hold dear. Second they can be seen as *implicit values*: something an observer infers is valued because it seems to be implied logically by what people do. The first kind of value can only be discerned by asking people to tell about it. The other kind of value, as an inference made about behavior, can be discerned without knowing what the actors themselves think. For example, an observer could see pupils being treated harshly and infer that the teacher valued toughness, authoritarianism, or adult domination, whether or not the teacher reported these values in an interview.

Because we did not ask teachers or children what their values were, we can say nothing about the beliefs that they hold. However, as interpreters we can conjecture about the values implied in their behavior. In doing so we shall confine our attention to one particular issue only, an issue which has been disputed philosophically for over two thousand years— the relating of the individual to his society.

Each child, the psychology books tell us, is a unique individual; yet our society has been branded a conforming one. We might ask then, what sort of uniqueness is valued in classrooms today? Our findings hint that the answer appears to be, paradoxically, individualism-in-conformity or, to put it in the terms of a wartime English ballad,

> You can do as you ruddy well like,
> So long as you do what you're told.

If individuality is valued in the classroom, it is valued privately. For public purposes, idiosyncratic individualism is frowned upon. The individual effort that gets commended is the one that is worthy of *all* pupils to be believed, and ergo, copies. Furthermore the range of behavior within which individuality may express itself is notoriously small. The social behaviors that may be manifested in the classroom are remarkably limited, remarkably confined. Task behaviors predominate; they consume most time, they demand most attention. It follows then that if task behaviors are defined exactly and prescribed exactly (after the fashion of programmed learning) individuality can only be manifested to the extent that pupil *A* gets further in the program than does pupil *B*. If task is defined in terms of knowing facts, then individuality can be manifested only to the extent that pupil *A* knows and pupil *B* does not know. Similarly if task is defined as understanding, we can only distinguish between individuals according to the extent of their understandings.

Now it might be claimed that the argument above begs the question and that what individuality really means is that pupils learn differently—it is the *process* of gaining facts and coming to understand that calls for the recognition of individuality, not the end product. We may accept this caveat momentarily although we reject its basic premises. If children learn differently we should expect to see recognition of this within the classroom situation. On the evidence of our study this is not the case. The predominance of the central system and the utilization of large audiences suggest that a pupil is a pupil is a pupil. It appears to be that feedback from any individual pupil is nearly always treated as representative of all pupils.

Given the organizational structure of schools, and the allocation of numbers of pupils to one teacher, it is difficult to see a way out of the impasse. Of course, individualized instruction purports to provide one solution to the learning process problem. However, as we saw, the end result of individualized task programs is either conformity or differential achievement. Is there some other way then in which individuality can be nurtured and expressed within the task domain? In order to attempt to answer this question, it is necessary to make a distinction between two concepts, education and training.

One of the insistent facts of life is that people have to be trained in order to be employed. Furthermore, increasing

knowledge and increasing population demands that this training should be more intensive and more specific. It follows that
anyone being prepared for a job needs an increasingly elaborate but *defined* set of appropriate prior experiences. Our
problems of accommodating individuality then might be met
by insuring that specialization proliferates and that each person is prepared for his specialist niche. To this extent training
is the appropriate kind of learning experience. However, vocational preparation does not constitute the sole function of today's schools. Schools, we are told, are supposed to produce
citizens who are sane, socially responsible, moral, and humane.
It could be argued that the training orientation is appropriate
to accomplish these purposes too, but such a prospect smacks
of "1984." Presumably, social responsibility is more than a
conditioned reflex. Presumably, morality is a reflection of
choice not an abrogation of it. Presumably, humanity is a
value manifested through conviction not habit. For these,
training is not enough; education is necessary.

We are forced then to ask two questions. First, what sort of
socialization process is already proceeding in classrooms? Second, what kind of classroom conditions would permit education, rather than training, to proceed? We shall take these
issues in order.

In the classrooms of our study, societal needs have appeared to prevail over individual needs. Effort is expended—
and successfully too—to ensure that pupils maintain the peace,
respect others, protect property, and strive for public approval. Considerable effort goes into inducting pupils into the
classroom society. At Grade I, in particular, the recognition of
what constitutes appropriate and inappropriate behavior is an
important part of the training process. It is still important in
Grade VI, but by Grade XI it has become a matter of little
consequence, at least as far as the expenditure of time is concerned.

What constitutes approved social behavior in the classroom? An observer might be excused if he imagined that *quietness* and *orderly behavior* were two predominant values. He
might even hazard a guess as to why these values predomi-
nated. For instance, if they liked, thirty pupils could generate
quite an amount of noise, certainly enough to distract each
other and possibly enough to distract other classes. The doubt

that the observer might have, however, is how functional or useful such values are from the point of view of other educational objectives. For instance, do requirements of this sort help or hinder creativity, intellectual enterprise, or social maturity? The observer might also wonder at the educational relevance of *waiting*—another phenomenon apparently valued in the classroom. He might also wonder why activity was not valued more. If he had read Dewey he might ask, whatever happened to "learning through doing"? Again he might wonder at the *dominance of the teacher,* and how and to what extent the rules acceptable to the teacher become acceptable to the child. Assuming that responsibility is something that is supposed to transfer to occasions beyond the classroom, he might also wonder how the "model" exhibited in the classroom can be used. For instance, having learned responsibility by fiat at school, are adults supposed to find authority figures that will in effect substitute for the teacher?

Assuming, then, that quietness, orderly behavior, waiting, and teacher dominance appear to be values reflected in today's classroom, what ideal classroom conditions would permit education rather than training to be pursued? At the risk of inviting a highly charged (but polemical) argument, the distinction between training and education is seen by us as the difference between *specifically* functional behavior and *generally* functional behavior. Training, in other words, tends to have a more limited reference. One can be trained to write, to ride a bicycle, to apply mathematical formulas, to perform a profession, and so on. What is characteristic of all these trainings is that there are known and specified "right" ways of doing these things. Presumably such skills do not transfer. One cannot draw because one has been trained to write, or ride a horse because one has been trained to ride a bicycle, or perform as an educational philosopher because one has been trained as an admiral.

However, there are certain functions that can be performed because of prior experience. We can learn Spanish (a little) better through having learned another foreign language. Knowledge of mathematics does help the novitiate statistician. The typist can become a card puncher relatively easily, and so on. Transfer in cases like these can result from two processes. Either the components of the activities are very similar so that little adaptation is needed, or else general principles relevant in the first instance are also relevant in the second. It is the latter of these two cases that determines the difference between education and training. Education as it is being used here refers to the ability to recognize such common elements and act accordingly. Obviously the greater the range of situations that can be covered by the material learned, the better the education.

In order to ensure breadth of education, two conditions need to be met, and only one of these is in the hands of the teachers. First of all, the "essence" or "general principles" of any defined field of study have to be discerned and made explicit. This is a job for subject-matter specialists.[1] Second, the teaching-learning transaction has to be conducted in such a way that knowledge is seen as generalizable, that is in such a way that transfer from one situation to another is apparent. It is not within the scope of this present discussion to elaborate in detail the ways in which this may be accomplished. However, in general terms, questioning and querying are both conducive to knowledge transfer. Again, divergent thinking— conjecture over "what if . . ." is likely to aid the process. Trying to encourage "mental leaps" to relate apparently different phenomena seems useful too. In other words, when task performance is extended to beyond knowing and even beyond understanding to general principles and laws, and when these principles and laws are seen as potentially useful beyond the specific situations in which they were invoked, then task converts from training to education.

In the discussions so far we have slipped easily from references to subject matters to references to socialization. This was deliberate because both are seen in the same way. Both have appropriate and defined behaviors that can demonstrate mastery. Both have specified contents, and both can be subjected to continuous question, evaluation, and reformulation. This last point has led us to wonder about the social situation of the contemporary classrooms. Our data showed that at Grade I children were "trained" to obey the rules. At Grade VI, they discussed the rules and rationalized them but at Grade XI, the

---

[1] Some of the new developments in mathematics and science proceed on the basis of this assumption.

matter was of no moment. If the classroom is supposed to be society in miniature, then what has happened to democracy? Why are pupils and teachers not constantly concerned with matters of social moment in the classrooms? It seems almost as if the pupils have deferred their involvement in this social situation in the anticipation that "sit in's," "love in's," and "protest" will give them their day of retribution later.

Varieties of Constraint
in a Nursery School*

PHILIP W. JACKSON
BERNICE J. WOLFSON

The difficulties young children encounter in nursery school are a natural source of concern to parents and teachers alike. In addition, these early experiences are of great interest to many others who are professionally engaged in the study of human development. Understandably, therefore, several investigators have sought to learn more about the discomfort associated with early school attendance and the conditions surrounding its occurrence (Swift, 1964). To date, however, studies in this area have been focused on fragmented aspects of the problem —on the difficulties connected with the child's separation from his parents (Heinicke, 1956) and on the description and treatment of acts of aggression between children (Appel, 1942; Muste & Sharpe, 1947; Body, 1955).

Although these episodes of severe stress and of interpersonal conflict are surely among the more dramatic happenings to be witnessed in a nursery school, they are by no means the only events that interfere with the natural flow of desire in the preschool environment. To reach a fuller understanding of the demands of school life, particularly as they are experienced by the very young, it is necessary to consider the minor upsets as

* Reprinted with permission from *Young Children*, Vol. XXIII, No. 6, September 1968. Copyright © 1968, National Association for the Education of Young Children, 1834 Connecticut Avenue, N.W., Washington, D.C. 20009.

Based upon research pursued under the auspices of the Early Education Research Center, a component of the National Laboratory on Early Childhood Education, supported by U.S. Office of Education.

well as the major traumata to which the inhabitants of class-rooms fall victim.

With this necessity in mind, the present study was designed to provide as broad a view as was possible of the constraints encountered by 97 three- and four-year-old children attending a relatively "traditional" nursery school. The major question underlying the investigation was simply: How often do these children undergo experiences that might be interpreted as disruptive or as interfering with the natural pursuit of their desires? Closely related to this question was the goal of developing a taxonomy that would serve to categorize the observed phenomena. The customary search for sex and age differences and for interaction effects was also undertaken.

Method

Setting

The observations were collected in the University of Chicago Laboratory Nursery School, which is housed in two adjacent three-storied buildings that were once private dwellings. The school enrolls 100 pupils and is in session on weekday mornings from 9 a.m. to noon. Six senior teachers and ten assistants comprise the instructional staff, giving the school a pupil/teacher ratio of about 6 to 1. The staff and students are divided into four units, each occupying one complete floor in one of the two buildings. Everyone shares a common playground as well as some of the third-floor rooms and basement areas. The enrollment in each unit is determined by the physical space available on each floor of the buildings. The smallest of the four units contains one senior teacher, two assistants, and 19 pupils; the largest contains two senior teachers, three assistants, and 34 pupils. Despite differences in total number, the pupil/teacher ratio in all four units is approximately equal.

The school is well equipped with the standard materials found in nursery school settings. In each unit small toys, blocks, puzzles and art materials are in abundance. The outdoor playground contains several pieces of climbing apparatus, slides, and wheel toys, as well as areas for digging, planting and sand play.

Program

The daily activities in each unit are under the direction of the senior teachers and, as a result, they vary somewhat from one unit to the next. Throughout the school, however, much time is spent in "free play" and most of the pupils spend at least an hour outdoors when the weather permits. In some of the units more emphasis is placed on group activities, such as singing, dancing, and story-telling, than in others, but these differences are not quickly noticeable to a casual visitor. In none of the units is there a systematic attempt to teach the basic skills of reading or arithmetic to the children. In contrast with the recent emphasis on cognitive training to be found in some nursery schools, the program at the University of Chicago Laboratory Nursery School, might best be described as "traditional." To the extent that the educational goals of socialization and intellectual mastery can be distinguished, the focus in this school is decidedly more on the former than on the latter.

Subjects

The children attending this nursery school are drawn predominantly from middle-class and upper middle-class families having some connection with the University of Chicago, either as faculty members or as fulltime staff. Typically, pupils enter the school at three years of age and remain for two years before being transferred to the kindergarten. The total population of the school contains about equal numbers of three- and four-year-olds, as does the composition of pupils within each unit. Although no intelligence test scores were available for these students, former graduates of the nursery school who were tested in the early elementary grades are reported to have an average IQ slightly above 120. There is no reason to believe that the present population differs significantly in intellectual ability from those who have previously attended the school.

Observations

The observational technique, developed by the authors, consisted of watching each child for a series of two-minute periods and recording any events that might be interpreted as interfering with the natural pursuit of the child's desire. The details of the procedure were as follows. Observers were scheduled to work in a unit beginning at a specified hour of the morning—9, 10 or 11 o'clock. Before the observer began his work, he was given a clipboard to which were attached, in alphabetical order, the names of all the pupils in the unit, listed separately by sex. The order of the lists was systematically altered so that sometimes boys' names came first and sometimes girls'. A stop watch was also attached to the board. When the observer entered the unit, he located the first child on his list, started the stopwatch and observed from a convenient position for two minutes, after which he moved on to the next child on the list. He continued in this manner until all the children in the unit had been observed. Absentees were re-scheduled for observation at the assigned times when they returned to school.

During each two-minute observation the observer recorded the activities in which the child was engaged—using a letter code referring to 29 categories. If the child under observation encountered any experience that might be interpreted as interfering with the natural flow of his activity, the observer wrote a brief description of the episode in the space beside the child's name. When he finished observing all of the children in the unit, the observer dictated a full account of each episode he had witnessed—identifying the child, the unit, the time of day, and the activity in which the child was engaged at the time. These dictaphone recordings were then transcribed, one episode to a card, in preparation for coding and analysis. All of the observers took part in a series of training sessions with the authors before the data collection began.

Each child was observed three times a morning—once during each hour between 9 and 10, 10 and 11, and 11 and 12 o'clock—for an entire week. In this way, 15 two-minute observations were obtained for every child in the school. Three children left the school during the period of observation and were deleted from the sample, leaving 97 children (50 boys, 47 girls) for whom the observations were complete.

Coding of Protocols

Seven categories, derived from a pilot study, were used in coding the observed episodes. The categories and their definitions were as follows.

Desire vs. Desire. These are episodes in which the child's pursuit of his desire is interfered with by the desire of another child. A typical instance is one in which two children are struggling over the ownership of a toy, although visible signs of a struggle need not appear. The essential condition is that a child's ongoing activity is in some fashion disrupted by the desire of another child. The following two episodes are illustrative.

Subject 18 was operating a lift-ladder on the fire engine and another boy put the fireman figure in the machine. Subject 18 stopped the push button mechanism and shouted, "Get that off!"

Subject 07 was sitting on a bar. Another child came along and tried to push her off. She cried.

Desire vs. teacher expectation. The source of interference in these episodes is the action of a teacher. A typical instance involves the child who is told to discontinue an activity because it conflicts with the teacher's personal standard of acceptable behavior. However, not all of these encounters involve specific prohibitions. For example, a child whose teacher coaxes him to leave the block area and to participate in a singing group might not have been told explicitly that he could not continue playing with the blocks. Nonetheless, his actions have been disrupted by the teacher's wishes. The following two episodes are illustrative.

Subject 24 wanted to get a toy from inside the basement but the teacher said, "No, you cannot go down there now."

Subject 10 was coloring with crayons when the teacher came along and said, "Look at all those crayons under your chair! George and Julie, clean up the crayons under your chairs, please."

Desire vs. inability. These are episodes in which the child's desire to do something is frustrated by his lack of ability. A typical instance involves the child who is trying to lift an object that is too heavy for him, or to operate a piece of equipment, such as a typewriter or a camera, without success. Success following moderate perseverance would not be classified in this category, but success requiring the intervention of an adult would be. The following two episodes are illustrative.

When he was undressing, subject 14 said, "I need some help getting this off," meaning his snow pants. The teacher helped him, then he wandered off.

Subject 10 was trying to climb on a chair that was mostly buried in snow against the wall of the playyard. She couldn't seem to get up on the chair without falling and finally stopped trying.

Desire vs. teacher overlook. This category includes episodes in which the teacher does not respond to the child's request for help or attention. A typical instance involves the child who wants to show the teacher something and she ignores him, either because she has not heard his request or because she is busy doing something else. If the teacher acknowledges the child's appeal and responds to it after only a few seconds delay, the episode is not classified. The following two episodes are illustrative.

Subject 03 picked up a picture and said, "Teacher, teacher." But the teacher did not hear and left the room.

Subject 19 asked if he could bring a cooky home. He asked this of the teacher three times. She gave no answer. She was busy talking to children across the table.

Desire vs. clutter, crowds. These episodes include those in which the child is jostled by his classmates or by adults without any apparent intention on their part to disrupt his activity. A typical instance involves the child who is assembling a jigsaw puzzle on the rug area when suddenly a passerby inadvertently scatters the pieces. The pushing and shoving that occur when several children are trying to look at a small object would also be included among these episodes. The following two episodes are illustrative.

The teacher was helping subject 28 take off her coat and another girl was in the way. Subject 28 pushed the girl aside, and said, "No."

Subject 17 was trying to explain something to a boy who was sitting across the table from him. The boy couldn't hear because there were two or three children between them talking. Subject 17 repeated the same phrase four times, each time getting louder, and the girl sitting between them was talking across the table and her voice was getting louder and louder too.

Desire vs. environmental limitation. These episodes include those in which the child expresses a desire for something that is not available. A typical instance involves the child who asks for more crackers during the juice period and there are no more to be had. Episodes are included under this category even when suitable substitutes for the desired object are found. The following two episodes are illustrative.

Subject 14 wanted to check out a book. The teacher told her to look for her card but the child could not find it.

Subject 12 asked, "Where are the marbles?" He had the box in which he usually found them. The teacher said, "I think someone took them home." Subject 12 wandered around seemingly looking for something to do.

Desire vs. institutional restriction. During these episodes a child's activity is disrupted by the teacher, not because of her personal beliefs about what should be going on, but because the institutional operation of the school demanded it. A typical instance is one in which the teacher tells the child to discontinue an activity because it is time for his bus to depart. The following two episodes are illustrative.

The teacher announced during the sand-play, "Mary, it's almost time to go home now. Go see if you have anything to take home." Subject 04 dutifully responded but her activity at the sand was interrupted by the teacher's announcement.

Subject 12 shouted out loud, "I want to play this." The teacher said, "It's time to get your coat on." He moved toward the door.

These seven categories encompass almost all of the interferences found during the pilot study. An eighth category, labeled, "Ambiguous," was added to make the system exhaustive and to provide an estimate of the total coverage of the first seven categories.

The protocols were coded by the authors and an assistant who had also served as one of the observers.[1] A set of 30 protocols were coded independently by the three judges. The amount of agreement between pairs of judges was found to be over 90 percent. For the final analysis each protocol was coded independently by two judges. The few disagreements that occurred were later reconciled in a joint meeting.

[1] The authors wish to thank Joan Bradbury for her assistance in coding the protocols. We are also grateful to David Wiley for his help in planning the statistical analysis of the data.

Results

Because the overall purpose of the study was to estimate the frequency of constraints in the life of a nursery school child, the gross statistics for the total sample are of paramount importance. In all, 587 episodes involving constraint were observed during approximately 48 hours of observation. This figure must be interpreted in the context of the specific procedures employed in the study.

One way of understanding this total frequency is by using it to estimate how many constraining episodes would have been observed if all the children had been looked at for only one minute, instead of 30. Assuming an even distribution of these experiences over time, we would expect to witness 1/30 of 587, or about 20 constraining episodes in a group of 97 children every minute of the day. If we also assumed that these experiences were randomly distributed among the children, (a less tenable assumption, to be sure), we would expect to find each child undergoing such an experience about once every five minutes. If we were to add to the frequency of personal experiences those that were merely witnessed by the children, the prominence of constraining episodes in the life of the nursery school child would, of course, be greatly increased.

Another way of coming to grips with the meaning of these data is to ask what they would lead us to expect if the amount of observation were much greater than the limits of the study allowed. Suppose, for example, every child had been observed for a full morning instead of for 30 minutes. Based on the total of 587 constraints in a half-hour of observation, we would expect to witness approximately 3,500 constraining experiences in this nursery school every morning. If it were possible to observe all subjects for a full year, the expected frequency would come close to 64,000 constraining episodes.

Whichever way we look at it, constraining episodes of one sort or another appear to be a commonplace feature of nursery school life, at least in the particular school under investigation. To move beyond this generalization, it is necessary to look more closely at the way in which these 587 episodes were distributed among the children and within the category system used to organize them.

A child at the median of the group of 97 children was observed to experience five constraints during one half hour of observations. The bottom 10 percent of the sample appears to have encountered two or fewer such experiences during the time in question, whereas the top ten percent underwent nine or more. The range of these frequencies indicates that few children, if any, were observed to go along completely unruffled during the entire set of observation. Conversely, an equally small number seemed to have been disrupted during each of the 15 two-minute periods. Moreover, the relative smoothness of the frequency curve does not reveal any sharp breaks between those who undergo a small number of these experiences and those who undergo many. Apparently, life proceeds more smoothly for some than for others, but the differences among children are more continuous than discrete.

Gross differences in the frequency of these events among the students were not related to sex or to age, nor did it seem to matter in which of the four units of the school the student was observed. The average number of constraints was 6.4 for the boys (with a standard deviation of 3.2) and 5.6 for the girls (with a standard deviation of 2.9). This difference was not statistically significant. The distribution of constraints across four age groups of the children is shown in Table 1. It is obvious, by inspection, that the total number of constraints is divided among the age groupings in almost exactly the same proportions as their representativeness in the total sample would lead us to expect.

TABLE 1
Distribution of Constraints among Four Age Groups

AGE GROUP	PERCENT OF SAMPLE	PERCENT OF CON- STRAINTS	DIFFERENCE
4-7 and older	31	32	−1%
4-1 to 4-6	26	25	+1%
3-7 to 4-0	29	30	−1%
3-6 and younger	14	13	+1%
Total	100	100	

The failure to find significant age differences is doubly significant because of the close relationship between age and years of school attendance. Almost all of the children four years of age and older were in their second year of nursery school at the time the observations were collected; whereas all those below age four were in their first year of school. Thus, it appears that neither age nor exposure to a nursery school environment significantly affects the number of constraints a young child will experience. At least insofar as these minor abrasions are concerned, school life does not seem to become easier for the more experienced. Of course, it is possible that the older children are more adroit in their handling of these mishaps, even though they experience them as frequently as do their younger classmates.

The distribution of the 587 constraining experiences within the eight categories is shown in Table 2. The categories in that table are arrayed in descending order of the proportion of events each contains. The percentages in Table 2 reveal that slightly more than half of all the constraining episodes involved some kind of a direct confrontation between the child and one of his classmates or the child and his teacher. These two categories, desire vs. desire, and desire vs. teacher expectation, occurred frequently enough to be experienced by each child about once every ten minutes throughout the school day. Apparently, nursery school is a place where people interfere with each other's activities much of the time.

TABLE 2
Distribution of Types of Constraining Experiences

TYPE	FREQUENCY	PERCENT
Desire	183	31.2
Teacher expectation	148	25.2
Inability	82	14.0
Teacher overlook	79	13.4
Clutter, crowds	28	4.8
Environmental limitation	23	3.9
Institutional restriction	23	3.9
Ambiguous	21	3.6
Total	587	100.0

But, as the percentages in Table 2 also indicate, the mere presence of other people is not sufficient to account for all of the abrasiveness of nursery school life. These figures tell us that almost once every half hour the nursery school child can be observed to be trying to do something that he is unable to do (desire vs. inability) and almost as frequently he can be found to be calling for adult help or attention without receiving it (desire vs. teacher overlook). In this crowded environment it is apparently possible to be quite alone with one's difficulties. Paradoxically, the presence of others may help to create these moments of individual helplessness, for the demands on the teacher often exceed her ability to satisfy them.

One way of rearranging the categories in Table 2 is by grouping together those that involve the intrusion of others into the child's private life space (desire vs. desire, desire vs. teacher expectation, desire vs. clutter, crowds, and desire vs. institutional expectations), and contrasting them with those that depict the child's encounter with personal or environmental limitation (desire vs. inability, desire vs. teacher overlook, desire vs. environmental limitation). Percentages of constraining experiences in these two groups are shown in Table 3. Percentages in that Table do not equal 100 because the category of "Ambiguous" has been omitted.

TABLE 3
Distribution of Two Major Classes of Constraining Experiences

CLASS	FREQUENCY	PERCENT
Invasion of personal life space	382	65.1
Encounters with personal and environmental limitations	184	31.4
Total	566	96.5

The numbers in Table 3 reveal that the children in the sample experienced intrusions into their personal life space about twice as often as they experienced encounters with personal or environmental limitations. In other words, the dominant form of constraint in the nursery school, at least in quantitative terms, seems to be that of having one's activities interfered with by someone else. Of greater relevance, however, than the relative frequency of these two classes of events (because both are present in abundance) is the difference in the strategies of adaptation each is likely to elicit.

When the desires of others intrude upon us the ensuing situation has combative overtones. The concepts of assault, defense, escape, surrender, and retreat are useful in describing what happens in these situations. The underlying range of accommodation extends from acquiescence to counter-aggression. Either implicitly or explicitly, these situations revolve around the fundamental ideas of ownership, competition, and individual rights. Almost invariably they concern a moral question. As experiences they are usually encountered abruptly and entail an interruption of an on-going activity.

In contrast to what happens during these transitory moments of invasion, the situation that ensues when we encounter our own shortcomings and those of our environment is of quite a different type. Under such circumstances the strategies of defense, retreat and surrender are of less relevance than are notions of dependency, rationalization, and control. The underlying range of adaptations extends from resignation to perseverance and does not contain the elements of interpersonal hostility characterizing the first set of adjustments. The central problem in this second set is how to live with the fact of unsatisfied desire, how to cope with the incomplete and unfinished quality of experience. If the first type of situation can be said to arouse moral issues, the second type could be said to give rise to questions concerning the inevitable conflict between human aspirations and external reality.

Though each of these two types of encounters seems to call for a relatively unique set of adaptive maneuverings, they have in common the fact that both involve the young child's coming to grips with what some would call "the stark realities of life." As we all know, people often *do* covet their neighbor's goods, demands frequently *do* exceed supplies, even calls for help sometimes *do* go unanswered. It comes as no surprise, therefore, to discover that three- and four-year-old children have begun to cope with these "natural" conditions. What is impressive is the fact that they are called upon so frequently to do so, even in environments specifically designed to meet their needs.

Given the frequency of these petty annoyances during the

young child's day in school, a person who had never visited a
nursery school might conclude that these are not very pleasant
places for three- and four-year-olds to spend their days. Yet
teachers and other adults who work in these environments
would doubtlessly argue that such a conclusion is unjustified,
at least on the basis of surface appearances. Many nursery
school children do seem to be enjoying themselves much of
the time and many show signs of reluctance when asked to
leave at the end of the day. Certainly the experience does not
look to be as disagreeable as the quantitative description of
these minor abrasions might lead us to expect. Despite their
abundance, these small discomforts seem to have their effects
cancelled out by some of the more positive aspects of school
life. Thus, we must not overemphasize their importance when
discussing the total quality of the child's life in school.

Also, the amount of unpleasantness associated with these
encounters can be easily exaggerated. Although shouts and
tears are sometimes clearly in evidence, often the children
undergoing these experiences exhibit no visible signs of annoy-
ance. When we consider that the victim often copes successfully with his experience—by routing the intruder or by finding a suitable substitute for an unsatisfied desire—it is even
possible to imagine that many of these episodes culminate in a
sense of victory and a feeling of competence.

Because of these complexities not only would it be unwise
to conclude that the total character of school life is made
unpleasant by the profusion of intrusive events, it would be
equally unwarranted to assume that nothing positive could
come from these experiences and, therefore, that they should
be eliminated if at all possible. But, conversely, neither does
our present state of knowledge allow us to move in the opposite direction and argue that the superabundance of these little
abrasions is good for children because it toughens them, so to
speak, for the harder knocks that lie ahead.

In the final analysis we must admit that we do not know
what these thousands of fleeting events do to the children who
experience them. The chief justification for cataloging their
occurrence is that they seem to comprise a salient feature of
the young child's experience while in school (and possibly
outside of it). Accordingly, the value of looking at these phenomena is not to discover the enduring impact of early school

experience but, rather, to help us see what life in nursery school is like.

We all know that childhood is a time of many skinned knees. If our data are correct, it is also a time of many skinned psyches. Even if most of these scratches leave no scars, they are a significant part of the "stuff" that makes a young child's life what it is.

References

Appel, M. H. Aggressive behavior of nursery school children and adult procedures in dealing with such behavior. *J. exp. Educ.*, 1942, 11, 185–199.

Body, M. K. Patterns of aggression in the nursery school. *Child Develpm.*, 1955, 26, 3–11.

Heinicke, C. M. Some effects of separating two-year-old children from their parents: a comparative study. *Human Relations*, 1956, 9, 105–176.

Muste, M. J. and Sharpe, D. F. Some influential factors in the determination of aggressive behavior in preschool children. *Child Develpm.*, 1947, 8, 11–28.

Swift, J. W. Effects of early group experience: the nursery school and day nursery. In M. L. Hoffman & L. W. Hoffman (Ed.), *Rev. of Child Develpm. Research*, 1964, I, New York: Russell Sage Foundation, 1964, 249–288.

Discussion

Classrooms are crowded places. Approximately thirty people inhabit a room which has far less space than a family enjoys in a house. We confine students to quarters in which their ability to stretch their feet, walk around, and spread out their possessions is limited. Furthermore, the ratio of students to teacher and to material is quite high, even in the most uncrowded classrooms.

The purpose of mentioning these conditions is not to generate criticism of our schools but rather to call attention to an aspect of classroom life we commonly overlook. An increasing number of researchers are finding that ecological conditions in the classroom, that is, the ways in which students are related to its physical environment, are powerful determinants of what students experience in school. An examination of the crowded social environment in classrooms is, therefore, important to our understanding of the process of schooling.

In most classrooms, several students must share the attention of one teacher. Moreover, certain students, teachers commonly complain, demand more than their fair share of time. This typically means that teachers find it necessary to discipline or give additional instructions to some students more than to others. The effect of this practice, as Jackson and Lahaderne point out, is to lessen even further the little contact many students receive from their teacher.

Because of the social traffic in classrooms, teachers devote a large portion of their energy to managing the flow of classroom activity rather than instructing students. This requires subjecting students to many directions and prohibitions as they move about the classroom. According to Jackson and Lahaderne, however, the extent to which students face a steady stream of commands is influenced by the classroom they are in and by their sex. It is probably no surprise to learn that some teachers are more controlling than are others and that boys are more frequent targets of teachers' managerial and control messages than are girls. But the latter finding, in particular, should not be lightly dismissed. We often say, as if it explains everything, that "boys will be boys." What we may not realize is that boys are expected in our culture to engage in independent action. Classrooms, though, are not designed well for private interests and pursuits. As a result, boys are ill prepared for the demands of communal living in school.

Kounin's research suggests that teachers do not need to manage students by constant warning and prohibitions. The key in dealing with crowded classrooms is not how teachers discipline but how they arrange and coordinate activities. If teachers can develop a learning program which has enough variety and challenge to it and if they can move students from one task to another smoothly and with momentum, the classroom can become an effective work setting despite its crowded conditions. Moreover, the mastery of group-management techniques, according to Kounin, frees teachers to spend time with children individually. This does not mean, however, that teachers can always achieve personal contact with students. When working with several students at a time, for example, they must keep their attention focused on the group rather than immerse themselves in a single child.

Of course, many teachers believe that work involvement and classroom control are best achieved by treating their students as a total unit. Adams and Biddle point out, however, that when a class is required to move as a whole group, quietness, orderly behavior, waiting, and the dominance of teachers become more important than activity and student responsibility. The net result of conducting classrooms in terms of these values is to deny expression of individuality. One student becomes indistinguishable from the rest.

Regardless of the values by which classrooms are organized for instruction, the problems of crowds remain. The nursery school in which Jackson and Wolfson did their research has an unstructured, informal educational program. Also, compared to other nursery schools, it has a wide variety of materials, a low teacher-student ratio, and a great deal of physical space. Nonetheless, many individual student's desires are thwarted there by the intrusions of classmates and teachers.[1]

---

[1] Berk has found that one way in which educational philosophy does make a difference is the source of interference with individual pursuits (Laura E. Berk, "The influence of variations in the nursery-school environment on frustrating events and modes of adaptation." Unpublished doctoral dissertation, University of Chicago, 1969). Her findings suggest that in schools where the educational program is highly structured, teachers interfere with the desires of individual students more often than

What this means is that it is virtually impossible for a single student to carve out of the classroom any physical or psychological privacy. There are simply too many people surrounding him.[2]

The impact on children of spending five hours a day in the classroom cannot be easily studied. Adults, moreover, cannot fully comprehend the experience because the conditions under which they work are rarely as crowded. By comparison, classrooms provide less freedom of movement, less personalized facilities, and more distraction than do most adult work settings. Despite our distance from classroom life, however, we might logically deduce that children have very little incentive to develop their own interests and plans in school. To have such incentive would require that individual students experience the classroom as a place for their own use. Fortunately, classrooms are changing, in part, due to a new breed of school architects. As a result of their involvement in the problems of classroom ecology, significant advances have been made in designing schools so that space can be used flexibly to create several types of physical settings in which students can learn. Thus, teachers and students in new schools will have a greater choice as to how any activity can be organized. In the meantime, of course, the existing limitations of thousands of schools inhibit the individual growth of students. The question is whether we can be our own architects, able to reconceptualize space in current school buildings to accommodate a variety of purposes, and thereby make the classroom a less depersonalizing climate in which to live and work.

---

do classmates. The opposite is true in schools where activities are relatively unplanned. Furthermore, in the former schools, students adapt to the limits placed on them most often with dependent, compliant behavior. In the latter schools, by contrast, students adjust to disrupted wishes by questioning why they were disrupted or giving reasons for the legitimacy of their desires.

[2] Interestingly, children are often beseeched to keep to themselves, not to talk with classmates and certainly to avoid showing their work to them. To ask children to ignore each other is, of course, equally impossible given the crowded social conditions in classrooms.

Part IV

THE THREAT
OF EVALUATION

How Children Fail–
An Excerpt*

JOHN HOLT

EDITOR'S NOTE: How Children Fail *is composed of a series of memos which John Holt originally wrote to a colleague in whose fifth-grade class he observed and taught. The experiences he describes took place in a private school with an excellent reputation. Two of these memos are presented here. Another memo is found in the next part of the book (Part V).*

December 3, 1958
The other day I decided to talk to the other section about what happens when you don't understand what is going on. We had been chatting about something or other, and everyone seemed in a relaxed frame of mind, so I said, "You know, there's something I'm curious about, and I wonder if you'd tell me." They said, "What?" I said, "What do you think, what goes through your mind, when the teacher asks you a question and you don't know the answer?"

It was a bombshell. Instantly a paralyzed silence fell on the room. Everyone stared at me with what I have learned to recognize as a tense expression. For a long time there wasn't a sound. Finally Ben, who is bolder than most, broke the tension, and also answered my question, by saying in a loud voice, "Gulp!"

He spoke for everyone. They all began to clamor, and all said the same thing, that when the teacher asked them a question and they didn't know the answer they were scared

---

half to death. I was flabbergasted—to find this in a school which people think of as progressive; which does its best not to put pressure on little children; which does not give marks in the lower grades; which tries to keep children from feeling that they're in some kind of race.

I asked them why they felt gulpish. They said they were afraid of failing, afraid of being kept back, afraid of being called stupid, afraid of feeling themselves stupid. Stupid. Why is it such a deadly insult to these children, almost the worst thing they can think of to call each other? Where do they learn this?

Even in the kindest and gentlest of schools, children are afraid, many of them a great deal of the time, some of them almost all the time. This is a hard fact of life to deal with. What can we do about it?

December 30, 1958

All fall long, I wondered why Jack fell down so much playing soccer. He is an agile, well-coordinated boy. His balance is good. People don't knock him over. Why was he on the ground so often? Suddenly, the other day, I had the answer.

I discovered it while trying to learn to control the tension that builds up in me when I practice the flute. Music is a good thing for teachers to study, because it creates in us the kind of tension that children live under all the time in the classroom, and that most adults have long forgotten. Incidentally, it is most interesting, when Gattegno explains the Cuisenaire rods to teachers, to see them under this very tension. They react to it very much like children, by getting sore at Gattegno, or fighting his ideas, by saying in elaborate language what fifth graders say when they are startled by a new idea—"This is crazy, nutty, cuckoo."

I have observed many times that children who can do one or two problems of a certain kind, with no trouble, collapse when given a big sheet of them. Something like this is true of exercises in music. When I am trying to play an exercise at (for me) high speed, I am under tension. If the exercise is short, I feel that I can get through it before tension gets the better of me. But if it is long, I am less confident from the start that I can get through without a mistake, and as I play, the inner voice that comments on what I am doing says: "All right so far; watch that G sharp; oops! narrow escape, you almost played F sharp instead of F natural, etc., etc." The voice gets louder and louder, until finally the communication channels are clogged up, coordination breaks down, and I make the mistake I have been fearing to make.

I haven't forgotten Jack and his falling down. One thing I have discovered is that there is a peculiar kind of relief, a lessening of tension, when you make a mistake. For when you make one, you no longer have to worry about whether you are going to make one. Walking a tightrope, you worry about falling off; once fallen off, you don't have to worry. Children, to whom making mistakes is acutely painful, are therefore under great tension when doing something correctly. Worrying about the mistakes they might make is as bad—no, worse—than worrying about the mistakes they have made. Thus, when you tell a child that he has done a problem wrong, you often hear a sigh of relief. He says, "I *knew* it would be wrong." He would rather *be* wrong, and know it, than not know whether he was wrong or not.

Well, the reason Jack falls down is that this relieves him, for a few seconds, of the great tension he is under when he plays soccer. Being small, he is afraid of crashing into bigger boys, but he is also afraid of showing his fear, and resolutely tries to play the game as he feels he should. This puts his nervous system under a strain that is too much for it. Being a boy, he can't pull out of the game, as a girl might do, or just get out of the way of bigger boys when they come at him. So, every now and then, he falls down, and thus gets an honorable rest period for a second or two.

This makes me think about written work. Some say that children get security from large amounts of written work. Maybe. But suppose every teacher in the school were told that he had to do ten pages of addition problems, within a given time limit and with no mistakes, or lose his job. Even if the time given were ample enough to do all problems carefully with time over for checking, the chances are that no teacher would get a perfect paper. Their anxiety would build up, as it does in me when I play the flute, until it impaired or wholly broke down their coordination and confidence. Have you ever found yourself, while doing a simple arithmetic problem, checking the answer over and over, as if you could not believe that you had done it right? I have. If we were under the gun as much as the kids in our classes are, we would do this more often.

Perhaps children need a lot of written work, particularly in math; but they should not get much of it at one time. Ask children to spend a whole period on one paper, and anxiety or boredom is sure to drive them into foolish errors. It used to puzzle me that the students who made the most mistakes and got the worst marks were so often the first ones to hand in their papers. I used to say, "If you finish early, take time to check your work, do some problems again." Typical teacher's advice; I might as well have told them to flap their arms and fly. When the paper was in, the tension was ended. Their fate was in the lap of the gods. They might still worry about flunking the paper, but it was a fatalistic kind of worry, it didn't contain the agonizing element of choice, there was nothing more they could do about it. Worrying about whether you did the right thing, while painful enough, is less painful than worrying about the right thing to do.

One way to keep down tension is to be aware of it. I told the math class that to let something go by in class without knowing what it means, and without saying anything, is like leaving something in Howard Johnson's on a long car trip. You are going to have to go back for it eventually, so the sooner the better. This foolish metaphor has helped the kids, or so they say. They have learned to recognize, if only a little, the feeling of panicky confusion that slowly gets hold of them. To be able to say, "I'm getting left at Howard Johnson's" helps them to control this feeling, and if it gets too much for them they can always tell me that they have been left behind; then I can do something about picking them up.

We must set a limit to the tension that we put children under. If we don't, they will set their own limits by not paying attention, by fooling around, by saying unnecessarily, "I don't get it." We should let them know in advance that they will not have to be under tension for an entire period, and that, if need be, they have the means to bring it to a stop.

Perhaps this is a reason why people like Gattegno, who go

around teaching demonstration math classes, get such spectacular results. The kids know that this is not real school, that this strange man is not their teacher, that if they make mistakes nothing serious will happen, and that, in any case, it will be over soon. Thus freed from worrying, they are ready to use their brains. But how can we run a class from day to day and keep that spirit? Can it be done at all?

On What Is Learned in School—An Excerpt*

ROBERT DREEBEN

EDITOR'S NOTE: On What is Learned in School *discusses the links between schools and other social institutions, particularly the family. In the excerpt presented here, Dreeben is analyzing how teachers, in comparison to parents, elicit desirable conduct from children.*

Sanctioning

In both family and school, certain patterns of action are encouraged and discouraged by rewards and punishments which take the form of both specific acts and more enduring patterns of action.

I assume that when enduring patterns of behavior are encouraged and discouraged, a sustained relationship between the persons involved must exist, one that involves more than the reward and punishment of specific acts on a *quid pro quo* basis. Whatever else its weakness, an arrangement based on exchange would require those involved to maintain such surveillance of each other that each desirable act received its reward and each undesirable one its punishment. As Durkheim and others have indicated, patterns of social life cannot continue if the contractual terms of each action must be settled each time.[1] In the family, the basis for encouraging and discouraging children's behavior lies in their dependence on

---

[1] Emile Durkheim, *The Division of Labor in Society*, translated by George Simpson, pp. 200–229, Free Press, New York (1949).

* Reprinted by special permission from R. Dreeben, *On What Is Learned in School*, 1968, 33–41, Addison-Wesley, Reading, Mass.

parents from earliest infancy and the mutual expression of love and affection; a relationship, in other words, analogous to good will in the economic sense. Although rewards for specific actions can replenish this bank of good will, the existence of the bank is not itself a reward nor is it filled only by rewarded acts. Rather, it is maintained by gratuitious support, friendliness, interest, sympathy, encouragement, and the like, not as responses to specific acts, but as indications of a more enduring solidarity. Punishment, then, even if severe, means one thing if administered in the context of a sustained relationship of affection and another where such feeling is absent.

Problems of reward and punishment confront teachers as well as parents. At the start of their schooling, the experiences children have had with rewards and punishment have been limited primarily to the family. Since classrooms are structured differently than families, as are the activities of the adults and nonadults in each setting, the problems of reward and punishment also tend to differ.

First, since children in classrooms outnumber those in families, teachers, for reasons of limited time and energy, cannot sanction each child as much or in the same manner that his parents can; a teacher must be able to control a class without sacrificing the school agenda to the imperatives of keeping some semblance of order. Moreover, a teacher does not have at his disposal those emotional resources for the exercise of authority that are characteristic of the family; resources based on intimate association in a very small group and on a prolonged relationship of warmth, nurturance, acceptance, withdrawal of affection, and even physical punishment. Second, pupils' academic performance is customarily sanctioned by means of the grades teachers assign according to the quality of specific units of work. There is nothing inherently rewarding or punishing in the letters, numbers, and words conventionally assigned as grades. Prior to their first encounter with school, children's behavior is not judged primarily on a specific task for specific sanction basis (and, if it is, only to a limited extent), and parents do not usually reward and punish their children with grades or other discrete symbolic forms of recognition. One central problem of early elementary schooling, then, is for teachers to establish grades *as* sanctions, that is, to get pupils to regard high grades as rewarding, low grades as punishing. To the extent that pupils do not learn to accept them as such, grades cannot serve the function of rewarding good performance and punishing poor. Secondary schools, and to some lesser extent the later years of elementary schools, operate according to the assumption—not always correct—that pupils have already come to accept the sanctioning quality of grades.

The problem confronting elementary school teachers, then, resembles that of parents with young children; to treat them so that they come to regard certain symbolic and physical expressions as rewards and punishments. As a prerequisite, the parents' initial job is to develop a relationship of love and nurturance with their children; analogously, the elementary school teacher's first job is to create among pupils a diffuse and positive attachment both to herself and to the school.

The Structural Basis of School Sanctions

In the first grade, a formal and prolonged process of separating children from the family begins. It does not involve severing or renouncing kinship ties nor does it require relinquishing the normative principles of family life, since most members of society remain part of some kinship unit throughout most of their lives. School does, however, put demands on pupils to give up, in certain situations, principles and patterns of behavior they have come to accept as family members; more precisely, it requires them to restrict the premises governing family life to conduct among kinsmen, and to adopt others—new, strange, and even painful—that apply to settings outside the family. At the outset, schooling may provide but few of the gratifications of family life, and then only in attenuated form, until pupils discover sources of gratification in schooling itself, an outcome by no means universal or inevitable.

It should not be assumed that schooling is by nature an alien experience nor one for which young children are entirely unprepared. They differ in their interest in and capacities for doing school work; some have learned the rudiments of the basic cognitive skills and have had experience in school-like social situations before entering the first grade. Many parents provide their children with opportunities to act independently, stress the importance of achievement and competence, and create a home environment in which reading, talking, and thinking have a prominent place. Yet even with prior preparation, school represents a considerable departure in a child's existence.

Little is known about how elementary teachers create gratifications for their pupils out of resources available in the school. They cannot assume that grades will be automatically rewarding, although undoubtedly some children have already learned to value grades before starting school. Also, by rigorously enforcing standards of self-reliance and achievement in the earliest grades and by expecting pupils to accept responsibilities incommensurate with their capacities, teachers may create undue pressure and discouragement for the pupils. Although a pupil can gain a sense of competence and gratification from his successes, extracting gratification from public failure poses a problem in psychological alchemy. Parents make allowances for their young children and help them with tasks beyond their existing capacities, but teachers, because of their responsibility for a class of like-aged pupils both as a collectivity and as an aggregate of individuals, are unable to give each one the special attention he may have grown accustomed to at home.

Aside from the fact that they lack the resources for sanctioning available to parents and cannot necessarily rely on the effectiveness of grades, teachers must confront certain technological weaknesses in their position. Little is known, for example, about how to persuade individuals gathered in a public place to be cooperative, how to diagnose one's own errors in the near absence of qualified observers or reasonably reliable methods of assessment, or how to create the desire among pupils to bring collective pressure on each other to advance the instructional enterprise.[2] In terms of power, the teacher's

[2] "Collective approval of power legitimates that power. People who consider that the advantages they gain from a superior's exercise of power outweigh the hardships that compliance with his demands imposes on them tend to communicate to each other their approval of the ruler and their feelings of obligation to him." Peter M. Blau, *Exchange and Power in Social Life*, p. 23, Wiley, New York (1964).

position is vulnerable. Ostensibly positive sanctions are often found problematic; not all pupils are drawn to the lure of grades, and nonacademic incentives may pale in comparison to the intrinsic pleasures of making life difficult for teachers. Ostensibly negative sanctions often bring diminishing returns; punishments meted out too often lose their punishing quality, and pupils who have survived the worst a teacher can dish out cease to be awed by what might be in store for them next time. In effect, the teacher, consciously or not, must rely to a considerable extent on personal resources for gaining the necessary respect and affection from the large number of pupils who assemble daily in classrooms.

The substance of sanctioning problems differs according to school level. At the elementary level, teachers must use their available resources so that pupils come to like school, accept the prevailing rules of the game, find gratification in doing school work, and learn to accept as rewarding the symbolic expressions that teachers intend them to experience as rewarding. At the secondary level, problems arise when teachers incorrectly assume that the elementary school has done its job; thus pupils will experience the sanctioning qualities of grades only if they have learned to acknowledge them as such during the elementary years.

Teaching involves a classic problem in the creation of goodwill; finding in the classroom some gratuitous pleasure not tied to *specific* acts in a relationship of exchange. There is a distinction, for example, between a teacher smiling when a pupil has done a particular task well and smiling as a characteristic demeanor with no direct connection to any specific (approved of) act. A form of expression such as the latter is not negotiated act-by-act (a smile for ten words spelled correctly), and, although it is not negotiable in this sense, a general relationship of friendliness between teacher and pupils may nevertheless affect the terms of exchange even if it is not such a term itself.[3] What the components of goodwill are

---

[3] Parsons treats this issue by distinguishing ". . . the *contingency* of what alter (the agent of care) does on what ego (the child) has done or is expected to do, . . ." from ". . . the component of *generalization*. There exist not merely discrete, disconnected sanctions, but a pattern of relatively systematic and organized sanctions. . . ." Talcott Parsons,

(e.g., whether the teacher likes the pupils, smiles, talks kindly, acts encouragingly, etc.), remains a matter of conjecture. Conditions for the creation of goodwill, however, probably include associations between persons that endure beyond each social transaction as well as the successful use of *generalized* resources such as the expression of positive emotion.[4]

There are several structural characteristics of classrooms, all discussed earlier, that when considered in combination, identify the resources available to teachers for sanctioning. I am concerned not with such rewards and punishments as grades, compliments, criticisms, and the like exchanged for specific manifestations of discrete skills and conduct, but with more generalized sanctions providing resources for the acquisition of norms. A classroom is a public place in that membership is collective and visible. Its nonadult members are alike in one crucial respect, their age. Age is crucial because it represents an index (even if inexact) of developmental maturity, and, by implication, of capacity.[5] (Pupils are roughly alike in other characteristics besides age, particularly in certain social attributes related to neighborhood residence.) Homogeneous age composition is important in two senses: (1) It provides classrooms with a built-in standard for comparison, a fixed point indicative of those pupil capacities directly relevant to the activities in which they are engaged. Each pupil, then, can be compared and can compare himself with all others because the comparisons can be anchored to the standard. (2) It allows each pupil the experience of finding himself in the same

"Social Structure and the Development of Personality: Freud's Contribution to the Integration of Psychology and Sociology," in *Social Structure and Personality*, p. 87, Free Press, New York (1964).

[4] Parsons, for example, commenting on Freud's contribution to understanding personality development, states: "[Childhood eroticism] can be regarded as, essentially, a built-in physiological mechanism of the *generalization* of internal reward. . . . Erotic pleasure seems to be essentially a diffuse, generalized 'feeling' of organic well-being which is not attached to any one discrete, instinctual need-fulfillment." Talcott Parsons, "Social Structure and the Development of Personality: . . ." p. 90.

[5] Perhaps the social expectations for and beliefs about the capacities of similar-aged children are narrower than their actual capacities (however these are measured). If so, age is an exaggeratedly "good" index of equal capacity even if the goodness is a self-fulfilling prophecy.

boat with others in terms of the characteristics of their social surroundings and in the way they are treated by teachers.

Since many classroom activities are judged in public, the pupil is bombarded with messages telling him how well he has done and (with a short inferential leap) how good he is. If he doesn't take the teacher's word for it, he need only look at the performance of others of the same age and in the same circumstances. The school, in effect, plays on his self-respect. Each pupil is exposed and vulnerable to the judgments of adults in authority and of his equals, those who resemble him in many respects.[6] If the child at home wonders whether he is loved, the pupil wonders whether he is a worthwhile person. In both settings he can find some kind of answer by observing how others treat him.

Given the standards for and patterns of behavior that children learn from their family experiences, the schools, in preparing them for adult public life, must effect changes of considerable magnitude, changes that require giving up certain patterns of conduct found gratifying in other settings and adopting new patterns whose gratifications may at best take the form of promissory notes. If knowledge about other forms of socialization is applicable to schooling, and there is no reason in principle why it should not be, the sanctions required must affect people's emotions deeply, as is true in some of the most demanding and stress-creating social situations involving psychological change: psychotherapy, religious conversion, brainwashing, deracination. It is my contention that the emotions aroused in schooling derive from events in which the pupil's sense of self-respect is either supported or threatened, and that school classrooms, permitting the public exposure and judgment of performance against a reasonably fixed reference point (age-adapted tasks), are organized so that the pupil's sense of personal adequacy, or self-respect, becomes the leverage for sanctioning. The effectiveness of the leverage, of course, is not determined by its availability, and many conditions will determine pupils' susceptibility to it.

[6] " 'Remember that you are as good as any man—and also that you are no better.' . . . [But] the man who is as good as his neighbors is in a tough spot when he confronts all of his neighbors combined." Louis Hartz, *The Liberal Tradition in America*, p. 56, Harcourt, New York (1955). The coerciveness of massed equals is not negligible.

Not all sanctions employed in school settings have the potentiality for arousing intense emotions, nor are they similarly diffuse in character. Some are contingent: grades, compliments, admonitions, chastisements in exchange for desirable and undesirable conduct; others are noncontingent: friendly greetings, gentleness, sympathy, sarcasm, bitchiness, and so on through the whole gamut of words, gestures, and postures indicating approval and disapproval. All represent resources at the teacher's disposal, used consciously or unconsciously, which influence the pupils in deciding whether or not they will find their early experiences at school enjoyable enough to act according to the standards governing school activities.

Life in Classrooms–
An Excerpt*

PHILIP W. JACKSON

EDITOR'S NOTE: Life in Classrooms *is an examination of the school as a setting for human activity. The book is especially concerned with the school's abrasive qualities as a social institution. In the excerpt below, Jackson discusses the evaluative climate of the elementary classroom.*

Every child experiences the pain of failure and the joy of success long before he reaches school age, but his achievements, or lack of them, do not really become official until he enters the classroom. From then on, however, a semi-public record of his progress gradually accumulates, and as a student he must learn to adapt to the continued and pervasive spirit of evaluation that will dominate his school years. Evaluation, then, is another important fact of life in the elementary classroom.

As we all know, school is not the only place where a student is made aware of his strengths and weaknesses. His parents make evaluations of him in the home and his friends do likewise in the playground. But the evaluation process that goes on in the classroom is quite different from that which operates in other settings. Accordingly, it presents the student with a set of unique demands to which he must adapt.

The most obvious difference between the way evaluation occurs in school and the way it occurs in other situations is that tests are given in school more frequently than elsewhere.

* From Chapter One, from *Life in Classrooms* by Philip W. Jackson. Copyright © 1968 by Holt, Rinehart and Winston, Inc. Reprinted by permission of Holt, Rinehart and Winston, Inc.

Indeed, with the exception of examinations related to military service or certain kinds of occupations most people seldom encounter tests outside of their school experience.[1] Tests are as indigenous to the school environment as are textbooks or pieces of chalk.

But tests, though they are the classic form of educational evaluation, are not all there is to the process. In fact, in the lower grades formal tests are almost nonexistent, although evaluation clearly occurs. Thus the presence of these formal procedures is insufficient to explain the distinctively evaluative atmosphere that pervades the classroom from the earliest grades onward. There is more to it than that.

The dynamics of classroom evaluation are difficult to describe, principally because they are so complex. Evaluations derive from more than one *source*, the *conditions of their communication* may vary in several different ways, they may have one or more of several *referents*, and they may range in *quality* from intensely positive to intensely negative. Moreover, these variations refer only to objective, or impersonal features of evaluation. When the subjective or personal meanings of these events are considered, the picture becomes even more complex. Fortunately, for purposes of the present discussion, we need to focus only on the more objective aspects of the student's evaluative experiences.

The chief *source* of evaluation in the classroom is obviously the teacher. He is called upon continuously to make judgments of students' work and behavior and to communicate that judgment to the students in question and to others. No one who has observed an elementary classroom for any length of time can have failed to be impressed by the vast number of times the teacher performs this function. Typically, in most classrooms students come to know when things are right or wrong, good or bad, pretty or ugly, largely as a result of what the teacher tells them.

But the teacher is not the only one who passes judgment. Classmates frequently join in the act. Sometimes the class as a whole is invited to participate in the evaluation of a student's

---

[1] There are, of course, the popular quizzes in newspapers and magazines which many people seem to enjoy answering. But these exercises, which might best be called "toy tests," are of little consequence when compared with the real thing that goes on in school.

work, as when the teacher asks, "Who can correct Billy?" or "How many believe that Shirley read that poem with a lot of expression?"[2] At other times the evaluation occurs without any urging from the teacher, as when an egregious error elicits laughter or an outstanding performance wins spontaneous applause.

There is a third source of evaluation in the classroom that is more difficult to describe than are the positive or negative comments coming from teachers and peers. This type of evaluation, which entails self-judgment, occurs without the intervention of an outside judge. When a student is unable to spell any of the words on a spelling test he has been apprized of his failure even if the teacher never sees his paper. When a student works on an arithmetic example at the blackboard he may know that his answer is correct even if the teacher does not bother to tell him so. Thus, as students respond to test questions or complete exercises in their workbooks, or solve problems at the blackboard, they inevitably obtain some information about the quality of their performance. The information is not always correct and may have to be revised by later judgments (Not everyone who thinks he has the right answer really has it!), but, even when wrong, evaluation can leave its mark.

The conditions under which evaluations are communicated add to the complexity of the demands confronting the student. He soon comes to realize, for example, that some of the most important judgments of him and his work are not made known to him at all. Some of these "secret" judgments are communicated to parents; others, such as IQ scores and results of personality tests, are reserved for the scrutiny of school officials only. Judgments made by peers often circulate in the form of gossip or are reported to persons of authority by "tattle-tales." Before he has gone very far in school the student must come to terms with the fact that many things are said about him behind his back.

---

[2] Jules Henry, an anthropologist, has witnessed signs of what he terms "a witch-hunt syndrome" in several elementary classrooms. A chief component of this syndrome is the destructive criticism of each other by the students, egged on, as it were, by the teacher. See his article, "Attitude organization is elementary school classrooms," . . . [p. 261 of this text—ed.].

Those judgments of which the student is aware are communicated with varying degrees of privacy. At one extreme is the public comment made in the presence of other students. In the elementary classroom in particular, students are often praised or admonished in front of their classmates. Perfect papers or "good" drawings are sometimes displayed for all to see. Misbehavior evokes negative sanctions—such as scolding, isolation, removal from the room—that are frequently visible. Before much of the school year has gone by the identity of the "good" students and the "poor" students has become public knowledge in most classrooms.

A less public form of evaluation occurs when the teacher meets privately with the student to discuss his work. Sometimes the student is called to the teacher's desk and sometimes the teacher walks around the room and chats with individuals while the class is engaged in seatwork. Often, however, these seemingly private conferences are secretly attended by eavesdroppers. Thus, it is quite probable, although it might be difficult to prove, that a student's nearest classmates are more intimately aware of the teacher's evaluation of him than are students sitting at a greater distance.

Writing is an even more private means of communicating evaluations than is the spoken word. The terse comment on the margin of a student's paper is the classic form of written evaluation. A variant of this situation occurs when the student answers a self-quiz in his workbook or textbook but does not report his score to anyone. On occasions such as these the student confronts the evaluation of his work in solitude.

Logically, evaluation in the classroom might be expected to be limited chiefly to the student's attainment of educational objectives. And, clearly these limits seem to hold insofar as most of the official evaluations go—the ones that are communicated to parents and entered on school records. But there are at least two other *referents* of evaluation quite common in elementary classrooms. One has to do with the student's adjustment to institutional expectations; the other with his possession of specific character traits. Indeed, the smiles and frowns of teachers and classmates often provide more information about these seemingly peripheral aspects of the student's behavior than they do about his academic progress. Moreover, even when the student's mastery of certain knowledge or skills is allegedly the object of evaluation, other aspects of his behavior commonly are being judged at the same time.

As every school child knows, teachers can become quite angry on occasion. Moreover, every school child quickly learns what makes teachers angry. He learns that in most classrooms the behavior that triggers the teacher's ire has little to do with wrong answers or other indicators of scholastic failure. Rather, it is violations of institutional expectations that really get under the teacher's skin. Typically, when a student is scolded by the teacher it is not because he has failed to spell a word correctly or to grasp the intricacies of long division. He is scolded, more than likely, for coming into the room late, or for making too much noise, or for not listening to directions, or for pushing while in line. Occasionally, teachers do become publicly vexed by their students' academic shortcomings, but to really send them off on a tirade of invective, the young student soon discovers, nothing works better than a partially suppressed giggle during arithmetic period.

The teacher, of course, is not the only source of nonacademic judgments. Evaluation that focuses on a student's personal qualities is as likely to come from his classmates as from anyone else. The student's classroom behavior contributes in large measure to the reputation he develops among his peers for being smart or dumb, a sissy or a bully, teacher's pet or a regular guy, a cheater or a good sport. Most students are fully aware that their behavior is being evaluated in these terms because they judge others in the same way. Classroom friendships and general popularity or unpopularity are based largely on such assessments.[3] Although some of these judgments are instantly communicated to the person being evaluated, others are related through intermediaries or friends. Some are so secret that even best friends won't tell.

[3] Watching these evaluations being made in the classroom (through huddled conferences and the surreptitious exchange of notes) one begins to wonder whether friendship is determined by the possession of special qualities, or whether the qualities are ascribed as a rationalization of friendship or enmity that already exists. In many instances it is almost as if the students were saying, "My friends are good guys and my enemies are tattle-tales and cheaters," rather than "Good guys are my friends and tattle-tales and cheaters my enemies." Doubtlessly both kinds of reasoning are in operation in most classrooms.

The teacher's evaluation of the personal qualities of his students typically deals with such matters as general intellectual ability, motivational level, and helpfulness in maintaining a well-run classroom. Such qualities are commonly mentioned on cumulative record folders in terse but telling descriptions. "Johnny has some difficulty with third grade material, but he tries hard," or "Sarah is a neat and pleasant girl. She is a good helper," or, simply, "William is a good worker," are typical of the thumb-nail sketches to be found in abundance in school records. Some teachers, particularly those who pride themselves on being "psychologically sophisticated," also evaluate their students in terms that relate more closely than do the ones already mentioned to the general concept of psychopathology. Aggressiveness and withdrawal are among the traits most frequently mentioned in this connection. Teachers also use the general labels of "problem child" or "disturbed child" for this purpose.

Quite naturally most of the evaluations that have to do with the student's psychological health are not communicated to the student and often not even to the child's parents. Less severe judgments, however, are often made publicly. In the lower grades it is not at all uncommon to hear the teacher, as she gazes over her class, say things like, "I see that John is a good worker," or "Some people (their identities obvious) don't seem to know how to follow directions," or "Liza has a listening face."

The separation of classroom evaluations into those referring to academic attainment, those referring to institutional adjustment, and those referring to possession of personal qualities should not obscure the fact that in many situations all three kinds of assessment are going on at one time. For example, when a student is praised for correctly responding to a teacher's question it may look as though he is simply being rewarded for having the right answer. But obviously there is more to it than that. If the teacher discovered that the student had obtained the answer a few seconds before by reading from a neighbor's paper he would have been punished rather than praised. Similarly, if he had blurted the answer out rather than waiting to be called on he might have received a very different response from the teacher. Thus, it is not just the possession of the right answer but also the way in which it was obtained that is being rewarded. In other words, the student is being praised for having achieved and demonstrated intellectual mastery in a prescribed legitimate way. He is being praised, albeit indirectly, for knowing something, for having done what the teacher told him to do, for being a good listener, a cooperative group member, and so on. The teacher's compliment is intended to entice the student (and those who are listening) to engage in certain behaviors in the future, but not simply in the repeated exposure of the knowledge he has just displayed. It is intended to encourage him to do again what the teacher tells him to do, to work hard, to master the material. And so it is with many of the evaluations that appear to relate exclusively to academic matters. Implicitly, they involve the evaluation of many "nonacademic" aspects of the student's behavior.

Evaluations, by definition, connote value. Accordingly, each can be described, at least ideally, according to the kind and degree of value it connotes. Some are positive, others are negative. Some are *very* positive or negative, others are less so. In the classroom, as every one knows, both positive and negative assessments are made and are communicated to students. Teachers scold as well as praise, classmates compliment as well as criticize.

The question of whether smiles are more frequent than frowns, and compliments more abundant than criticisms, depends in part, of course, on the particular classroom under discussion. Some teachers are just not the smiling type, others find it difficult to suppress their grins. The answer also varies dramatically from one student to the next. Some youngsters receive many more negative sanctions than do others, and the same is true with respect to rewards. Conditions also vary for the sexes. From the early grades onward boys are more likely than are girls to violate institutional regulations and, thus, to receive an unequal share of control messages from the teacher. All of these inequalities make it difficult to describe with great accuracy the evaluative setting as it is experienced by any particular child. All that can be said with assurance is that the classroom environment of most students contains some mixture of praise and reproof.

Because both the teacher and his fellow classmates may

evaluate a student's behavior, contradictory judgments are possible. A given act may be praised by the teacher and criticized by peers, or vice versa. This may not be the normal state of affairs, to be sure, but it does happen frequently enough to bear comment. A classic example of this kind of a contradiction was observed in one second grade classroom in which a boy was complimented by his teacher for his gracefulness during a period of "creative" dancing while, at the same time, his male classmates teased him for acting like a sissy. This example calls attention to the fact that students are often concerned with the approval of two audiences whose taste may differ. It also hints at the possibility that the conflict between teacher and peer approval might be greater for boys than for girls. Many of the behaviors that the teacher smiles upon, especially those that have to do with compliance to institutional expectations (e.g., neatness, passivity, cleanliness), are more closely linked in our society with feminine than with masculine ideals.

From all that has been said it is evident that learning how to live in a classroom involves not only learning how to handle situations in which one's own work or behavior are evaluated, but also learning how to witness, and occasionally participate in, the evaluation of others. In addition to getting used to a life in which their strengths and weaknesses are often exposed to public scrutiny, students also have to accustom themselves to viewing the strengths and weaknesses of their fellow students. This shared exposure makes comparisons between students inevitable and adds another degree of complexity to the evaluation picture.

The job of coping with evaluation is not left solely to the student. Typically the teacher and other school authorities try to reduce the discomfort that might be associated with some of the harsher aspects of meting out praise and punishment. The dominant viewpoint in education today stresses the pedagogical advantages of success and the disadvantages of failure. In short, our schools are reward-oriented. Thus, teachers are instructed to focus on the good aspects of a student's behavior and to overlook the poor. Indeed, even when a student gives a wrong answer, today's teacher is likely to compliment him for trying. This bias toward the positive does not mean, of course, that negative remarks have disappeared from our schools. But there are certainly fewer of them than there might be if teachers operated under a different set of educational beliefs.

When harsh judgments have to be made, as they often must, teachers often try to conceal them from the class as a whole. Students are called up to the teacher's desk, private conferences are arranged before or after school, test papers are handed back with the grades covered, and so on. Sometimes, when the judgments are very harsh, they are not reported to the student at all. Students are rarely told, for example, that they have been classified as "slow learners" or that the teacher suspects them of having serious emotional problems. Such evaluations, as has been pointed out, are usually the carefully guarded secrets of the school authorities.

School practices covering the communication of positive evaluations are probably less consistent than are those covering negative judgments. Although there is a common tendency to praise students whenever possible, this tendency is usually tempered by the teacher's desire to be fair and "democratic." Thus, the correct answers and perfect papers of students who almost always do good work may be overlooked at times in the interest of giving less able students a chance to bask in the warmth of the teacher's admiration. Most teachers are also sensitive to the fact that lavish praise heaped upon a student may arouse negative evaluations ("teacher's pet," "eager beaver") from his classmates.

Although the student's task in adjusting to evaluation is made easier by common teaching practices, he still has a job to do. In fact, he has three jobs. The first, and most obvious, is to behave in such a way as to enhance the likelihood of praise and reduce the likelihood of punishment. In other words, he must learn how the reward system of the classroom operates and then use that knowledge to increase the flow of rewards to himself. A second job, although one in which students engage with differing degrees of enthusiasm, consists of trying to publicize positive evaluations and conceal negative ones. The pursuit of this goal leads to the practice of carrying good report cards home with pride, and losing poor ones along the way. A third job, and, again, one that may be of greater concern to some students than to others, consists of trying to win the approval of two audiences at the same time. The problem, for some, is how to become a good student while remaining a good guy, how to be at the head of the class while still being in the center of the group.

Most students soon learn that rewards are granted to those who lead a good life. And in school the good life consists, principally, of doing what the teacher says. Of course the teacher says many things, and some of his directions are easier to follow than others, but for the most part his expectations are not seen as unreasonable and the majority of students comply with them sufficiently well to ensure that their hours in the classroom are colored more by praise than by punishment.

But only in very rare instances is compliance the only strategy a student uses to make his way in the evaluative environment of the classroom. Another course of action engaged in by most students at least some of the time is to behave in ways that disguise the failure to comply: in short, to cheat. It may seem unduly severe to label as "cheating" all the little maneuvers that students engage in to cloak aspects of their behavior that might be displeasing to the teacher or their fellow students. Perhaps the term should be reserved to describe the seemingly more serious behavior of trying to falsify performance on a test. But this restriction bestows greater significance than is warranted to test situations and implies that similar behavior in other settings is harmless or hardly worthy of notice.

Yet why should a student who copies an answer from his neighbor's test paper be considered guilty of more serious misbehavior than the student who attempts to misinform by raising his hand when the teacher asks how many have completed their homework assignment? Why is cheating on a test considered a greater breach of educational etiquette than is faking interest during a social studies discussion or sneaking a peek at a comic book during arithmetic class? The answer, presumably, is that performance on tests counts for more, in that it is preserved as a lasting mark on the student's record. And that answer might justify the differences in our attitudes toward these various practices. But it should not permit us to overlook the fact that copying an answer on a test, feigning interest during a discussion, giving a false answer to a teacher's query, and disguising forbidden activities are all of a piece. Each represents an effort to avoid censure or to win unwarranted praise. Such efforts are far more common in the classroom than our focus on cheating in test situations would have us believe. Learning how to make it in school involves, in part, learning how to falsify our behavior.

There is another way of coping with evaluations that warrants mention even though it is not deserving of the term "strategy." This method entails devaluing the evaluations to a point where they no longer matter very much. The student who has adopted this alternative over those of complying or cheating has learned how to "play it cool" in the classroom. He is neither elated by success nor deflated by failure. He may indeed try to "stay out of trouble" in the classroom and thus comply with the teacher's minimal expectations, but this is principally because getting into trouble entails further entanglements and involvement with school officials and other adults, a situation that he would prefer to avoid.

Classroom Rewards
and Intellectual Courage*

MELVIN L. SILBERMAN

John Holt and Philip Jackson describe the classroom as a place which discourages intellectual risk taking. Students realize very early in their school careers that teachers attach attractive rewards to classroom success and unpleasant penalties to classroom failure. Their responses to maximizing success and minimizing failure include ingenious designs such as provoking the teacher's attention when they know the right answer and hiding behind another student when they are not sure.

The study reported here attempts to support empirically the negative relationship between reward seeking and intellectual courage. It is contended that when a student desires extrinsic classroom rewards (for example, good grades, prizes, and praise), his experience in school tells him to steer clear of unfavorable evaluation. Two ways of avoiding negative impressions were studied: hiding weaknesses and mistakes; and rejecting intellectual challanges.

Method

The data were collected in four fifth-grade, public-school classrooms located in an upper-middle-class suburb. All four teachers were women. Their classes did not differ appreciably in achievement. Each student filled out a questionnaire designed to measure his desire for external classroom rewards. The questionnaire consisted of fifteen situations in which a

* This article was written expressly for this book and is published here for the first time.

hypothetical student is involved in a conflict between desiring an external reward or rejecting it. Two of the items, for example, are:

Mary and Jane both had read ten books. They were tied for the lead in a contest for who could read the most books during the year. There was a prize for the winner. During the last week of school, Mary went to the library to get another book to read. She found a book which she had wanted to read for a long time, but the book was in such great demand that the library never had it in. The book was very long, however. Mary knew that she could read two books during the time it would take to read this long one.

If you were Mary, would you pass up reading this book?

Dan discovered that his teacher added up his test score incorrectly. She gave him a 91, but it should have been a 95. Either score would get an A. If you were Dan, would you report the error to the teacher?

Students were asked to respond in one of four ways:

1. Yes, I think I would.
2. I'm not sure, but I think I would.
3. I'm not sure, but I think I would not.
4. No, I think I would not.

Numerical values assigned to the four responses were $+2$, $+1$, -1, and -2. It was assumed that the higher the score, the greater a desire for seeking external rewards.

Each teacher was asked to read descriptions of students' behaviors which express fear of exposing weaknesses and accepting intellectual challenges. The former description includes behaviors such as hiding mistakes at the blackboard, changing incorrect answers on ungraded seatwork, and failing to inform a teacher when something is not understood. The latter description consists of behaviors such as not being willing to express new ideas, rigidly adhering to immature ways of doing arithmetic, and preferring easy reading to more advanced books. The teacher was then asked to report as objectively as possible how frequently each of her students engaged in each general class of behavior. Numerical values assigned to the response categories were: "frequently" = 2, "occasionally" = 1, "almost never" = 0.

Results

The mean scores for each class group on the student questionnaire are summarized in Table 1.

TABLE 1
Mean Scores on Student Questionnaire

CLASS A $N = 28$	CLASS B $N = 29$	CLASS C $N = 30$	CLASS D $N = 27$	TOTAL $N = 114$
15.7	8.2	11.2	19.8	12.5

Since the scores could theoretically range from —30 to +30, it is clear that the desire for external rewards in this population of students is significant. At the same time we should note that class groups differ somewhat as to how much they seek such rewards. Perhaps their teachers also differ as to the amount of encouragement they give to reward seeking.

The correlations between the scores on the student questionnaire and the teachers' reports on hiding weaknesses for each class group are contained in Table 2.

TABLE 2
Correlations between Reward Seeking and Hiding Weaknesses

CLASS A $N = 28$	CLASS B $N = 29$	CLASS C $N = 30$	CLASS D $N = 27$	TOTAL $N = 114$
.51[b]	.39[a]	.42[a]	.47[a]	.45[a]

[a] $p < .01$.
[b] $p < .001$.

The .45 correlation for the entire sample supports the hypothesis that the greater his desire for external rewards, the more likely the student will hid his weaknesses from the teacher. The probability of this relationship is strengthened by the fact that the differences among the correlation coefficients for each class group are slight. This suggests that the relationship between reward seeking and hiding weaknesses does not depend on particular classroom conditions within a school.

The correlations between the scores on the student questionnaire and the teachers' reports on rejecting intellectual challenge are stated in Table 3.

TABLE 3
Correlations between Reward Seeking and Rejecting Intellectual Challenge

CLASS A $N = 28$	CLASS B $N = 29$	CLASS C $N = 30$	CLASS D $N = 27$	TOTAL $N = 114$
.62[a]	.57[a]	.56[a]	.64[a]	.60[a]

[a] $p < .001$.

The correlation of .60 for the entire sample indicates that the greater their desire for classroom rewards, the more likely students will reject intellectual challenges. Again, we find that the correlations among class groups are remarkably similar. They are also higher than those reported for the relationship between reward seeking and hiding weaknesses.

Discussion

Students, we have found, are generally responsive to the external rewards which pervade the classroom. The more responsive they are, however, the more unwilling they appear to be to reveal their deficiencies to teachers and to take a chance with more difficult material. The most plausible explanation for these findings is that students do not feel safe enough in the classroom to grow intellectually. They believe that exposing weaknesses and undertaking intellectual challenges will penalize them in their quest for classroom rewards. As a result, they fail both to consolidate current knowledge and to seek out new experiences.

It is somewhat surprising that rejection of intellectual challenge, in particular, has such a strong association with a desire for classroom rewards. A student who craves the teacher's approval is possibly more concerned with losing it than gaining it. By that I mean he is more interested in protecting himself from providing new grounds for the teacher's displeasure than taking active steps to impress him. Therefore, he does not attempt new learning activities which might jeopardize his tenuous status even further.

It would be invalid to conclude that the problems revealed in this study would be solved only if teachers would reward students who show their mistakes and take on new challenges. Knowing what the teacher rewards means knowing what he expects. Consequently, this solution merely adds to the pile of extrinsic rewards which entice and yet scare students. The crucial need is to create conditions which allow students to grow and learn because they choose to rather than because they must satisfy their teachers.

Discussion

Our official reason for evaluating students is to determine whether they can advance to more difficult work. But, evaluation is also used to encourage and direct involvement in current learning activities. It is further employed to influence students to follow institutional rules and procedures. Even if our intention is to guide students by helpful criticism or to motivate them by the promise of reward, students are bound to infer from our evaluations of their work and behavior how we view them as people. Since we have so many reasons to evaluate students, it would not be an exaggeration to say that school, for most of them, is where one is continually being appraised.

The power to make frequent judgments about a student's worth cannot be taken lightly. According to Holt, students, even in the most progressive schools, are greatly affected by the teacher's evaluative power. Holt was surprised to learn that his students felt "under the gun" much of the time in school. They lived under constant tension that their mistakes and failings would be revealed. He believes that many children want more than anything to find relief from this tension even if it means the teacher's disapproval. They will hand in their work without checking it or hurry through an important test in order to "get it over with."

Why are students so threatened by the teacher's judgments? It might be assumed that a student's major fear in school is his report card. Thus, every evaluation made by the teacher indicates to a student the grades he will be taking home to his parents. Dreeben's discussion of school sanctions suggests, however, that students have more immediate fears than grades. He points out that teachers typically evaluate students in front of their classmates. Since a classroom is usually populated by a homogeneous age group, each student is in a position to know how he stands in comparison to his peers. Every time his teacher judges him, his sense of self-esteem hangs in the balance. As Dreeben expresses it, the teacher is able to "play on a student's self-respect" by his ability to support or threaten it. It is not the praise or criticism itself which creates the fear, but the uncertainty as to which

one will be received. Jackson's description of classroom evaluation supports Dreeben. He stresses that the teachers' evaluative remarks are generally communicated publicly. A student's
own failures are seldom private. The student comes to sense
that his classmates are counting along with him how the
praises and criticisms he has received total up for the day.

If students wish to escape this tension, they must find ways
to protect themselves from the threat which classroom evaluation poses. The strategies they use depend on the intensity of
that threat. Those whose position in the class pecking order is
secure continue to comply with the academic and social expectations which brought them the teacher's praise in the first
place. But as Jackson points out, to stay on the teacher's "good
side" may at times require feigning involvement, hiding mis-
deeds, and misinforming the teacher. The less secure the student, the more likely he is forced to engage in this "cheating."
However, active attempts to impress the teacher are often too
risky for students to whom school is an especially threatening
experience. So, these students must minimize failure by deny-
ing the importance of success much like the boy, described by
Holt, who falls down on the soccer field to avoid the tension of
playing against bigger classmates.

My study of classroom rewards identifies some of these
same adaptations to the evaluative climate in schools. Many
students will hide their weaknesses and shy away from new
and challenging learning experiences because they are afraid
of inviting the teacher's disapproval. They learn in school not
to take a chance or to explore precisely because they desire
the extrinsic rewards teachers can offer. Students realize that
their teacher watches and judges every action against a con-
fusing set of standards. They must "play it safe" because there
are so many ways in which they can present a bad impression
of themselves.

When we witness students in school laughing, daydreaming, or complaining, it is hard to believe that many of them are
apprehensive. The problem of observing the apprehension created by classroom evaluation is that children respond to it in
ways which disguise their real fears. Nevertheless, it is visible
if one looks closely enough. It is reflected best in the choices
apprehensive students make in the classroom. If the teacher's

judgments did not threaten them, they would choose to use their mental energies to tackle new ideas rather than scheme how to hide their shortcomings.

School is a place where children are not accepted at their present stage of development. Growth is expected. But, children grow only after they feel safe; that is, they will seek out new knowledge most fully when they are convinced that penalties will not be invoked if they fail. Failure itself is not anxiety producing. The persistence which infants show in their attempts to master the environment suggests that human beings are not naturally afraid of failure. It becomes problematic, though, when a person believes he will lose something of value to him (for example, approval, good grades, a special privilege) if he does not succeed. The only way to relieve a child's anxiety about the teacher's evaluations is to assure him that they will not be held against him. The problem is whether students can be evaluated so that their successes and failures are viewed as helpful information rather than as indications of reward and punishment.

Part V

STUDENT POWERLESSNESS

How Children Fail–
An Excerpt*

JOHN HOLT

July 27, 1958

It has become clear over the year that these children see
school almost entirely in terms of the day-to-day and hour-to-
hour tasks that we impose on them. This is not at all the way
the teacher thinks of it. The conscientious teacher thinks of
himself as taking his students (at least part way) on a journey
to some glorious destination, well worth the pains of the trip.
If he teaches history, he thinks how interesting, how exciting,
how useful it is to know history, and how fortunate his students will be when they begin to share his knowledge. If he
teaches French, he thinks of the glories of French literature, or
the beauty of spoken French, or the delights of French cook-
ing, and how he is helping to make these joys available to his
students. And so for all subjects.

Thus teachers feel, as I once did, that their interests and
their students' are fundamentally the same. I used to feel that
I was guiding and helping my students on a journey that they
wanted to take but could not take without my help. I knew the
way looked hard, but I assumed they could see the goal almost
as clearly as I and that they were almost as eager to reach it. It
seemed very important to give students this feeling of being
on a journey to a worthwhile destination. I see now that most
of my talk to this end was wasted breath. Maybe *I* thought the
students were in my class because they were eager to learn
what I was trying to teach, but they knew better. They were

in school because they had to be, and in my class either because they had to be, or because otherwise they would have had to be in another class, which might be even worse.

Children in school are like children at the doctor's. He can talk himself blue in the face about how much good his medicine is going to do them; all they think of is how much it will hurt or how bad it will taste. Given their own way, they would have none of it.

So the valiant and resolute band of travelers I thought I was leading toward a much-hoped-for destination turned out instead to be more like convicts in a chain gang, forced under threat of punishment to move along a rough path leading nobody knew where and down which they could see hardly more than a few steps ahead. School feels like this to children: it is a place where *they* make you go and where *they* tell you to do things and where *they* try to make your life unpleasant if you don't do them or don't do them right.

For children, the central business of school is not learning, whatever this vague word means; it is getting these daily tasks done, or at least out of the way, with a minimum of effort and unpleasantness. Each task is an end in itself. The children don't care how they dispose of it. If they can get it out of the way by doing it, they will do it; if experience has taught them that this does not work very well, they will turn to other means, illegitimate means, that wholly defeat whatever purpose the task-giver may have had in mind.

They are very good at this, at getting other people to do their tasks for them. I remember the day not long ago when Ruth opened my eyes. We had been doing math, and I was pleased with myself because, instead of telling her answers and showing her how to do problems, I was "making her think" by asking her questions. It was slow work. Question after question met only silence. She said nothing, did nothing, just sat and looked at me through those glasses, and waited. Each time, I had to think of a question easier and more pointed than the last, until I finally found one so easy that she would feel safe in answering it. So we inched our way along until suddenly, looking at her as I waited for an answer to a question, I saw with a start that she was not at all puzzled by what I had asked her. In fact, she was not even thinking about it. She was coolly appraising me, weighing my patience, waiting for that next, sure-to-be-easier question. I thought, "I've been had!" The girl had learned how to make me do her work for her, just as she had learned to make all her previous teachers do the same thing. If I wouldn't tell her the answers, very well, she would just let me question her right up to them.

Schools and teachers seem generally to be as blind to children's strategies as I was. Otherwise, they would teach their courses and assign their tasks so that students who really thought about the meaning of the subject would have the best chance of succeeding, while those who tried to do the tasks by illegitimate means, without thinking or understanding, would be foiled. But the reverse seems to be the case. Schools give every encouragement to *producers,* the kids whose idea is to get "right answers" by any and all means. In a system that runs on "right answers," they can hardly help it. And these schools are often very discouraging places for *thinkers.*

Until recently it had not occurred to me that poor students thought differently about their work than good students; I assumed they thought the same way, only less skillfully. Now it begins to look as if the expectation and fear of failure, if strong enough, may lead children to act and think in a special way, to adopt strategies different from those of more confident children. Emily is a good example. She is emotionally as well as intellectually incapable of checking her work, of comparing her ideas against reality, of making any kind of judgment about the value of her thoughts. She makes me think of an animal fleeing danger—go like the wind, don't look back, remember where that danger was, and stay away from it as far as you can. Are there many other children who react to their fears in this way?

The Modern High School: A Profile*

EDGAR Z. FRIEDENBERG

Not far from Los Angeles, though rather nearer to Boston, may be located the town of Milgrim, in which Milgrim High School is clearly the most costly and impressive structure. Milgrim is not a suburb. Although it is only fifty miles from a large and dishonorable city and a part of its conurbation, comparatively few Milgrimites commute to the city for work. Milgrim is an agricultural village which has outgrown its nervous system; its accustomed modes of social integration have not yet even begun to relate its present, recently acquired inhabitants to one another. So, though it is not a suburb, Milgrim is not a community either.

Milgrim's recent, fulminating growth is largely attributable to the rapid development of light industry in the outer suburbs, with a resulting demand for skilled labor. But within the past few years, futher economic development has created a steady demand for labor that is not skilled. In an area that is by no means known for its racial tolerance or political liberalism, Milgrim has acquired, through no wish of its own, a sizable Negro and Puerto Rican minority. On the shabby outskirts of town, a number of groceries label themselves Spanish-American. The advanced class in Spanish at Milgrim High School makes a joyful noise—about the only one to be heard.

Estimates of the proportion of the student body at Milgrim who are, in the ethnocentric language of demography, nonwhite, vary enormously. Some students who are clearly middle-class and of pinkish-gray color sometimes speak as if they themselves were a besieged minority. More responsible staff

* *Commentary*, 36, 1963, 373–380. Reprinted from *Commentary*, by permission; copyright © 1963 by the American Jewish Committee.

members produce estimates of from 12 to 30 per cent. Observations in the corridors and lunchrooms favor the lower figure. They also establish clearly that the non-whites are orderly and well behaved, though somewhat more forceful in their movements and manner of speech than their light-skinned colleagues.

What is Milgrim High like? It is a big, expensive building, on spacious but barren grounds. Every door is at the end of a corridor; there is no reception area, no public space in which one can adjust to the transition from the outside world. Between class periods the corridors are tumultuously crowded; during them they are empty. But at both times they are guarded by teachers and students on patrol duty. Patrol duty does not consist primarily in the policing of congested throngs of moving students, or the guarding of property from damage. Its principal function is the checking of corridor passes. Between classes, no student may walk down the corridor without a form, signed by a teacher, telling where he is coming from, where he is going, and the time, to the minute, during which the pass is valid. A student caught in the corridor without such a pass is sent or taken to the office; there a detention slip is made out against him, and he is required to remain after school for two or three hours. He may do his homework during this time, but he may not leave his seat or talk.

There is no physical freedom whatever at Milgrim. Except during class breaks, the lavatories are kept locked, so that a student must not only obtain a pass but find the custodian and induce him to open the facility. Indeed Milgrim High's most memorable arrangements are its corridor passes and its johns; they dominate social interaction. "Good morning, Mr. Smith," an attractive girl will say pleasantly to one of her teachers in the corridor. "Linda, do you have a pass to be in your locker after the bell rings?" is his greeting in reply. There are more classifications of washrooms than there must have been in the Confederate Navy. The common sort, marked just "Boys" and "Girls," are generally locked. Then there are some marked, "Teachers, Men" and "Teachers, Women" unlocked. Near the auditorium are two others marked simply, "Men" and "Women," which are intended primarily for the public when the auditorium is being used for some function. During the school day cardboard signs saying "Adults Only" are placed on these doors, Girding up my maturity, I used this men's room during my stay at Milgrim. Usually it was empty; but once, as soon as the door clicked behind me, a teacher who had been concealed in the cubicle began jumping up and down to peer over his partition and verify my adulthood.

He was not a voyeur; he was checking on smoking. At most public high schools, students are forbidden to smoke, and this is probably the most common source of friction with authorities. It focuses, naturally, on the washrooms which are the only place students can go where teachers are not supposed to be. Milgrim, for a time, was more liberal than most; last year its administration designated an area behind the school where seniors might smoke during their lunch period. But, as a number of students explained to me during interviews, some of these seniors had "abused the privilege" by lighting up before they got into the area, and the privilege had been withdrawn. No student, however, questioned that smoking was a privilege rather than a right.

The concept of privilege is important at Milgrim. Teachers go to the head of the chow line at lunch; whenever I would attempt quietly to stand in line the teacher on hall duty would remonstrate with me. He was right, probably; I was fouling up an entire informal social system by my ostentation. Students on hall patrol also were allowed to come to the head of the line; so were seniors. Much of the behavior that Milgrim depends on to keep it going is motivated by the reward of getting a government-surplus peanut butter or tuna fish sandwich without standing in line.

The lunchroom itself is a major learning experience, which must make quite an impression over four years time. There are two large cafeterias which are used as study halls during the periods before and after the middle of the day. The food, by and large, is good, and more tempting than the menu. The atmosphere is not quite that of a prison, because the students are permitted to talk quietly, under the frowning scrutiny of teachers standing around on duty, during their meal—they are not supposed to talk while standing in line, though this rule is only sporadically enforced. Standing in line takes about a third of their lunch period, and leaves plenty of time for them to eat what is provided them. They may not, in any case, leave the room when they have finished, any more than they could leave a class. Toward the end of the period a steel gate is swung down across the corridor, dividing the wing holding the cafeterias, guidance offices, administrative offices, and auditorium from the rest of the building. Then the first buzzer sounds, and the students sweep out of the cafeteria and press silently forward to the gate. A few minutes later a second buzzer sounds, the gate is opened, and the students file out to their classrooms.

During the meal itself the atmosphere varies in response to chance events and the personality of the teachers assigned supervisory duty; this is especially true in the corridor where the next sitting is waiting in line. The norm is a not unpleasant chatter; but about one teacher in four is an embittered martinent, snarling, whining, continually ordering the students to stand closer to the wall and threatening them with detention or suspension for real or fancied insolence. On other occasions, verbal altercations break out between students in the cafeteria or in line and the *student* hall patrolmen. In one of these that I witnessed, the accused student, a handsome, aggressive-looking young man, defended himself in the informal but explicit language of working-class hostility. This roused the teacher on duty from his former passivity. He walked over toward the boy, and silently but with a glare of contempt, beckoned him from the room with a crooked finger and led him along the corridor to the administrative office: the tall boy rigid in silent protest, the teacher, balding and stoop-shouldered in a wrinkled suit, shambling ahead of him. The youth, I later learned, was suspended for a day. At some lunch periods all this is drowned out by Mantovani-type pop records played over the public address system.

What adults generally, I think, fail to grasp even though they may actually know it, is that there is no refuge or respite from this: no coffee-break, no taking ten for a smoke, no room like the teachers' room, however poor, where the youngsters can get away from adults. High schools don't have club rooms; they have organized gym and recreation. A student cannot go to the library when he wants a book; on certain days his schedule provides a forty-five-minute library period. "Don't let anybody leave early," a guidance counselor urged during a group-testing session at Hartsburgh, an apparently more permissive school that I also visited. "There really isn't any place for them to go." Most of us are as nervous by the age of five as we will ever be, and adolescence adds to the strain; but one thing a high-school student learns is that he can expect no provision for his need to give in to his feelings, or swing out in his own style, or creep off and pull himself together.

The little things shock most. High-school students—and not just, or even particularly, at Miligrim—have a prisoner's sense of time. They don't know what time it is outside. The research which occasioned my presence at Milgrim, Hartsburgh, and the other schools in my study required me to interview each of twenty-five to thirty students at each school three times. My first appointment with each student was set up by his guidance counselor; I would make the next appointment directly with the student and issue him the passes he needed to keep it. The student has no *open* time at his own disposal; he has to select the period he can miss with least loss to himself. Students well-adapted to the school usually pick study halls; poorer or more troublesome students pick the times of their most disagreeable classes; both avoid cutting classes in which the teacher is likely to respond vindictively to their absence. Most students, when asked when they would like to come for their next interview, replied, "I can come any time." When I pointed out to them that there must, after all, be some times that would be more convenient for them than others, they would say, "Well, tomorrow, fourth period" or whatever. But hardly any of them knew when this would be in clock time. High-school classes emphasize the importance of punctuality by beginning at regular but uneven times like 10:43 and 11:27, which are, indeed, hard to remember; and the students did not know when this was.

How typical is all this? The elements of the composition— the passes, the tight scheduling, the reliance on threats of detention or suspension as modes of social control are nearly universal. The usurpation of any possible *area* of student initiative, physical or mental, is about as universal. Milgrim forbids boys to wear trousers that end more than six inches above the floor, and has personnel fully capable of measuring them. But most high schools have some kind of dress regulation; I know of none that accepts and relies on the tastes of students.

There are differences, to be sure, in tone; and these matter. They greatly affect the impact of the place on students. Take, for comparison and contrast, Hartsburgh High. Not fifteen miles from Milgrim, Hartsburgh is an utterly different community. It is larger, more compact, and more suburban; more of a place. Hartsburgh High is much more dominantly middle class and there are few Negroes in the high school there.

First impressions of Hartsburgh High are almost bound to be favorable. The building, like Milgrim, is new; unlike Milgrim's, it is handsome. External walls are mostly glass, which gives a feeling of light, air, and space. At Hartsburgh there is none of the snarling, overt hostility that taints the atmosphere at Milgrim. There are no raucous buzzers; no bells of any kind. Instead, there are little blinker lights arranged like the Mexican flag. The green light blinks and the period is over; the white light signals a warning; when the red light blinks it is time to be in your classroom. Dress regulations exist but are less rigorous than at Milgrim. Every Wednesday, however, is dress-up day; boys are expected to wear ties and jackets or jacket-sweaters, the girls wear dresses rather than skirts and sweaters. The reason is that on Wednesday the school day ends with an extra hour of required assembly and, as the students explain, there are often outside visitors for whom they are expected to look their best.

Students at Hartsburgh seem much more relaxed than at Milgrim. In the grounds outside the main entrance, during lunch period, there is occasional horseplay. For ten minutes during one noon hour I watched three boys enacting a mutual fantasy. One was the audience who only sat and laughed, one the aggressor, and the third—a pleasant, inarticulate varsity basketball player named Paul—was the self-appointed victim. The two protagonists were protraying in pantomime old, silent-movie type fights in slow motion. The boy I did not know would slowly swing at Paul, who would sink twisting to the ground with grimaces of anguish; then the whole sequence would be repeated with variations, though the two boys never switched roles. In my interviews with Paul I had never solved the problem arising from the fact that he was eloquent only with his arms and torso movements, which were lost on the tape recorder, and it was a real pleasure to watch him in his own medium. This was a pleasure Milgrim would never have afforded me. Similarly, in the corridors at Hartsburgh I would occasionally come upon couples holding hands or occasionally

rather more, though it distressed me that they always broke
guiltily apart as soon as they saw me or any adult. One of my
subjects, who was waiting for his interview, was dancing a
little jig by himself in the corridor when I got to him. This was
all rather reassuring.

It was also contrary to policy. There is a regulation against
couples holding hands and they are punished if caught by the
kind of teacher who hates sexuality in the young. The air and
space also, subtly, turn out to be illusions if you try to use
them. Hartsburgh High is built around a large, landscaped
courtyard with little walks and benches. I made the mistake of
trying to conduct an interview on one of these benches. When
it was over we could not get back into the building except by
disturbing a class, for the doors onto this inviting oasis can
only be opened from inside, and nobody ever goes there. Since
the courtyard is completely enclosed by the high-school building, this arrangement affords no additional protection from
intruders; it merely shuts off a possible place for relaxation.
The beautiful glass windows do not open enough to permit a
body to squirm through and, consequently, do not open
enough to ventilate the rooms, in which there are no individual controls for the fiercely effective radiators. Room tempera-
ture at Hartsburgh is a matter of high policy.

Teachers do not hide in the washrooms at Hartsburgh; but
the principal recently issued a letter warning that any student
caught in the vicinity of the school with "tobacco products"
would be subject to suspension; students were directed to
have their parents sign the letter as written acknowledgment
that they were aware of the regulation and return it to school.
Staff, of course, are permitted to smoke. At Hartsburgh a former teacher, promoted to assistant principal serves as a fulltime disciplinarian, but students are not dragged to his office
by infuriated teachers, as sometimes happens at Milgrim. Instead, during the first period, two students from the school
Citizenship Corps go quietly from classroom to classroom with
a list, handing out summonses.

Along with having a less rancorous and choleric atmosphere than Milgrim, Hartsburgh seems to have more teachers
who like teaching and like kids. But the fundamental pattern
is still one of control, distrust, and punishment. The observable
differences—and they are striking—are the results almost en-

tirely, I believe, of *structural* and demographic factors and occur despite very similar administrative purposes. Neither principal respects adolescents at all or his staff very much. Both are preoccupied with good public relations as they understand them. Both are inflexible, highly authoritarian men. But their situations are different.

At Milgrim there is a strong district superintendent; imaginative if not particularly humane, he is oriented toward the national educational scene. He likes to have projects, particularly in research guidance. Guidance officers report through their chairman directly to him, not to the building principal; and the guidance staff is competent, tough, and completely professional. When wrangles occur over the welfare of a student they are likely to be open, with the principal and the guidance director as antagonists; both avoid such encounters if possible, and neither can count on the support of the district office; but when an outside force—like an outraged parent—precipitates a conflict, it is fought out. At Hartsburgh, the district superintendent is primarily interested in running a tight ship with no problems. To this end, he backs the authority of the principal whenever this might be challenged. The guidance office is vertigial and concerned primarily with college placement and public relations in the sense of inducing students to behave in socially acceptable ways with a minimum of fuss.

In these quite different contexts, demographic differences in the student bodies have crucial consequences. At Milgrim, the working-class students are not dominant—they have not quite enough self-confidence or nearly enough social savvy to be—but they are close enough to it to be a real threat to the nice, college-bound youngsters who set the tone in their elementary and junior high school and who expect to go on dominating the high school. These view the rapid influx of lower-status students as a rising wave that can engulf them, while the newcomers, many of whom are recent migrants or high-school transfers from the city, can remember schools in which they felt more at home.

The result is both to split and to polarize student feeling about the school, its administration, and other students. Nobody likes Milgrim High. But the middle-class students feel that what has ruined it is the lower-class students, and that the punitive constraint with which the school is run is necessary to keep them in line. In some cases these students approach paranoia: one girl—commenting on a mythical high school described in one of our semi-projective research instruments —said, "Well, it says here that the majority of the students are Negro—about a third" (the actual statement is "about a fifth").

The working-class students are hard-pressed; but being hard-pressed they are often fairly realistic about their position. If the Citizenship Corps that functions so smoothly and smugly at Hartsburgh were to be installed at Milgrim, those who actually turned people in and got them in trouble would pretty certainly receive some after-school instruction in the way social classes differ in values and in the propensity for non-verbal self-expression. At Milgrim, the working-class kids know where they stand and stand there. They are exceptionally easy to interview because the interviewer need not be compulsively non-directive. Once they sense that they are respected, they respond enthusiastically and with great courtesy. But they do not alter their position to give the interviewer what they think he wants, or become notably anxious at disagreeing with him. They are very concrete in handling experience and are not given to generalization. Most of them seem to have liked their elementary school, and they share the general American respect for education down to the last cliché—but then one will add, as an afterthought, not bothering even to be contemptuous, "Of course, you can't respect *this* school." They deal with their situation there in correspondingly concrete terms. Both schools had student courts last year, for example, and Hartsburgh still does, though few students not in the Citizenship Corps pay much attention to it. Student traffic corpsmen give much attention to it. Student traffic corpsmen give out tickets for corridor offenses, and these culprits are brought before an elected student judge with an administrative official of the school present as adviser. But Milgrim had a student court last year that quickly became notorious. The "hoody element" got control of it, and since most of the defendants were their buddies, they were either acquitted or discharged on pleas of insanity. The court was disbanded.

The struggle at Milgrim is therefore pretty open, though

none of the protagonists see it as a struggle for freedom or could define its issues in terms of principles. The upper-status students merely assent to the way the school is run, much as middle-class white Southerners assent to what the sheriff's office does, while the lower-status students move, or get pushed, from one embroilment to the next without ever quite realizing that what is happening to them is part of a general social pattern. At Hartsburgh the few lower-status students can easily be ignored rather than feared by their middle-class compeers who set the tone. They are not sufficiently numerous or aggressive to threaten the middle-class youngsters or their folkways; but, for the same reason, they do not force the middle-class youngsters to make common cause with the administration. The administration, like forces of law and order generally in the United States, is accepted without deference as a part of the way things are and work. Americans rarely expect authority to be either intelligent or forth-right; it looks out for its own interests as best it can. Reformers and trouble-makers only make it nervous and therefore worse; the best thing is to take advantage of it when it can help you and at other times to go on living your own life and let it try to stop you.

This is what the Hartsburgh students usually do, and, on the whole, the results are pleasant. The youngsters, being to some degree ivy, do not constantly remind the teachers, as the Milgrim students do, that their jobs have no connection with academic scholarship. Many of the teachers, for their part act and sound like college instructors, do as competent a job, and enjoy some of the same satisfactions. The whole operation moves smoothly. Both Milgrim and Hartsburgh are valid examples—though of very different aspects—of American democracy in action. And in neither could a student learn as much about civil liberty as a Missouri mule knows at birth.

What is learned in high school, or for that matter anywhere at all, depends far less on what is taught than on what one actually experiences in the place. The quality of instruction in high school varies from sheer rot to imaginative and highly skilled teaching. But classroom content is often handled at a creditable level and is not in itself the source of the major difficulty. Both at Milgrim and Hartsburgh, for example, the students felt that they were receiving competent instruction and that this was an undertaking the school tried seriously to handle. I doubt, however, that this makes up for much of the damage to which high-school students are systematically subjected. What is formally taught is just not that important, compared to the constraint and petty humiliation to which the youngsters with few exceptions must submit in order to survive.

The fact that some of the instruction is excellent and a lot of it pretty good *is* important for another reason; it makes the whole process of compulsory schooling less insulting than it otherwise would be by lending it a superficial validity. Society tells the adolescent that he is sent to school in order to learn what he is taught in the classroom. No anthropologist and very few high school students would accept this as more than a rationalization; but rationalizations, to be at all effective, must be fairly plausible. Just as the draft would be intolerable if the cold war were wholly a piece of power politics or merely an effort to sustain the economy, so compulsory school attendance would be intolerable if what went on in the classrooms were totally inadequate to students' needs and irrelevant to their real intellectual concerns. Much of it is, but enough is not, to provide middle-class students, at least, with an answer when their heart cries out "For Christ's sake, what am I doing here?"

But far more of what is deeply and thoroughly learned in the school is designed to keep the heart from raising awkward, heartfelt issues—if design governs in a thing so subtle. It is learned so thoroughly by attendance at schools like Milgrim or even Hartsburgh that most Americans by the time they are adult cannot really imagine that life could be organized in any other way.

First of all, they learn to assume that the state has the right to compel adolescents to spend six or seven hours a day, five days a week, thirty-six or so weeks a year, in a specific place, in charge of a particular group of persons in whose selection they have no voice, performing tasks about which they have no choice, without remuneration and subject to specialized regulations and sanctions that are applicable to no one else in the community nor to them except in this place. Whether this law is a service or a burden to the young—and, indeed, it is both, in varying degrees—is another issue altogether. As I

have noted elsewhere,[1] compulsory school attendance functions as a bill of attainder against a particular age group. The
student's position is that of a conscript, who is protected by
certain regulations but in no case permitted to use their breach
as a cause for terminating his obligation. So the first thing the
young learn in school is that there are certain sanctions and
restrictions that apply only to them; that they do not participate fully in the freedoms guaranteed by the state, and that
*therefore, these freedoms do not really partake of the charac-
ter of inalienable rights.*

Of course not. The school, as schools continually stress,
acts *in loco parentis;* and children may not leave home because their parents are unsatisfactory. What I have pointed
out is no more than a special consequence of the fact that
students are minors, and minors do not, indeed, share all the
rights and privileges—and responsibilities—of citizenship.
Very well. However one puts it, we are still discussing the
same issue. The high school, then, is where you really learn
what it means to be a minor.

For a high school is not a parent. Parents may love their
children, hate them, or like most parents, do both in a complex
mixture. But they must nevertheless permit a certain intimacy
and respond to their children as persons. Homes are not run
by regulations, though the parents may think they are, but by
a process of continuous and almost entirely unconscious emotional homeostasis, in which each member affects and accom-
modates to the needs, feelings, fantasy life, and character
structure of the others. This may be, and often is, a terribly
destructive process; I intend no defense of the family as a
social institution. But children grow up in homes or the remnants of homes; are in physical fact dependent on parents, and
too intimately related to them to permit their area of freedom
to be precisely defined. This is not because they have no rights
or are entitled to less respect than adults, but because intimacy conditions freedom and growth in ways too subtle and
continuous to be defined as overt acts.

Free societies depend on their members to learn early and
thoroughly that public authority is not like that of the family;
that it cannot be expected—or trusted—to respond with sensi-

[1] See "An Ideology of School Withdrawal," June 1963.

tivity and intimate perception to the needs of individuals but must rely basically, though as humanely as possible, on the impartial application of general formulae. This means that it must be kept functional, specialized, and limited to matters of public policy; the meshes of the law are too coarse to be worn to the skin. Especially in an open society, where people of very different backgrounds and value systems must function together, it would seem obvious that each must understand that he may not push others further than their common undertaking demands, or impose upon them a manner of life that they feel to be alien.

After the family, the school is the first social institution an individual must deal with—the first place in which he learns to handle himself with strangers. The school establishes the pattern of his subsequent assumptions as to what relations between the individual and society are appropriate and which constitute invasions of privacy and constraints on his spirit—what the British, with exquisite precision, call "taking a liberty." But the American public school evolved as a melting pot, under the assumption that it had not merely the right but the duty to impose a common standard of genteel decency on a polyglot body of immigrants' children and thus insure their assimilation into the better life of the American dream. It accepted, also, the tacit assumption that genteel decency was as far as it could go. If America has generally been governed by the practical man's impatience with other individuals' rights, it has also accepted the practical man's determination to preserve his property by discouraging public extravagance. With its neglect of personal privacy and individual autonomy the school incorporates a considerable measure of Galbraith's "public squalor." The plant may be expensive—for this is capital goods; but little is provided graciously, liberally, simply as an amenity, either to teachers or students, though administrative offices have begun to assume an executive look.

The first thing the student learns, then, is that as a minor, he is subject to peculiar restraints; the second is that these restraints are general, not limited either by custom or by the schools' presumed commitment to the curriculum. High-school administrators are not professional educators in the sense that a physician, an attorney, or a tax accountant are professionals. They do not, that is, think of themselves as practitioners of a specialized instructional craft, who derive their authority from its requirements. They are specialists in keeping an essentially political enterprise from being strangled by conflicting community attitudes and pressures. They are problem-oriented, and the feelings and needs for growth of their captive and unenfranchised clientele are the least of their problems; for the status of the "teenager" in the community is so low that even if he rebels, the school is not blamed for the conditions against which he is rebelling. He is simply a truant or a juvenile delinquent; at worst the school has "failed to reach him." What high-school personnel become specialists in, ultimately, is the *control* of large groups of students even at catastrophic expense to their opportunity to learn. These controls are not exercised primarily to facilitate instruction, and particularly, they are in no way limited to matters bearing on instruction. At several schools in our sample boys had been ordered—sometimes on the complaint of teachers—to shave off beards. One of these boys had played football for the school; he was told that, although the school had no legal authority to require him to shave, he would be barred from the banquet honoring the team unless he complied. Dress regulations are another case in point.

Of course these are petty restrictions, enforced by petty penalties. American high schools are not concentration camps. But I am not complaining about their severity; what disturbs me is what they teach their students concerning the proper relationship of the individual to society, and in this respect the fact that the restrictions and penalties are unimportant in themselves makes matters worse. Gross invasions are more easily recognized for what they are: petty restrictions are only resisted by "troublemakers." What matters in the end is that the school does not take its own business of education seriously enough to mind it.

The effects on the students are manifold. The concepts of dignity and privacy, notably deficient in American adult folkways, are not permitted to develop here. The school's assumption of custodial control of students implies that power and authority are indistinguishable. If the school's authority is not limited to matters pertaining to education, it cannot be derived from its educational responsibilities. It is a naked, empirical fact, to be accepted or controverted according to the possibilities of the moment. In such a world, power counts more than legitimacy; if you don't have power, it is naïve to think you have rights that must be respected . . . wise up. High school students experience regulation only as control, not as protection; they know, for example, that the principal will generally uphold the teacher in any conflict with a student, regardless of the merits of the case. Translated into the high-school idiom, *suaviter in modo, fortiter in re* becomes "If you get caught, it's just your ass."

Students do not often resent this; that is the tragedy. All weakness tends to corrupt absolutely. Identifying, as the weak must, with the more powerful and frustrating of the forces that impinge upon them, they accept the school as the way life is and close their minds against the anxiety of perceiving alternatives. Many students like high school; others loathe and fear it. But even the latter do not object to it on principle; the school effectively obstructs their learning of the principles on which objection might be based; though these are among the principles that, we boast, distinguish us from totalitarian societies.

Yet, finally, the consequence of continuing through adolescence to submit to diffuse authority that is not derived from the task at hand—as a doctor's orders or the training regulations of an athletic coach, for example, usually are—is more serious than political incompetence or weakness of character. There is a general arrest of development. An essential part of growing up is learning that, though differences of power among men lead to brutal consequences, all men are peers; none is omnipotent, none derives his potency from magic, but only from his specific competence and function. The policeman represents the majesty of the state, but this does not mean that he can put you in jail; it means, precisely, that he cannot —at least not for long. Any person or agency responsible for handling throngs of young people—especially if he does not like them or is afraid of them—is tempted to claim diffuse authority and snare the youngster in the trailing remnants of childhood emotion which always remain to trip him. Schools succumb to this temptation, and control pupils by reinvoking the sensations of childhood punishment, which remain effective because they were originally selected, with great unconscious guile, to dramatize the child's weakness in the face of authority. "If you act like a bunch of spoiled brats, we'll treat you like a bunch of spoiled brats," is a favorite dictum of sergeants, and school personnel, when their charges begin to show an awkward capacity for independence.

Thus the high school is permitted to infantilize adolescence; in fact, it is encouraged to by the widespread hostility to "teen-agers" and the anxiety about their conduct found throughout our society. It does not allow much maturation to occur during the years when most maturation would naturally occur. Maturity, to be sure, is not conspicuously characteristic of American adult life, and would almost certainly be a threat to the economy. So perhaps in this, as in much else, the high school is simply the faithful servant of the community.

There are two important ways in which it can render such service. The first of these is through its impact on individuals; on their values, their conception of their personal worth, their patterns of anxiety, and on their mastery and ease in the world —which determine so much of what they think of as their fate. The second function of the school is Darwinian; its biases, though their impact is always on individual youngsters, operate systematically to mold entire social groups. These biases endorse and support the values and patterns of behavior of certain segments of the population, providing their members with the credentials and shibboleths needed for the next stages of their journey, while they instill in others a sense of inferiority and warn the rest of society against them as troublesome and untrustworthy. In this way the school contributes simultaneously to social mobility and to social stratification. It helps see to it that the kind of people who get ahead are the kind who will support the social system it represents, while those who might, through intent or merely by their being, subvert it, are left behind as a salutary moral lesson.

Children's Privacy and Compulsory Schooling*

JOANNE REYNOLDS BRONARS

A development of the notion of privacy as an individual human right can be traced through Western culture from Greek times to the present. The meaning of the concept has been a continuously changing one. For example, at one time private property rights referred only to tangible property, but now refer also to the privacy of ideas.[1] Morris Ernst cites the appearance of an article, "The Right of Privacy," *Harvard Law Review*, December, 1890, as a key event in the development of the principle of privacy in American legal thought. The article, written by Louis Brandeis and Samuel Warren, introduced the idea of "the right to be let alone." One section of the article states:

> *The common law secures to each individual the right of determining, ordinarily, to what extent his thoughts, sentiments and emotions shall be communicated to others. . . . The right is lost only when the author himself communicates his production to the public—in other words, publishes it. . . . The protection offered to thoughts, sentiments, and emotions . . . is merely an instance of the more general right of the individual to be let alone. It is like . . . the right not to be maliciously prosecuted, the right not to be defamed. In each of these rights . . . there inheres the quality of being owned or possessed—and . . . there may be some propriety in speaking of these rights as property. But, obviously, they bear little resemblance to what*

[1] See discussion of the historical development of the concept of privacy in Western culture in Hannah Arendt's *The Human Condition*. New York: Doubleday, 1959.

* *Teachers College Record*, 68, 1966, 33–41. Reprinted with permission from the publisher and the author.

> *is ordinarily comprehended under that term. The principle*
> *which protects . . . all . . . personal productions, not against*
> *theft and physical appropriation, but against publication in*
> *any form, is in reality . . . the principle . . . of an inviolate*
> *personality.*[2]

A linking of the notion of personal privacy to that of an individual's inviolate personality draws upon a body of thought regarding the sacredness of the person that goes back to the Old Testament. In Leviticus, for example, we are instructed to reason with our neighbor and show toward him reverence, love, and just behavior. The doctrines of natural law and natural rights advanced the notion of the sacredness of personality as did the Kantian imperative that we treat others as ends and not as means. In *The Sense of Injustice,* Edmond Cahn suggests that progress in civil law has involved an extension of the term "person" to more and more categories of individuals, such as slaves, women, and children.[3]

Children and Privacy Rights

The development of the principle of privacy has not included a consideration of the meaning of privacy rights as applied to children. This is not surprising since, not long ago, children had no rights at all. In his 1910 preface to *Misalliance,* George Bernard Shaw remarked that children were in some sense slaves with no rights and liberties.[4] Since that time, child labor laws and laws against child beating or neglect have somewhat mitigated this condition in the United States. But such legislation deals mainly with the child's physical welfare. The question of children's privacy rights involves the right to protection against psychological, as well as physical damage. The term "psychological damage" is used to refer to such conditions as the loss of peace of mind, or a sense of

[2] Ernst, Morris and Alan Schwartz. *Privacy: The Right to be Let Alone.* New York: Macmillan, 1962.

[3] Cahn, Edmond. *The Sense of Injustice,* New York: New York University Press, 1949.

[4] Shaw, George Bernard. *The Collected Works of George Bernard Shaw.* New York: William H. Wise Co., 1930, V. XIII.

being the victim of injustice. Here the issues are less clear than those involving physical injury, as are those involving the privacy of thought as opposed to tangible property rights. Some legal precedents have been set with regard to a consideration of children's psychological welfare. The Supreme Court decision on school segregation, for example, took into account such factors as feelings of inferiority, impairment of motivation to learn, and retardation of mental development. Judicial decisions in child-custody cases also take into account the factor of psychological damage.

Grounds for These Rights

Children's rights to privacy might be argued on legal, psychological, religious, or moral grounds. One might argue, for example, that since legal precedents have been set for granting privacy rights to the adult members of our society, some of the rights ought to be extended to children, assuming that we regard them as persons whose selfhood is to be respected. The psychological grounds would involve such factors as the child's image of himself, his intellectual and emotional development, or his social consciousness in relation to the quality and degree of privacy afforded to him. We can only speculate about what such correlations might be, for an examination of psychological literature fails to reveal any studies about the subject of privacy. It would be reasonable to suppose, however, that if children are given no opportunity to experience the meaning of privacy in at least some of its forms, they will not be prepared to expect, demand, or defend their privacy rights as adults, nor to respect the rights of others.

In this paper it shall be assumed that children have rights to some forms of privacy on moral grounds. When Warren and Brandeis argue that we have as our birthright a right to be let alone, they argue that the right to life has come to mean the right to enjoy life, which involves protection against all violations of our being. It is believed that children should enjoy life in the same respect as persons in their own right.

The analysis of privacy that follows will be limited to the context of compulsory schooling which, it is believed, has considerable influence upon children's notions of selfhood and of social membership and which, furthermore, constitutes enforced groupishness. There are, however, other important dimensions of children's privacy which demand analysis, such as the question as to whether children should receive publicity through the mass media because their parents' lives are judged to be of public interest, e.g., children of criminals, political figures or social reformers.

Compulsory School

David Reisman remarks that children learn early in their lives that they are to have no secrets from peers and adults. He suggests that parents may help their children to become autonomous individuals by letting them learn that they have a right to make choices "between those leisure situations in which they wish to be intimate with others and those in which intimacy is merely the demand of an authority, parental or groupish."[5] Compulsory schooling produces such enforced intimacy, for a body of students is compelled to come together in a designated place for a designated time for purposes established by the adult members of society. Groupings of students are made on the basis of such criteria as place of residence, age, and academic achievement, and assigned to a teacher. Clearly these are not criteria that would be used by children in establishing voluntary groupings, nor is the teacher-pupil relationship like that described by Paul Goodman in his analysis of the ideal teaching situation in which teachers with something to teach and students who want to learn from them come together in a free relationship for as long as is mutually agreed upon.[6] Edgar Friedenberg makes clear the full force of compulsory school attendance when he reminds us that it is provided for by a law which does not bind the school to any obligation which the student can enforce:

[5] Riesman, David, et al. *The Lonely Crowd.* New York: Doubleday, 1953.
[6] Goodman, Paul. *Community of Scholars.* New York: Random House, Inc., 1962.

He cannot petition to withdraw if the school is inferior, does not maintain standards, or treats him brutally. . . . His position is purely that of a conscript who is protected by certain regulations but in no case permitted to use their breach as a cause for terminating his obligations.[7]

The element of constraint in compulsory schooling seems to be one important factor in making schooling a moral matter and in giving significance to the subject of privacy in the school.

Protection of Property

The most obvious aspect of privacy in the school is that of the protection of private property. What sorts of things are to be regarded as a child's property and how are his ownership rights to be protected? The items in a child's possession are generally of two kinds—those lent to him by the school authorities for his temporary use, such as textbooks and paint brushes, and those brought from home. Some place is then provided where these items may be stored, such as a desk or, in rarer instances, a locker which the student may lock. Where no locks are provided the protection of each child's property is a moral one. Teachers may lecture to the class on the importance of each child taking good care of the school property in his possession and of leaving other people's things alone. Rules may be set up such as, "No going into another child's desk without asking permission" and penalties exacted for infringement of the rules. There is often a lack of clarity, however, as to who is to grant the permission and under what circumstances and who is to come under the penalty. Should the teacher be the one to grant the permission? This is often the case, as when a teacher says, "Yes, you can borrow Jane's crayons in order to finish your picture. Jane, lend Peter your crayons." If the crayons are school property does this mean that the disposition of that property is at all times to be at the

[7] Friedenberg, Edgar. *Coming of Age in America.* New York: Random House, Inc., 1963.

disposal of the school authorities, or should the child have some choice in the matter during the time that the crayons have been assigned to him?

The child's rights regarding his own possessions must also be made clear. Many teachers place a premium upon what is called "learning to share" and often assume the right to say, "Jill, you brought three pencils from home and John needs one. I want you to give him one of your pencils." If Jill replies, "I don't want to give one of my pencils away," the teacher may shame her into changing her mind or may take one of her pencils and give it to John. Conversely, a first grade teacher was heard to remark, "Remember, in our classroom you are not allowed to share your snacks." Does learning to share mean turning over one's possessions to someone else or withholding them from others whenever the teacher requests that it be done? Should a child be allowed to say, "Only I have the right to determine who shall use, or even see my possessions?" What are the circumstances under which a child's possessions are inviolate as opposed to those under which other values are to have precedence? For example, the teacher may reserve the right to confiscate a penknife which a child has brought to school in defiance of the teacher's rulings and which is judged to be a danger to others, but perhaps the teacher does not have the right to tear up a child's comic book because he was looking at it during a math lesson. A teacher might reserve the right to go through a child's desk in order to look for a missing item, but does she have the right to go through the desk in order to borrow a book or to show the child's work to a parent? Generally a teacher's desk is "off limits" to others. What is needed is some clarity as to when children have the right to keep their possessions inviolate.

Individual Solitude

Privacy rights have generally involved the right of the individual to remove himself at times from public scrutiny. "A man's home is his castle." Father's den is his private realm. A closed bedroom door means, "Do not enter," or at least,

"Knock first." The organization of the school militates against the opportunity being provided for children to get off by themselves for any part of the school day to read, work, think, or just to be alone. Most of the day is spent in one room of a box-like shape and crowded with students. Friedenberg makes his point about a typical high school where even the toilets are locked during class breaks, where the students may only use the library at scheduled times and where there is no place comparable to a faculty room where students may get away from adults, or from each other.

We do not really know to what extent children in a group situation need or desire periods of aloneness or to what extent they learn not to want aloneness. Teachers seem to believe that children do not like to be apart from the group, for isolation from the group is generally used as a punishment for misbehavior. Thus the implication is that aloneness is an unde-sireable thing which children will not willingly seek. Perhaps there is a relationship here between the idea of isolation as a punishment and the idea that a child who is alone (by his own choosing) and quiet must be doing something wrong. The following questions might help us clarify the issues of a child's right to physical privacy at school:

How is the individual's right to physical privacy related to maturity? Is this a privilege to be earned as a function of responsible behavior, or do we consider some opportunity for aloneness to be a natural right of children?

Can distinctions be made between learning experiences which are better carried on alone as opposed to those which are group experiences?

What are the purposes for which we would consider it legitimate for a student to seek solitude? How would such purposes compare with the purposes for which adults seek solitude?

In what way does the classroom program as planned by the teacher provide or deny opportunities for solitude?

What meanings does solitude have other than physical aloneness? Does that which we generally term and condemn as daydreaming play a function in allowing a child in the classroom to achieve aloneness when physical isolation is not possible? Would we permit a child to say, "I've got to think through a problem; I don't want to listen to the story you are reading," or "Don't call on me during the discussion"? In other words, is there ever a legitimate place for inattention on the part of individual children?

Freedom to be Unobserved

An aspect of privacy closely related to individual solitude is the right of the individual to choose those aspects of his being and of his behavior which he will or will not reveal to others. When this right is violated we say that he is being spied upon. The intent of the spy is to gain information about an individual without his knowledge, and thus, he is invading the individual's privacy. Any examination of the question of the privacy rights of children in school requires an examination of the forms of spying which have become a part of school practice.

One group of spying techniques involves the detection of supposed wrongdoing on the part of students when they are not being directly supervised. Examples of surreptitious supervision by means of techniques of spying are:

> The use of two-way P.A. systems whereby someone may tune in on a classroom and listen to what is going on.
> The use of closed-circuit TV to keep watch over study halls.
> The placing of adult spies in student bathrooms.

Such practices are reported by Friedenberg and by Myron Brenton in *The Privacy Invaders.* If we consider the end-in-view (that of the detection of misbehavior) to be a necessary one within the school context, then we need to examine the issue of means-ends relationships. To what extent does the end justify the means? Whose decisions are reflected in the techniques of spying that are employed? Are the moral issues different from those regarding the use of techniques to spy upon adults?

A more subtle problem regarding means-ends relationships is that raised by the use of spying techniques in the school in order to learn something about the behavior of children, as, for example, the use of the one-way screen observation room. Here the intent may be to observe children behaving naturally and spontaneously in a way in which they would not have if someone were watching them. The information gained might be used by students of child development, psychologists, physiologists, teachers, or anthropologists, as a part of scholarly research.

The fact that the intent here may be altruistic in character —it will benefit the child or mankind—does not alter the fact that the child is being spied upon. It is perhaps even more important that we raise questions about our practices where we consider our motives to be pure.

Can a clear justification be offered for each use of observation rooms? What kinds of controls are to be exercised with regard to who is permitted to observe a child?

What kinds of controls are to be placed upon the use of the information gained so that the children involved are in no way penalized? For example, are observations to be a source of conversation in the teacher's lunchroom?

Do scholars and scientists have the right to find out anything and everything about children's behavior? Students of child behavior have raised questions about the limits to be placed upon what they do to children in order to study their behavior where what they do might result in physical or psychological harm. There is also discussion needed regarding the limits to be placed upon what we have a right to know about children's private lives.

Choice and Disclosure

The use of techniques of observation is only one of the ways in which we gain information about children. We also gain it by asking questions. The use of question and answer is one of the traditional techniques of teaching and testing. The teacher puts certain questions to the student which call for oral or written replies. If the student knows the answer it is expected that he will be willing and even eager to give it. We assume that a child will accept as one of his roles in school that of demonstrating his competence in various subject areas by correctly replying to certain questions put to him. Therefore, we would scarcely expect him to answer the question, "What is the capital of Mexico?" by saying, "I do not choose to tell you." However, the expectation that children will reply when called upon is often transformed into the prescription that it is the child's duty to answer all questions put to him by adults. (Consider, for example, how disturbed adults become when a child will not reply to the blunt query, "What's your name?") In order to make clear the legitimate role of testing and of question asking in the educative process, we need to examine the kinds of questions put to children in school. We will then be in a position to better determine whether some of them might constitute invasions of a child's privacy and so warrant the legitimate reply, "I do not choose to tell you."

The Questions We Ask

Some of the categories of questions put to children are:

1. Objective fact questions such as, "What is the capital of Mexico?" or "How much is 3×4?"
2. Speculative questions such as, "How do you think that sap rises in trees?" or "How might our life be different if we had no measurement systems?"
3. Logical questions such as, "If three apples coat fifteen cents, how much will twice as many cost?"
4. Questions calling for individual judgment such as, "What conditions would you set up that would test your hypothesis?"
5. Value questions such as, "Should fist-fighting be considered an acceptable way to settle arguments?" or "Who was a greater president, Washington or Lincoln?"
6. Objective personal data questions such as, "How much do you weigh?" or "What does your father do for a living?"
7. Subjective personal data questions such as, "What is your favorite color?" or "Who is your best friend and why?" or "Why do you love your mother?"

Questions which fall under the last three categories need examination in terms of the kinds of personal revelations that are called for. We generally classify as personal data information which:

> might expose us to ridicule
> might make us the victim of blackmail
> might cause others to hold us in lower esteem

might be against the law
might have a sacred aspect
might be that which we choose to reveal only to treasured
friends or loved ones.

Having a private life means, among other things, exercising
some control over the disposition of such data, which may
include attitudes about sex, religious views, secret enthusiasms, or illegal activities. To what extent are children to have
a private life in these terms? It is assumed that the more a
teacher knows about a student, the better he will teach him.
This assumption needs to be questioned on epistemological
grounds and upon ethical grounds. In the latter case we might
ask:

> To what extent does the end—informed teaching—justify
> requiring a child to reveal personal data which he has not
> volunteered?
> What kinds of data do children consider to be personal data?
> If some probing is to occur, what distinctions should be drawn
> between private and public probing, so that the child is not
> made vulnerable to attack, ridicule, or embarrassment?

Problematic Practices

School practices, such as the following, ought at least to be
examined:

> Personality tests administered to children on a group basis
> include questions about fears, sex problems and home life. The
> questions under the "family life" section of one test include the
> following:
> "Do you prefer to keep your friends away from home because
> it is not attractive?"
> "Are the people in your home too quarrelsome?"
> "I get less understanding at home than elsewhere." [true or
> false][8]

A teacher introduced the idea that different colors produce
different emotional reactions and asked the children to express

[8] Gross, Martin. *The Brain Watchers*. New York: Random House,
Inc., 1962.

their feelings about a particular color. As the children worked she read their papers over their shoulders, and at one point said, "Stop your work, class; I want Jane to read her beautiful thoughts about the color green." When Jane demurred the teacher took her paper and read it to the class.

Fourth graders were asked to practice using descriptive phrases by writing Mother's Day compositions on "Why I love my mother," and sharing the compositions with the class.

Sixth graders were required to make personal poetry anthologies, which were to be given to the teacher for examination and marking. Then each child had to read a favorite poem to the class.

Second graders wrote compositions about, "Who is my best friend in class and why," and the compositions were posted on the bulletin board.

Would we allow a child to respond to any of these assignments by saying, "It's none of your business?" A teacher might attempt to justify some of them by arguing that he was helping a child identify and express those feelings and reactions toward the world which belonged to his growing system of values. However, even if we consider it a valid classroom task to help children form or clarify their values, we might want to make a distinction between helping children become aware of the value dimension of their lives and having access to the actual content of their intimate thoughts and feelings.

Children's Confidences

There are times when a child chooses to confide in a teacher and to disclose information which we might judge to be of a personal nature. This raises the issue of how that confidence is to be regarded. We have made certain stipulations regarding the nature of the professional relationship between priest and confessor, lawyer and client, and doctor and patient; but we have not clearly established the nature of the professional relationship between teacher and student. Decisions are needed about such issues as:

> What are the ethics involved in allowing teachers to send to newspapers or book publishers remarks that children make, such as "cute sayings" or mistakes in grammar?

Should teachers be free to quote students' remarks to colleagues?
Should teachers ever judge it right to withhold from parents or
the principal confidences volunteered by children, and if so,
under what circumstances?

These are aspects of the general question, "What is the
meaning of confidential data in a school setting?" Teachers are
not now clear about the meaning and disposition of confidential data. Report cards are generally distributed in envelopes,
but test marks are often posted on the bulletin board. Sometimes, children are directed to announce out loud marks received on a piece of work, so that they may be recorded.
Other kinds of data that may be displayed publicly, so that
children may compete with one another or so that visitors may
see what progress has been made, include reading progress
charts, individual behavior commendation charts, or charts indicating who ate a good breakfast. Children's weights may be
announced publicly during weighing-in time, but color-blind-
ness tests are usually given privately. Children are often asked
to state their father's occupation, but not his earnings.

Files officially labeled as "confidential" are not open to
children or to their parents, a restriction which has recently
been challenged; but they follow a child all through school
and into his occupational life. In clarifying the meaning of
confidential data and the ethics involved in its disposition, we
need to question the grounds for publicizing any such personal
data whose disclosure might violate a child's privacy.

Creative Products

In the passage from the Brandeis article quoted earlier it
was stated that an individual's right to privacy extends to the
disposition of his creative products. He may choose to hide
them away, to show them to a few friends, or to hang them in
a gallery. In the latter case he knowingly subjects his work to
public scrutiny and criticism. When a child produces work in
school, however, he is not given such choices. First of all he is
often told when he must work and for how long. "You have
half an hour to work on a Haiku poem." The teacher may
dictate the subject matter to be dealt with such as, "Write a

composition about spring." Penalties may be exacted if certain rules are not followed as the child works. A teacher gave instructions about drawing figures without facial detail so that the focus could be upon action. When one child added features to his faces the teacher tore up his drawing in front of the class. When the child's work is completed he is generally compelled to show it to the teacher and to the rest of the class, as in the case of the Mother's Day compositions. Then the child's work may be publicly evaluated by the teacher and/or by his classmates, who tell "what's good about it" and "what's not good about it."

In *Culture Against Man,* Jules Henry reports an incident where a boy was asked to read an original story to the class and was then beaten down by the flood of trivial criticisms with which his classmates picked the story apart.[9] Finally the teacher may take possession of the child's work and display it in the room or in the hall, on the assumption that every child will want his work displayed.[10] Thus, what children are expected to do are to engage in creative endeavors on command, to make public all of their art products and to submit them to uninvited criticism.

These modes of guiding creative effort need examination. Should we assume that it is the teacher's responsibility to assess the quality of a child's creative efforts? If we do assume so, is there a need to make a distinction between process and product? That is, might a teacher focus upon the skill with which a child handles tools and materials, such as paint brushes, metaphors, or carving knives, while considering the substantive content of the child's creative work to be none of her or anyone else's business? Would such a shift in focus require the formulation of a new set of evaluative criteria? Should children want, much less be required, to display everything they create? Should the development of critical thinking involve having children evaluate their classmates' compe-

[9] Henry, Jules. *Culture Against Man.* New York: Random House, Inc., 1963.

[10] For example, in her book, *Teaching Art to Children.* (Boston: Allyn and Bacon, 1963) Blanche Jefferson states that the showing of a completed art project is "a final rewarding part of creative work." Therefore, some kind of display of every child's work is to be planned as part of an art project.

tencies of inner visions? To be sure, children submit themselves to each other's judgments when they enter a baseball
game, a running contest, or a debating group, but here the
rules for making judgments are reasonably clear and the involvement in the activity a voluntary one. It is this element of
choice that permits a child to protect his privacy. The central
issue to be explored is the place of this element of choice in
daily classroom life if children's rights to privacy are to be
respected.

Choosing Privacy

If the protection of privacy is to become a concern of the
school then not only must it become a subject for consideration by teachers, but it must also become a subject for consideration by the children themselves. We can guide children's
thinking in this area only after we have clarified the issues
regarding the privacy needs and rights of children in terms of
their legal, psychological, moral, and pedagogical dimensions.
Then we may be able to help children protect their uniqueness
and the privacy of their inner lives by helping them distinguish between aspects of their being which must be involved
in cooperative group living and those aspects which one nur-
tures in solitary places and reveals only to those chosen few
one invites to share them.

Perceptions
of Decision-Making
in Elementary-School
Classrooms*

BERNICE J. WOLFSON
SHIRLYN NASH

Every day in every classroom countless decisions, major and minor, are made. The research reported here was designed to study teachers and pupils' perceptions of the opportunities for decision-making in the classroom.[1]

Specifically, we wanted to answer the following questions: How do children and teachers perceive their roles in classroom decisions? Do all children in a class agree on the opportunities the classroom offers pupils for making their own decisions? Are the opportunities the children agree on the same opportunities their teacher believes he provides? Where disagreement exists, what kinds of decisions are involved?

These questions are important for at least two reasons. First, in our daily lives we are constantly involved in making decisions. Second, the child's awareness of opportunities to make decisions is, we believe, related to his feelings of independence and of power to control his environment. Because statements of educational goals stress the development of in-

---

[1] This article is based on a paper presented at the annual meeting of the American Educational Research Association, Chicago, Illinois, February, 1968.

* *The Elementary School Journal*, 69, 1968, 89–93. Copyright © 1968 by the University of Chicago. Reprinted with the permission of the publisher and the authors.

dependence, we wanted to know teachers' and pupils' perceptions of decision-making. Who do they think makes decisions in the classroom? The pupils? The teachers? The class? Someone else?

In a previous study we examined perceptions of decision-making in a first-grade classroom.[2] The major finding was that the children differed widely in their perceptions of decision-making roles. Also, their perceptions, on the average, differed from their teacher's. By the end of the school year, a second administration of the questionnaire revealed that children saw themselves making more decisions and their teacher making fewer decisions, although there were still differences between perceptions of the teacher and his pupils.

The present investigation, part of a larger in-service project, involved eight elementary-school classrooms. Six were primary classrooms, each including first-, second-, and third-grade children. Two were intermediate classrooms, each including fourth-, fifth-, and sixth-grade children.

The children, two hundred in all, and their teachers responded to a fifty-item questionnaire. Some items had to do with classroom management (for example, Who decides what desk or seat you can sit in? Who decides who cleans the blackboards?) Other items had to do with the planning and scheduling of academic activities (for example, Who decides the plans or work for the day? Who decides when it's reading time?)

In the primary grades, the questionnaire was administered orally and individually to the children. In the intermediate grades, the children completed the questionnaire by themselves. Each teacher completed the questionnaire independently during the same weeks his pupils were interviewed. For each item, the subjects were asked to identify whether the child, the class, the teacher, or someone else was usually responsible for the decision. Responses were gathered twice, first in October and again in May.

The responses of the children in each class were totaled and a mean frequency was obtained for each category. The

    [2] Bernice J. Wolfson and Shirlyn Nash. "Who Decides What in the Classroom?" *Elementary School Journal,* 65 (May, 1965), 436–38.

mean frequency for the pupils of each class was compared with their teacher's frequency in each category.

The major finding in our analysis was the wide discrepancy between each teacher and his pupils in their perceptions of the number of decisions pupils make (category Child). These data are summarized in Table 1. The teachers saw more decisions resting with the children than their pupils did. Even the class range, which was wide, seldom showed a child placing more items in the category Child than his teacher did.

Table 1
Comparison of Pupils and Their Teacher on Number of Items Placed in Category, Child (October and May) [a]

		PUPILS				TEACHER	
					Difference		
	October		May		between	Number	
Class	Mean	Range	Mean	Range	Means	October	May
A	13.1	5–20	18.1	5–30	+5.0	37	31
B	12.4	4–20	18.7	8–26	+6.3	22	29
C	18.4	8–26	25.4	9–32	+7.0	32	30
D	18.0	6–26	20.0	7–26	+2.0	30	26
E[b]	20.9	11–33	20.8	14–27	− .1	18	25
F[b]	16.6	12–30	20.4	13–31	+3.8	28	27
G	18.4	11–27	27.3	16–39	+8.9	28	40
H	14.1	2–26	22.8	7–35	+8.7	31	30

[a] The questionnaire, Who Decides, contains fifty items.
[b] Intermediate-level classes. Others are primary level.

We expected that the May administration of the questionnaire would show an increase in the number of decisions pupils perceived they could make. Our findings in our previous study showed such an increase. Also, it seemed reasonable to assume that as pupils and teacher worked together during the year they would come to know one another better. The pupils would see more opportunities for making decisions, and the teachers might offer more. In the May administration, seven of the eight classes moved in this direction, as Table 1 shows, in mean differences as well as ranges.

Even when pupils had high agreement (80 per cent) on a particular item, the teacher's perception frequently differed from his pupils'. However, some classes showed more agreement with their teacher than others did. Table 2 summarizes the amount of agreement for all categories.

TABLE 2
Agreement among Pupils and between Pupils and Their Teacher on All Categories

		NUMBER OF ITEMS[a]		
Class		High Agreement (80 per cent) among Pupils	Teacher Agreed with class	Teacher Disagreed with class
A	October	31	16	15
	May	30	16	14
B	October	27	19	8
	May	29	15	14
C	October	21	11	10
	May	34	28	6
D	October	22	17	5
	May	31	27	4
E[b]	October	18	11	7
	May	27	22	5
F[b]	October	14	11	3
	May	22	17	5
G	October	24	18	6
	May	25	22	3
H	October	23	14	9
	May	20	15	5

[a] Total number of items on questionnaire, Who Decides, was fifty.
[b] Intermediate-level classes. Others are primary level.

No significant differences were found between boys' and girls' responses. However, a small but consistent trend suggested that girls perceived themselves making more decisions than boys perceived themselves making. Analysis of the data by age also revealed no significant differences.

What is the substantive nature of the discrepancy between the perceptions of teacher and pupils? To answer this question, we examined items on which 80 per cent of the pupils in six of the eight classes agreed. There were ten such items. With which did their teachers agree? With which did they disagree? Items that show high agreement among pupils and between pupils and their teacher seem to have two characteristics. First, the activities involved are highly visible and frequent as illustrated by the items: Who decides: when you can get a drink? when you can get up to throw something away? when you can sharpen your pencil? Second, the decisions involved are logically in the child's control, as illustrated by the items: Who decides: what you can read during your free time? who your special friends in school will be?

Items that drew high agreement from pupils but disagreement with their teacher did not seem to follow any obvious pattern. Responses to certain items may show a disparity between teacher's and pupils' perceptions because those decisions are sometimes made by pupils, sometimes by teachers, and sometimes by others. This explanation may apply to responses to the item: Who decides what story your teacher will read to the class? Sometimes individual pupils make suggestions; sometimes the teacher asks the class for its wishes. Nevertheless, the pupils perceive the decision as the teacher's. The disparity between teacher's and pupils' perceptions may have another source: the questions may involve an activity that the class has not experienced, as illustrated by the item: Who decides where to go on a class trip? Still another source of this disparity may be differences in interpretation. The item: Who decides the rules in your room? is probably open to various interpretations.

In summary, then, we found that all teachers disagreed with their pupils on some items on which pupils in their class showed high agreement (see Table 2). In addition, the extensive range of pupil responses (see Table 1) reveals many pupil disagreements and also disagreements with their teachers.

Discussion

We were particularly struck with the major finding: that teachers see pupils making many more decisions than the pupils perceive themselves making. Three possible explanations suggest themselves.

One explanation is related to the nature of the questionnaire and the complexity of classroom life. When the teacher was responding to the question, "Who usually decides?" he undoubtedly was thinking of the class as a whole. When the pupil was answering, he was responding from a more limited viewpoint based on his personal experience plus any broader context he might be aware of in the classroom. It seemed clear from spontaneous comments made during the interviews that some pupils were much more aware of existing alternatives than other pupils were.

Another possible explanation of this finding lies in social theories of institutional life. From this point of view the discrepancy between teachers and their pupils is rooted in differences in perceptions of power commonly held by different classes of people in institutions. The pupils (the subservient class) see themselves as having less power than the teachers (the ruling class) believe the pupils have. There can be no doubt that the teacher is commonly viewed as the director and controller of classroom events.

A third explanation is related to the likelihood that teachers seldom check their perceptions against their pupils' perceptions. This lack of communication may contribute to the extensive differences in perceptions of decision-making in the classroom. On the one hand, children may not be aware of the opportunities to decide for themselves; on the other hand, the teacher may communicate indirectly the idea that decisions have to satisfy him even though he thinks that he allows children to decide.

It is not clear what combination of factors leads to this difference between the perceptions of teachers and their pupils. The importance of this finding rests on our assumption that children's perceptions of opportunities to make their own decisions are related to feelings of independence and of power to control their environment.

Consider the great range within each class in the number of items the pupils feel they can decide for themselves (Table 1). We cannot conclude that this disagreement represents, primarily or solely, a large number of misperceptions. Rather, we must assume that it also represents differences in perceptions of authority-roles and in classroom experience. From an educational point of view, it would be desirable to help children grow in awareness of the various decisions they may make for themselves. Certainly our eight classes differ greatly in this respect. Looking at ranges on the post-test, we see that in Class G, an intermediate class, the number of decisions perceived as being made by the child reached 39. The lowest number perceived in that group was 13. The next highest range, from 13 to 31, was in Class F, also an intermediate class. The widest spread, 7 to 35 and 5 to 30, occurred in primary classrooms.

In each classroom, the teacher himself must answer the questions: If I perceive that children are free to make more decisions than they perceive, am I really making opportunities available to them? How can I help children grow in awareness of the opportunities for decision-making that are available to them in the classroom?

Two Classrooms*

TONY KALLET

I want to describe two classrooms in which I have worked during the past few years: one is in England, one in the United States. In what follows I am relying on memory abetted by some notes and, while I realize the impossibility of attaining objectivity, I shall try to keep closely to factual statements unless I clearly label what I am saying as opinion. The names of the schools and teachers are fictitious.

First Grade at the Meadow School, U.S.A.

During the fall and winter of 1962 I spent about four months as an apprentice teacher in Miss Jones' first grade at the Meadow School. Miss Jones was an experienced teacher who had been at Meadow for many years. There were 21 children in her class and in addition to Miss Jones and me there was a part-time assistant teacher.

The children, almost all of whom had been in the school since they were four, came primarily from upper middle-class homes. Their fathers were university professors, lawyers, doctors, businessmen: the school was a private one and tuition was fairly high, although there were one or two children in the class on scholarship. With a single exception the children were near their sixth birthdays at the beginning of the year. One boy of seven was repeating the first grade for academic reasons. (He had been in the other section of the class, with a different teacher the previous year.)

* *This Magazine is About Schools*, 1, 1966, 45–59. This article first appeared in *This Magazine is About Schools*, 56 Esplanade St. E., Rm. 301, Toronto 1, Ontario. Subscription $3.50 per year.

The two sections of the first grade shared a building. In addition to Miss Jones' classroom, in her half of the building, there was a workshop, through a door at the rear. The main classroom was about twenty by thirty feet in size (if memory serves me) with windows along one wall and two doors leading to the outside, the main entrance at the rear and a door at the side opening onto the playground. The desks, each labelled with a child's name, were arranged in a sort of horseshoe, a column down each side of the room and two rows at the rear. There was some open space behind the last row, including a small alcove containing a piano, bookshelf, cupboard, and table. Along the wall opposite the windows were open lockers and cubbies for the children's coats and personal belongings. Two children shared each locker and cubby. At the front of the room was a blackboard and, in the open end of the horseshoe, there was a table which might be used in teaching. The teacher's desk was in a front corner and was not much used except for storage. Another desk at the back was shared by the assistant and me. Along the wall under the windows were tables and shelves for plants, some small building blocks and various science materials—leaves, shells, stones, a magnifying glass, etc.

The first graders at Meadow did not stay all day. School began at 8:40 and ended at noon. During the second term half the class stayed one afternoon a week in alternate weeks. The morning was divided into several periods, each lasting between fifteen or twenty minutes and half an hour. The last period might be somewhat longer, perhaps forty or forty-five minutes. The best way to give an impression of the class in action might be to describe a composite day. (While I believe this description to be accurate in general, there may be errors in specific details, such as the precise length of various periods.)

The children, who might have arrived at school from eight o'clock on, were called to their desks when it was time to begin, and the attendance was taken, a child being sent with the slip to the main office. On Monday, Miss Jones or I would ask for volunteers for a number of jobs to be done during the week, including watering the plants, taking the attendance slip to the office, being line leader (to head up the line when children moved from the classroom to another part of the school), and so forth. Morning "chores" were usually followed by a few minutes during which children could come to the front of the room and share with the class any news they might have, or show items of interest which they had brought with them. At nine o'clock the science specialist might come in for half an hour of science, often bringing a variety of things with her: I remember particularly a live iguana, and there was always her dog. On another day the children would go to the music room for half an hour of singing and dancing. The first period on still another day might be devoted to "Central Subject" which, in this class, was Pre-historic Man. Once a week the school day began with an assembly in the main hall.

At about nine-thirty it might be time for mathematics. Each child had a bag of Cuisenaire rods hung on his own hook at the front of the room (where his reader was also stored) and the children might be asked to get these and take them to their desks. Sometimes they were allowed a few minutes of free play with the rods, and then Miss Jones would demonstrate a type of problem, or perhaps call a few children to the front of the room to try it. Activities with the rods were fairly closely supervised by the teacher and specific tasks were set. On other occasions the children would do problems on worksheets which had been prepared and duplicated by Miss Jones. She would again demonstrate or have several children demonstrate, the kind of problem to be done, and there might be discussion of the principles involved. When the children had finished a paper they would take it to the back of the room and place it in a tray on my desk to be corrected and, if there were mistakes, handed back the next day for revision. Sometimes there was a selection of papers available and children could work through as many as they wished. During the mathematics period, as during the writing period which followed, the two or three adults would move around the room answering questions. Children were not, in general, permitted to move around the room or talk with one another during work periods, although they were free to go to the toilet. It was expected that during "academic" periods, except when there was class discussion, the only conversation would be between a child and a teacher.

Twenty minutes of mathematics might be followed, sometimes after a break of two or three minutes during which children could stretch and walk around and talk, by a writing period. During most of the first term this was largely devoted to presenting a new letter and sound, discussing the formation of the letter (children would be called to the board to practice making it), playing various games involving the new sound. The children would then be given papers on which the letter had been formed, and they would trace and copy it.

A reading period might follow at about 9:50 or ten o'clock. Soon after the term began, the children were divided into three reading groups, according to Miss Jones' estimation of their ability. During the term children might be moved from one group to another. Each group would go with a teacher to a different part of the room: one group went into the workshop. The reader was of the "Dick and Jane" type and the procedure was for each child in turn to read a few lines aloud. Flash cards with words from the readers were often used and various reading games might be played from time to time, but the main activity was reading aloud from the books. (I found it exceptionally difficult to maintain discipline, especially when I was working with the "slowest" group. Occasionally it would be necessary to ask a child to remain behind after the reading period, which meant that he would miss part of recess.) Later in the term, when many children had gained some proficiency in reading, this "round robin" reading period was supplemented by another which was somewhat freer. The children would choose a book from a selection at the back of the room, and their choice would be approved and recorded by the teacher. As children read the teachers would again circulate, listening to them read, helping them select new books, and so forth. Children who had finished a particular book might sometimes listen to other children read from it. At the beginning of the second term, these reading and writing periods were further supplemented by a period (during the afternoon session in alternate weeks) when children were introduced to composition. They might be given a sentence to start them off or the teacher might suggest a theme or a question.

After reading, at about 10:20 or 10:30, it was recess time and the children would go into the playground where they would find the other first grade class and the second graders. They could use a slide, swings, climbing apparatus, a ball, large wooden blocks for building, etc. Most of the teachers of the four classes were in the playground during recess: there might be sixty or eighty children and four or five adults present.

Recess, which generally lasted fifteen or twenty minutes, was followed by milk and crackers which had been set out by one of the teachers. Following this mid-morning snack, at about eleven o'clock, there was a rest period. Each child would get a mat from a storage fixture at the back of the room and lie down: one of the teachers would read to the class. (Again, I found this a situation in which it was difficult, at times, to maintain discipline. Children wanted to talk or move their mats together and this was frowned upon unless it could be done without too much distrubance. I often had to stop reading to speak to children who were disturbing the class.)

After rest a child would be appointed "mat caller" and would call the other children, one at a time, to put their mats away. The last period of the morning might be devoted to art (once a week) or music in the classroom with the music teacher (also once a week), to some reading aloud, or to work on one of the subjects which had not been touched upon earlier: I recall that mathematics was sometimes done at this time, but never reading or writing.

At the end of the morning the children would put on their coats and line up at the back of the room. When the line was quiet the class would move off, the line leader and a teacher at the head of it, to the main building where the children would be met by their parents. I should note that children were not permitted to talk when in line moving from one place to another, although at times this rule was not too strictly enforced.

I want now to summarize my impressions of Miss Jones' class. It was, generally speaking, a fairly tightly controlled situation. The individual child had few decisions to make at any point. The daily schedule was posted next to the blackboard in front of the room, showing the order of activities for the day, and children knew, or should have known, what was expected of them. There was time during the day for discussion, but almost never was this child-to-child discussion: it was discussion with the teacher as the focus and children talking to her. The degree of tightness of control can be illustrated by my recollection that once, after having given the mathematics lesson, I was criticized by Miss Jones for having allowed two children in the back row to slide their desks together. In my recollection (distorted, beyond question, by the passage of time and by intervening events) discipline problems loom large. There were one or two children who were distinct "problems" and often I felt that there was an undercurrent of things about to get out of hand. Miss Jones was so experienced that the situation rarely flew apart when she was in charge of the class, but even she had to work quite hard to keep the lid on what so often seemed to be a pot about to boil.

Symptomatic of the tightness of control was the rule about not talking when in line: indeed, the concept of moving children around in a line in itself indicates a fair degree of control being imposed. At the Meadow School, and as far as I could tell throughout the school, decisions typically were made by adults for children. In the first grade this meant that reading groups were determined by the teacher, the seating arrangement was determined by the teacher, and the order of activities during the day and the amount of time spent on each was determined by the teacher. Within a given lesson, children had little say about what they did: they were presented with a task and they carried it out. In writing, the letter-of-the-day was already on their paper. In reading the teacher assigned the lines each child was to read. The freest periods during the week were the music periods but here again the problems of discipline, of simply keeping the noise down to a manageable level, were often so great that the exceptionally gifted woman who taught music seemed at times almost defeated by the task of keeping these twenty-odd children in order. Control was again indicated by the need (and it was a real need—or should I say it *became* a real need because it was assumed to be a real need) to have several teachers on duty in the playground during recess. Control again was in the fore when, on that single day in alternate weeks during the second term, half of the children stayed for lunch and a teacher was assigned to each table of five. (The pattern of one or two teachers to six or eight children at meals prevailed throughout the school.)

Some children appeared to manage quite well despite all this control but for others, especially the "problem" children, I often felt that the control was too much, that they were being held too tightly in check, that too little was permitted them in the way of free behavior, that their problems were, in part, being created rather than mitigated by control. No, this is not quite an accurate statement: I said "I often felt," whereas in fact I can see this now, in retrospect, but while I was in the classroom it did truly seem that every single control imposed was necessary if anything was to be accomplished.

An Infant Class at Hillside County Primary School, England

During the autumn term of 1963 I spent several hours a week observing, and working informally with children, in Miss Smith's class at Hillside. I was in no sense an official teacher of the class at any time and so my experience with the class was not only less extensive than my experience with the first grade at Meadow but also different in kind. In both situations, however, I was able to do a lot of looking and listening.

Miss Smith was a first-year teacher, just out of the Froebel Educational Institute in London: this was her first class. The children in the class, one of three parallel infant classes in the school, came from families living in the school district, a prosperous suburb in the Midlands of England. Like the children at Meadow, most of these children came from middle class homes, although many more of the fathers were in business than in the professions. There were, among the fathers, a good number of artisans, highly skilled, well-paid workers in the light industries of . . . the neighboring city. The children in the class ranged in age, at the beginning of the year, from four years ten months to six years nine months. That is, it was a vertically grouped class comprising children of all the ages covered by the term "Infant." For the youngest children this was their first term in school: the oldest might have been in school four or five terms. Because of the intake of new five-year-olds three times a year, and because children move into the Junior school only once a year, the class grew from about thirty children in September to about forty in April. During the period I was with the class the number was about thirty, or perhaps one or two more.

The room, about the same size as the first grade classroom at Meadow but without the workshop space, was attractive but crowded. On the far side were windows and a french door leading to a grassy playing field. The main entrance led off a corridor which was also used as a makeshift activity area: part of the corridor was enclosed and part open on one side. In the building were the other two infant classes and a junior class, the headmaster's office, a small library, and the girls' and boys' lavatories, the latter also serving to house the woodworking bench and tools.

There were no desks in the classroom, but rather four or five groups of trapezoidal tables in pairs or in threes. Each group was associated not with specific children but with activities. Some of the tables were mainly for writing, others for number work, still others for arts and crafts, and so forth. In the back of the room next to the corridor was a Wendy (play) House equipped with toy furniture, dolls, tableware, etc. Next to this was a table often used by the teacher and a storage table on which the children's writing books were kept. Under the windows were tables for number apparatus, a sand table and a water table. Along the front wall was the library, partially screened from the rest of the room by a divider: the books were in racks on the wall and there were several chairs turned to face the wall. Next to the library were two double painting easels. Interspersed among all these pieces of equipment were several storage units. A table along the corridor wall was used part of the morning as a "milk bar."

The school day at Hillside began at nine o'clock and continued until 3:45, with a dinner break from noon until 1:30. The day usually began with a short religious service (required by law) which was held in one of the three infant rooms. Following this the children returned to their own classroom and Miss Smith marked the register and took the names of the children staying for dinner. She then went through a list of the various activities available in the room and asked children to raise their hands for the one they wanted to start the day with: for each activity there was a maximum permissible number of children. Among the choices would be painting, building with blocks, reading, writing, woodwork, sand and water play, Wendy House, clay or model-making, and any special activities Miss Smith might have set up. When all the children had chosen, they went off and got to work. Their choices were only starting points in some cases and during the course of the morning children might move from one part of the room, one activity, to another as they finished what they were doing.

Conversely, a child might choose to spend the entire morning, or even the whole day, working at a single project. As space became available in one place (for example, a child might leave the Wendy House) other children could move in. Aside from the initial choice the process of selection of an activity was informal. Miss Smith might, on occasion, ask a particular child or a small group to do something she had in mind but the children were largely left to make their own choices, within the limitations of space and equipment. The afternoon was organized in much the same way and at the end of the day Miss Smith would call the class together for a period of discussion, or she might read aloud to them.

Considering the number of things going on and the number of children in the room, the atmosphere in Miss Smith's class was generally calm and collected. (I should point out that seldom were all the children in the room at the same time: there would be one or two in the corridor, one or two in the library around the corner—where more "advanced" books were kept and which was open to both infants and juniors— and one or two at the woodworking bench in the boys' lavatory.) Most of the children in the classroom would be moving about, talking quietly and doing a good job of keeping out of each other's way: only rarely did Miss Smith have to request that the noise level be kept down. The sheer density of children and apparatus meant that now and again a tower of blocks would come crashing down or someone's paints would be upset or water would slosh onto the floor but this caused little confusion: the child involved picked up the pieces or mopped up, and went on working.

In this classroom reading, writing, mathematics were not treated as separate "subjects" and it took me quite a while to discover just how, for example, a child learned to read. An important element, I am sure, was that reading was "in the air": there were always older children reading and writing and I often saw a little one sitting near a big one trying to imitate his acitivity. Upon entering the class in his first term each child was given a large, unlined "free writing book" with his name on the cover. He was free to do what he liked in this book: part of the "free" in "free writing" stemmed from the child's growing awareness that what he put in this book was his own and would not be corrected by the teacher—save in cases of complete incomprehensibility. At first most children drew pictures with pencil or crayon. Now and then Miss Smith might discuss what the child was doing with him and perhaps write a sentence or two in the book, which the child was to trace or copy. Soon he would be given a small notebook to serve as his personal dictionary, to supplement word cards on the wall and a homemade class dictionary. He might, when he asked for a word, be requested to guess what the first sound was, or later Miss Smith would ask him what letter he thought the word began with. Phonetic skills were developed but the process was informal. (There was, however, nothing informal about the detailed records Miss Smith kept of representative examples of each child's work throughout the year.) There was, as I have said, a library corner and a library room nearby. The younger children, perhaps at first mainly because they saw older ones doing it, would go over and take a book to look at. Miss Smith would come by now and then and read with someone or listen to someone read. There seemed to be little anxiety about reading: children were encouraged to read and to write as they wished, and a considerable number of them wished to often. Books the children wrote would be prominently displayed and read by other children, which may also have been an important source of motivation. Perhaps as a result, in part, of the low anxiety level Miss Smith appeared to have about reading and writing there seemed to me only one or two of the older children who were not reading at a level one might deem appropriate for their age, and the mass of free writing these fives and sixes and sevens turned out was astonishing.

There was little formal number work in this infant class although, since the room was full of material with mathematical potential, much of which was attractive, a fair number of children were using some sort of number-related equipment almost all the time. Among the available apparatus were Cuisenaire rods, MAB blocks, geometric sorting sets, attribute blocks, counting apparatus including beads and abacii, scales, liquid measures, and so forth.

Painting, model making, clay, collage, paper cutting and folding, all these were, it seemed to me, accorded as high status in the scheme of things as reading and writing and mathematics: I felt that the amount of time Miss Smith spent on the arts in the course of a morning was about equal to that she spent on "the R's." There was invariably a quartet of children at the easels, someone working with clay, someone else out at the woodworking bench. The Wendy House was in continuous use, was, indeed, perhaps the most popular single activity for the younger children and some of the older ones. An adjunct to play in the Wendy House was a fine collection of dress-up clothes and it was not at all unusual for a child, boy or girl, to put on an outlandish costume and traipse around the room, or down the corridor, to show it to his or her friends: there always seemed to be laughter and high spirits in the Wendy corner which at times infected much of the rest of the room to good advantage.

In the midst of all of this Miss Smith might one moment be discussing a model rocket with two or three boys and the next be listening to a seven-year old read, or perhaps she would simply stand for a minute or two and watch a child building a tower with some blocks, asking a question, making a comment or not as the situation seemed to warrant. She never seemed rushed or harried and her calm most often communicated itself to the children, whose general enthusiasm and high spirits seldom got away from them. The range of matters to which Miss Smith attended in the course of a day was as varied as the number of things going on in the room and yet, with all this, she was able to keep fairly well in mind, I felt, the general direction of each child's activities not, perhaps, minute by minute or even day by day but certainly over a longer and possibly more meaningful span of time: her training in observation and recording of specifics seemed to stand her in very good stead indeed in this complex situation.

An important element in Miss Smith's approach to teaching seemed to me that she did not readily label children as "problems." She seemed aware that thinking in terms of "problems" often helped create them, and she was willing and able to accept a fairly wide range of behavior and achievements as falling within a "normal" range.

The contrast between Miss Jones' class and Miss Smith's could not be greater, although I certainly do not mean to imply that nothing good happened in the former and nothing untoward ever happened in the latter. In Miss Jones' class most decisions were made for the children by an adult: in

Miss Smith's class each child had continually to decide for himself what he was going to do and, once having decided, he had to implement his choice, being given a lot of room to do things right—or "wrong." In Miss Jones' class there was, I felt, a subtle but powerful undercurrent of competitiveness. For example, the reading groups, which were based upon the teacher's judgment of each child's ability, gave children a chance to demonstrate a quick intolerance of those who did not read so fluently, who needed help with a new work. In Miss Smith's classroom the proliferation of activities and equipment often meant that no two children would be working at the same task, thus making competition difficult (although probably not impossible for some children from middle class homes). When several children were doing the same thing, like as not they would be working together. Vertical grouping made cooperating easy and natural, as older children would, quite spontaneously it seemed, pitch in and help younger ones in countless ways from spelling a word to tying an apron.

A most striking difference between the two learning situations was in the self-reliance of the children. It often seemed that in Miss Jones' class, and in Meadow school in general, children were deliberately protected from the need to rely on themselves. For example, on painting day, Thursday each week, Miss Jones and I would spend twenty minutes or so before school pouring the paint into muffin tins, a tin for each child. We would put each child's name on a piece of paper and, when painting time came around at the end of the morning we would hand out the paper and the paints. We did the washing up afterwards. (Indeed, and I blush to admit that at the time I saw nothing wrong with it, in this classroom we even sharpened the children's pencils once a week.) In Miss Smith's class a child who had decided to paint took out the canisters of paint, poured out the powder, added water, got a brush, painted, put away the paint, and cleaned up his tins. Naturally, there was help available for the younger ones who needed it—either help by Miss Smith or, more often, by one of the older children. By the time they were six, almost all of these children had mastered a wide variety of housekeeping skills without the exercise of which the situation simply would not have been viable. The general assumption in Miss Jones' class, unspoken, of course, was that adults knew best and children took and did what was given to them. In Miss Smith's class children quickly came to realize that they were expected to seek out and cope with self-chosen aspects of a richly complex environment, and that the teacher and other children would help when necessary—but not take over the job and hence preclude learning.

There is little question in my mind that in many aspects of their work the children in Miss Smith's class were achieving results which surpassed those of the children at Meadow. Most of the six-year-olds who had been in school two or three terms were writing copiously and often quite creatively, almost always illustrating what they wrote—or writing about what they drew. They wrote stories, poems, even little plays. Indeed, I would judge that the writing of many of these children surpassed in both quantity and quality that being done by the children two years older at Meadow. An important reason, of course, was that they were writing when they chose and about subjects they chose and that they were writing for other children, not just the teacher, to read. It is harder to compare the mathematics work since nothing formal was done in Hillside until the children reached the junior part of the school. Certainly Miss Smith's children were having a variety of experience with mathematical materials and all sorts under conditions which made discovery possible. The art seemed to me at least as creative at Hillside as at Meadow and there was, of course, vastly more of it since so much more time was devoted to it and it was so highly valued as an activity.

Here then, are two classrooms as they were . . . a number of years ago. I imagine that neither Miss Jones nor Miss Smith is teaching now just as she was teaching then, but based upon my experience in the two rooms as I have tried to portray them, I have little doubt which provided more suitable conditions for children to explore and grow, which provided children with more scope for important learning, which manifested in everything that went on a greater respect for and acceptance of the uniqueness of each child.

Discussion

It has been frequently noted that schools parallel so-called "total institutions" such as mental hospitals and prisons in certain ways.[1] Students, like mental patients, are removed from the outside world for a considerable period of time to participate in a tight schedule of imposed activities. Like prisoners, they are involuntary members of the institutions to which they go. Finally, students, like the inmates of these other institutions, are placed in large groups and supervised by personnel whose job is to see to it that everyone does what is required of him.

Schools, of course, are progressive versions of these total institutions. Students can make certain choices for themselves and punishment for wrongdoing is seldom harsh. Nonetheless, school personnel have broad discretionary jurisdiction over students. They can decide what content will be in the curriculum as well as what disciplinary action to take when students do not follow rules and regulations. Even in schools where students have a voice in these matters, the privilege to do so can be withdrawn at any time. If students are dissatisfied with the school's decisions, they have no official power to press their grievances. In short, school authorities are very much in control.

Interestingly, children do not generally balk at the prospect of going to school each day. School is accepted as a part of life; students do not seem to mind that they are compelled to attend. From this observation, however, teachers are misled into believing that students are with them in a joint endeavor. But Holt maintains that children perceive school mainly as a series of tasks imposed on them, to be rid of in the shortest possible order. Students are rarely asked to be a part of the initial planning of these tasks nor are they even consulted as to whether these tasks are meaningful to them. Their apparent acceptance of school may, therefore, reflect their own powerlessness to reject what transpires there.

In fact, one of the most important things learned in school

---

[1] The characteristics of total institutions are discussed by Erving Goffman in his book *Asylums* (New York: Anchor Books, 1961).

according to Friedenberg is what it is like to be a minor. He describes, for example, how high schools reinterpret basic student rights as privileges which, if abused, can be withdrawn. Thus, students in one of the schools he visited were allowed to smoke behind the school during lunch period, but since some students lit their cigarettes before they arrived in the designated area, their "privilege" to smoke was taken away. At the same time, he observed that teachers routinely assume privileges of seniority such as cutting to the head of the cafeteria line. As minors, students have few means of redress when teachers abuse their authority.

High school, he believes, is also a poor preparation for later experiences in the work world. Through policies which tightly control physical freedom and student initiative, it teaches adolescents to accept living under a public authority that disregards "personal privacy and individual autonomy." The result is that students form a fundamentally wrong concept of how public authority should function.

Bronars extends many of Friedenberg's concerns to life in elementary classrooms. Because we compel children to go to school and associate with certain people, she feels that we have a moral obligation to protect children's rights, especially their right to privacy. This is not as simple a responsibility as it first appears. So many classroom phenomena potentially intrude on children's sense of privacy that quite a few completely escape attention. Bronar's list of "hidden" invasions of privacy occurring in school indicates how frequently we violate children's right to be left alone. One possible reason for our lapses is that we sometimes invade privacy in the belief that it is good for the children when, in fact, it is merely necessary for the school's functioning. The failure to make this distinction clouds the issues involved in our attempt to honor children's personal rights.

One of the inferences children may draw from the school's pervasive authority over them is that no areas of choice are open. This seems to be confirmed by the study conducted by Wolfson and Nash. The findings indicate that even when decision-making opportunities are seemingly available in school, children are unaware of them. It appears as if students perceive school as a place in which they have little power and hence, when they are given some, they do not sense it. In other words, students seem to have a poor image of themselves as autonomous agents. They take their subservient status so much for granted that they cannot picture themselves as capable of seizing a decision-making opportunity that comes their way. This is why Bronars believes that the school has a responsibility to help its students become aware of their rights and choices.

One of the common fears, however, in giving students greater control in school is that they will not act responsibly. Kallet believes that this fear is unfounded. Children in a British infant school, from his observations, were capable of choosing activities for themselves without creating confusion and chaos. Moreover, the school's informal approach enabled them to learn from each other and rely on themselves. By contrast, in an American private school, restrictions were placed on moving and talking, activities were closely supervised, and decisions were rarely left to children. Students who attended this school, according to Kallet, were more intolerant of each other and less self-reliant than their British counterparts.

The concern that children make wise choices may be partly invalid to begin with. It suggests that children are prone to make personally irresponsible decisions. Yet, Maslow states that "if free choice is *really* free and if the chooser is not too sick or frightened to choose, he will choose wisely, in a healthy and growthward direction, more often than not."[2] The real problem may not be whether children can be trusted with freedom but whether it is possible in schools to allow each student to be fully free to make his own choices.

In recent years, increased attention has been given to questions concerning the school's authority over its students. Attempts have been made to lessen the distance between teachers and students, to relax regulations concerning physical appearance and other personal matters, and to reduce the number of academic requirements to which a student must adhere. But, as welcome as these liberalizing efforts may be, they have

[2] Abraham H. Maslow, *Toward a Psychology of Being*, 2d Edition (Princeton, N.J.: Nostrand Company, Inc., 1968), p. 48.

not changed the basic powerlessness of students. It is questionable whether a school can be run like a political democracy. On the other hand, by assuming the right to be autocratic, school personnel deny students the opportunity to achieve some meaningful direction over their own lives.

Part VI

PEER GROUP
TENSIONS

Attitude Organization
in Elementary School
Classrooms*

JULES HENRY

The word *organization* in this paper is used to stand for order
and determinateness as distinguished from disorder and ran-
domness. The emotions and attitudes of prepubertal children
in our culture are not, on the whole, directed toward generalized social goals, but focused rather on the peer group and
parents. From the point of view of an observer who has in
mind the larger social goals, like the maintenance of stable
economic relations, common front against the enemy, maintenance of positive attitudes toward popular national symbols,
and so on, the emotions and attitudes of prepubertal children
in our culture may be viewed as lacking order. The adult, on
the other hand, is supposed to have so organized his tendencies to respond to the environment that his emotions, attitudes,
and activities subserve over-all social goals. While it is true
that attitudes and feelings are bent toward social goals even
from earliest infancy, (Henry and Boggs, 1952), many institutions combine to organize these attitudes and feelings so that
ultimately a social steady state will be maintained. The elementary school classroom in our culture is one of the most
powerful instruments in this effort, for it does not merely sustain attitudes that have been created in the home, but reinforces some, de-emphasizes others, and makes its own
contribution. In this way it prepares the conditions for and

* Jules Henry, "Attitude Organization in Elementary School Classrooms,"
The American Journal of Orthopsychiatry, 27, 1957, 117–133. Copyright
© 1957, the American Orthopsychiatric Association, Inc. Reproduced by
permission of the publisher and author.

contributes toward the ultimate organization of peer- and parent-directed attitudes into a dynamically interrelated attitudinal structure supportive of the culture.

This organizing process is comparable to, though not identical with, the *re*organization of atttitudes and resources that takes place as a society shifts from a peacetime to a wartime footing. During a period of peace in our society, adult hostility and competitiveness may be aimed at overcoming competition in business or social mobility, while love and cooperation are directed toward family and friends, and toward achieving specific social economic ends *within* the society. With the coming of war the instruments of government seek to direct hostility and competitiveness toward the enemy, while love and cooperation are directed toward the armed forces, civilian instruments of war (price controls, rationing, civilian officials, etc.), and national symbols. From the point of view of an observer *within the war machine,* the civilian attitudes at first seem random and unorganized. He wants to change them so that from *his point of view* they will seem organized. The situation is similar, though not identical with respect to the child: to an observer inside the head of even some psychotic children, attitudes and behavior may seem organized. But to the observer on the outside, whose focus is on social goals, the child seems *un-* or *dis*-organized. The prime effort of the adult world is *to make child attitudes look organized to adults.* The emphasis in this paper is on the description of the process of organizing child attitudes as it can be observed in some middle-class urban American classrooms.

The Witch-Hunt Syndrome

One of the most striking characteristics of American culture since the settlement has been the phenomenon of intragroup aggression, which finds its pathological purity of expression in witch hunts (Starkey, 1949). It comes as a frightening surprise to democratic people to find themselves suddenly in terror of their neighbors; to discover that they are surrounded by persons who carry tales about others while confessing evil of themselves; to perceive a sheeplike docility settling over those whom they considered strong and autonomous. The *witch-hunt syndrome* therefore, as constituting one of the key tragedies of democracy, is selected for the elucidation of the organization of attitudes in our culture. In this witch's brew *destructive criticism* of others is the toad's horns; *docility* the body of the worm; *feelings of vulnerability* the chicken heart; *fear of internal (intragroup) hostility* the snake's fang; *confession of evil deeds* the locust's leg; and *boredom and emptiness* the dead man's eye. The witch-hunt syndrome is thus stated to be a dynamically interrelated system of feelings and actions made up of destructive criticism of others, docility, feelings of vulnerability, fear of internal aggression, confession of evil deeds, and boredom.

The witch-hunt syndrome in full panoply was observed in but one of the dozen classrooms in four schools studied in the research which I discuss here. Thus it seems a relatively rare phenomenon. But the question I set myself to answer is, How could it occur at all? What are the attitudes, present in the children, that were organized by this teacher into the syndrome? How could she do it? With what materials did she work? She did not create out of nothing the attitudes she manipulated in her "Vigilance Club" in this fourth-grade classroom in a middle-class American community. She had to have something to start with. The argument of this paper will be that the feelings and tendencies to action which this teacher organized into the witch-hunt syndrome in her class are present in an *un*organized state in other classrooms. Given a certain type of teacher, he or she will be able to develop into a highly specialized, tightly integrated system in his classroom those attitudes which are present in differently organized state in the children in all classrooms. Let us now look at a meeting of the Vigilance Club.

> 1.   In the extreme back of the room is a desk called the "isolation ward." A child has been placed there for disciplinary reasons. The Vigilance Club of the class is holding a meeting. . . . Officers are elected by the group. The purpose of the club is to teach children to be better citizens. The order of procedure is as follows: the president . . . bangs her gavel on the desk and . . . says, "The meeting of the Vigilance Club will come to order." Each child then takes from his or her desk a booklet whose title is *All About Me* . . . and places it on top of

his desk. The vice-president calls the name of a child, gets the child's booklet, and places it on the teacher's desk. The president then calls on the child and asks, "————, have you been a good citizen this week?" The president says, "Name some of the good things you have done," and the child tries to recall some, like opening doors for people, running errands, etc. Next the president asks the class if it remembers any good things the child has done. Each point is written in the child's booklet by the teacher. The president then . . . says to the child, "Name the bad things you have done. . . ." The child reports the wrongs he has committed during the week, and the class is asked to contribute information about his behavior. This too is written in the booklet by the teacher, who also reprimands the student, registers horror, scolds, etc. . . . When one child reports a misdemeanor of another the teacher asks for witnesses, and numerous children sometimes volunteer. . . . The child in the "isolation ward" reported some good deeds he had done; the children reported some more, and the isolated child was told he would soon be released. . . . [During this meeting some children showed obvious pleasure in confessing undesirable behavior. One child, by volunteering only good things of the students, seemed to be using the situation to overcome what seemed to the observer to be her unpopularity with the class.][1]

Before analyzing this protocol for the attitudes present in it, it will be well to look at some events that occurred in this classroom on another day.

2.   During the game of "spelling baseball" a child raised her hand and reported that Alice and John had been talking to each other. This occurred when neither child was "at bat." The teacher asked Alice if this was so, and she replied that it was, but John denied having spoken to Alice. The teacher said that John must have listened to Alice, but he denied this too. Then the teacher asked whether there had been any witnesses, and many hands were raised. Some witnesses were seated on the far side of the room, and hence could not have seen Alice and John from their location in the room. All those testifying had "seen" Alice talking, but denied John's guilt. Alice was sent to

---

[1] In order to prevent identification of teachers and children, the names of my student observers are not used.

the "bull pen," which meant that she had to sit on the floor behind the teacher's desk, and could no longer participate in the game. . . .

3. Mary raised her hand and said, "It hurts me to say this. I really wish I didn't have to do it, but I saw Linda talking." Linda was Mary's own teammate, had just spelled a word correctly, and had gone to first base. The teacher asked Linda if she had talked, and Linda said, "No, I just drew something in the air with my finger. . . ." She was sent to the "bull pen."

In these examples we see intragroup aggression; docility of the children in conforming, with no murmur of protest, to the teacher's wishes; and confession of "evil." In such a situation children develop feelings of vulnerability and fear of detection. Let us now look for these phenomena in classrooms presided over by teachers who seem to represent the more normal American type, in comfortable, middle-class, white communities: teachers who are conscientious and reasonably gentle, but creatures of their culture, and humanly weak. We begin not with internal aggression as expressed in spying and talebearing, but with the milder, though closely related phenomenon of carping, destructive criticism. While this occurs throughout the sample, I give here examples only from a fifth-grade classroom in the same school system.

4. Bill has given a report on tarantulas. As usual the teacher waits for volunteers to comment on the child's report.

Mike: The talk was well illustrated, well prepared. . . .

Bob: Bill had a piece of paper [for his notes], and teacher said he should have them on cards. . . .

Bill says he could not get any cards.

Teacher says that he should tear the paper next time if he has no cards.

Bob: He held the paper behind him. If he had had to look at it, it wouldn't have looked very nice.

5. Betty reports on Theodore Roosevelt.

A child comments that it was very good but she looked at her notes too much.

Teacher remarks that Betty had so *much* information.

Bob: She said "calvary" [instead of "cavalry"].

6. Charlie reads a story he made up himself: "The Unknown Guest." One dark, dreary night . . . on a hill a house stood. This

house was forbidden territory for Bill and Joe, but they were
going in anyway. The door creaked, squealed, slammed. A
voice warned them to go home. Spider webs, dirty furniture . . .
Bill wanted to go home. They went upstairs. A stair cracked.
They entered a room. A voice said they might as well stay and
find out now; and their father came out. He laughed and they
laughed, but they never forgot their adventure together.
Teacher: Are there any words that give you the mood of the
story? . . .
Lucy: He could have made the sentences a little better. . . .
Teacher: Let's come back to Lucy's comment. What about his
sentences?
Gert: They were too short. . . .
Charlie and Jeanne are having a discussion about the position
of the word "stood."
Teacher: Wait a minute, some people are forgetting their
manners. . . .
Jeff: About the room: the boys went up the stairs and one
"cracked"; then they were in the room. Did they fall through
the stairs or what?
Teacher suggests Charlie make that a little clearer.
Lucy: If he fell through the step. . . .
Teacher: We still haven't decided about the short sentences.
Perhaps they make the story more spooky and mysterious.
Gwynne: I wish he had read with more expression instead of
all at one time.
Rachel: Not enough expression.
Teacher: Charlie, they want a little more expression from you.
I guess we've given you enough suggestions for one time.
(Charlie does not raise his head, which is bent over his desk
as if studying a paper.) Charlie! I guess we've given you
enough suggestions for one time, Charlie, haven't we? (Charlie
half raises his head, seems to assent grudgingly.)

The striking thing about these examples is that the teacher
supports the children in their carping criticism of their fellows.
Her performance in this is not, however, consistent; but even
where, as in Example 6, she seems at one point to try to set
herself against the tide of destruction, by calling attention to
the possible artistry in Charlie's short sentences, she ends up
supporting the class against him, and Charlie becomes upset.
Thus the teacher, by rewarding the children's tendencies to
carp, reinforces them. Teachers, however, are able to make their

own contributions to this tendency. The single example given below will serve as illustration:

> 7. Joan reads us a poem she has written about Helen Keller . . . which concludes with the couplet:
>> "Helen Keller as a woman was very great;
>> She is really a credit to the United States."
> Teacher (amusedly): Is "states" supposed to rhyme with "great"? When Joan murmurs that it is, the teacher says, "We'll call it poetic license."

From time to time one can see a teacher vigorously oppose tendencies in the children to tear each other to pieces. The following example is from the sixth grade:

> 8. The Parent-Teachers Association is sponsoring a school frolic, and the children have been asked to write jingles for the publicity. For many of the children the experience of writing a jingle seems painful. They are restless, bite their pencils, squirm around in their seats, speak to their neighbors, and from time to time pop up with questions like, "Does it have to rhyme, Mr. Smith?" . . . At last Mr. Smith says, "All right, let's read some of the jingles now." Child after child says he "couldn't get one"; but some have succeeded. One girl has written a very long jingle, *obviously the best in the class.* However, instead of using Friday as the frolic day she used Tuesday, and several protests were heard from the children. Mr. Smith defended her. "Well, so she made a mistake. But you are too prone to criticize. If *you* could only do so well!"

It will be observed that all the examples are taken from circumstances in which the child's self-system is most intensely involved; where his own poetry or prose is in question, or where he has worked hard to synthesize material into a report. It is precisely at the points where the ego is most exposed that the attack is most telling. The numerous instances in the sample, where the teachers, by a word of praise or a pat on the head, play a supportive role, indicate their awareness of the vulnerability of the children. Meanwhile, as I have pointed out, the teachers often fall into the trap of triggering or supporting destructive impulses in the children.

The carping criticism of one's peers is a form of intragroup aggression, which can be quite threatening and destructive. Tale-bearing, however, countenanced by some teachers more than by others, can be an overwhelming threat to autonomy. While telling on others can be organized into the patrol-monitor complex (prestige through controlling and telling), useful perhaps in maintaining order in large school populations, its operation within the classroom may have serious consequences. Let us look at a couple of examples.

> 9. Second grade. As teacher asked the children to clear their desks one boy raised his hand, and when called on said, "Jimmy just walked by and socked me on the head."
> Teacher: Is this true?
> Jimmy: He hit me first.
> Teacher: Why don't you both take seats up here (in front of the room). I'm not sure people like you belong in the second grade.
> 10. Sixth grade special class for bright students.
> The children are working on their special nature study projects. Joseph passes where Ralph is working. Ralph (to teacher): Joseph is writing too much on his birds.
> Teacher: Joseph, you should write only a few things.

In our sample, telling on other children in the classroom is infrequent outside the class in which the Vigilance Club was formed. Destructive criticism is the preferred mode of attack in most classrooms. The ease with which tendencies to attack peers can be organized into telling on others, however, is illustrated by the monitor-patrol complex, and by the Vigilance Club (Example 3).

Competition

Competition is an important element in the witch-hunt syndrome. Since witch hunts involve so often obtaining the attention and approval of some powerful central figure, the examples of competitiveness that I shall cite illustrate how approval and attention seeking occur as the child attempts to beat out his peers for the nod of the teacher. It would be easy to cite examples from protocols of the merciless laughter of children at the failures or gaucheries of their classmates. I am interested, however, more in showing the all-pervading character

of the phenomenon of competition, *even in its mildest forms.*
The first example is from a fourth-grade music lesson:

> 11.   The children are singing songs of Ireland and her neigh-
> bors from the book *Songs of Many Lands.* . . . Teacher plays
> on piano while children sing. . . . While children are singing
> some of them hunt in the index, find a song belonging to one
> of the four countries, and raise their hands before the previous
> song is finished in order that they may be called on to name
> the next song. . . .

Here singing is subordinated, in the child, to the competitive wish to have the song he has hunted up in the index
chosen by the teacher. It is merely a question of who gets to
the next song in the index first, gets his hand up fast, and is
called on by the teacher.

The following examples also illustrate the fact that almost
any situation set by the teacher can be the occasion for release
of competitive impulses:

> 12.   The observer enters the fifth-grade classroom.
> Teacher: Which one of you nice polite boys would like to take
> [observer's] coat and hang it up? (Observer notes: From the
> waving hands it would seem that all would like to claim the
> title.)
> Teacher chooses one child . . . who takes observer's coat. . . .
> Teacher: Now children, who will tell [observer] what we have
> been doing?
> Usual forest of hands . . . and a girl is chosen to tell. . . .
> Teacher conducted the arithmetic lesson mostly by asking,
> "Who would like to tell . . . the answer to the next problem?"
> This question was usually followed by the appearance of a
> large and *agitated* forest of hands; apparently *much com-
> petition to answer.*

Thus the teacher is a powerful agent in reinforcing competition.

It has already been pointed out that carping criticism helps
to settle in the child a feeling of vulnerability and threat. In
this connection it is significant that *the failure of one child is
repeatedly the occasion for the success of another.* I give one
illustration below from the same class as the one from which I
have taken Example 12.

13. Boris had trouble reducing $^{12}\!/_{16}$ to lowest terms, and could get only as far as $^{6}\!/_{8}$. Much excitement. Teacher asked him quietly [note how basically decent this teacher is] if that was as far as he could reduce it. She suggested he "think." Much heaving up and down from the other children, all frantic to correct him. Boris pretty unhappy. Teacher, patient, quiet, ignoring others, and concentrating with look and voice on Boris. She says, "Is there a bigger number than 2 you can divide into the two parts of the fraction?" After a minute or two she becomes more urgent. No response from Boris. She then turns to the class and says, "Well, who can tell Boris what the number is?" Forest of hands. Teacher calls Peggy. Peggy gives 4 to be divided into $^{12}\!/_{16}$, numerator and denominator.

Where Boris has failed Peggy has been triumphant; *Boris's failure has made it possible for Peggy to succeed.*

This example and also Example 6 are ones in which the discomfort of the child was *visible,* and such instances may be multiplied. They illustrate how vulnerable the children feel in the presence of the attacks of the peer group in the classroom. But since these are children who face the world with serious anxiety to begin with, the classroom situation sustains it. Let us look at some stories created by these very children, and read by them to their classmates. We have already seen one, Example 6, Charlie's story of "The Unknown Guest." Here are *all* the stories read to their classmates by these children during an observation period.

14. (a) Charlotte's story: "Mistaken Identity." One day last year my family and I went to the hospital to visit somebody. When we were coming out and were walking along my father hit me. I came up behind him to hit him back, but just as I was about to do it I looked back and he was behind me! I was going to hit the wrong person!
(b) Tommy's story: "The Day Our House Was Robbed." [Observer has recorded this in the third person.] He was coming home from school one afternoon. He knew his Mom was away that afternoon. He started to go in the side door, but decided, he doesn't know why, to go round the back. He found the door open, went into the kitchen, looked into the front room where he saw a thief. Tommy "froze stiff" (chuckle of appreciation from the class), ran out, shouted, "Stop thief" as the man ran out after him. He went to a neighbor, rang the bell,

called his mother at the store. The cops came, asked questions, but the man had gotten away with $99 and his mother's watch. If he had gone in the side door he would not have had a chance to see the man. Changing to the back door "may have saved my life." [Teacher's only remarks about this story were: 1) instead of having said "froze stiff," Tommy should have said, "froze stiff as something"; 2) he should have left out the word "then" in one place; 3) he could have made the story clearer; 4) he changed from the past to the present tense.]

(c) Polly's story: "Custard the Lion." Custard the Lion was the most timid animal in Animal Town. The doctors couldn't cure him. Then they found a new medicine. It had strange effects, but Custard wanted to try it. When he did he felt very queer. (Child gives details of queer feeling.) But he soon realized he wasn't afraid of anything. [Teacher's first remark: "You didn't let us hear the last sentence."]

(d) Dan's story: "The Boy Hero." Bill wanted to be a fireman, so he went to the firehouse. The Chief was telling him to go home when the bell clanged. While the Chief was getting into the engine, he didn't see that Bill was getting on too. (Class or teacher picks up flaw in sentence and it is reread correctly.) The Chief said O.K. as long as Bill was aboard, "But you're not to get into no mischief." (Class choruses, "Any. . . .") Everyone was out of the fire except a little girl and her doll. The firemen cannot figure out what to do, but Bill, seeing a tree near the house, climbs it over the protests of the firemen. He misses the girl on his first try, but gets her on the second. While sliding down the tree she slips and almost falls, but grabs Bill's pants, and they make it to safety. . . . [Children's remarks center on position of "clang, clang, clang" in the story. Teacher talks about how to use direct quotations, which, it seems, Dan had not used properly.]

(e) Bertha's story: Title not recorded. The story is about Jim who was walking home past the Smith's house one night and heard a scream. Penny Smith came out and said there was a robber in the house. When the cops came they found a parrot flying around in there, and Penny's parents told her to shut the parrot up before she read mystery stories again. [This story was followed by much carping criticism, which was terminated by the teacher's telling Bertha to change the story to suit the class.]

These stories contain elements of anxiety and even of terror. As each child finishes, the carping criticism of students and teacher then reminds him of his vulnerability. As the child sends out his cloud of fear, it returns with the leaden rain of hostility.

Docility

It comes as a somewhat shocking surprise, perhaps, to middle-class parents, to find their children described as "docile." Yet we have already seen the perfection of docility in the Vigilance Club, and we shall presently see its manifold forms in more normal classrooms.

> 15. First grade. The children are to act out a story called "Pig Brother," which is about an untidy boy. The teacher is telling the story. One boy said he did not like the story, so the teacher said he could leave if he did not wish to hear it again, but the boy did not leave.
>
> 16. In gym the children began to tumble, but there was much restless activity in the lines, so the teacher had all the children run around the room until they were somewhat exhausted before she continued the tumbling.
>
> 17. Second grade. The children have been shown movies of birds. The first film ended with a picture of a baby bluebird. Teacher: Did the last bird ever look as if he would be blue? The children did not seem to understand the "slant" of the question, and answered somewhat hesitantly, yes.
> Teacher: I think he looked more like a robin, didn't he?
> Children, in chorus: Yes.

Item 17 is one of a large number of instances, distributed throughout all grades, in which the children exhibit their docility largely through giving the teacher what he wants. Thus in the elementary schools of the middle class the children get an intensive eight-year-long training in hunting for the right signals and giving the teacher the response wanted. The rest of the examples of docility document this assertion.

> 18. Fourth grade. (a) An art lesson.
> Teacher holds up a picture.
> Teacher: Isn't Bob getting a nice effect of moss and trees?
> Ecstatic Ohs and Ahs from the children. . . .
> The art lesson is over.
> Teacher: How many enjoyed this?

Many hands go up.

Teacher: How many learned something?

Quite a number of hands come down.

Teacher: How many will do better next time?

Many hands go up.

(b) Children have just finished reading the story "The Sun Moon and Stars Clock."

Teacher: What was the highest point of interest—the climax?

The children tell what they think it is. Teacher is aiming to get from them what *she* considers the point of climax, but the children seem to give everything else but.

Bobby: When they capture the thieves.

Teacher: How many agree with Bobby?

Hands, hands.

19.   Fifth grade. This is a lesson on "healthy thoughts," for which the children have a special book depicting, with appropriate illustrations, specific conflictful incidents among children. The teacher is supposed to discuss each incident with the children in order to help them understand how to handle their emotions.

One of the pictures is as follows: A sibling *pair* is illustrated by *three* boys: 1) One has received a ball. 2) One is imagined to react with displeasure. 3) One is imagined to react benignly and philosophically, saying, "My brother couldn't help being given the football; we'll use it together."

Teacher: Do you believe it's easier to deal with your thoughts if you own up to them, Betty?

Betty: Yes it is, if you're not cross and angry.

Teacher: Have you any experience like this in the book, Alice? Alice tells how her brother was given a watch and she envied him and wanted one too; but her mother said she wasn't to have one until she was fifteen, but now she has one anyway.

Teacher: How could you have helped—could you have changed your thinking? How could you have handled it? What could you do with mean feelings?

Alice seems stymied. Hems and haws.

Teacher: What did Susie (a character in the book) do?

Alice: She talked to her mother.

Teacher: If you talk to someone you often then feel that "it was foolish of me to feel that way. . . ."

Tommy: He had an experience like that, he says. His cousin was given a bike and he envied it. But he wasn't "ugly" about it. He asked if he might ride it, and his cousin let him, and then, "I got one myself; and I wasn't mean, or ugly or jealous."

Before continuing it will be well to note that since the teacher does not say Alice was wrong the children assume she was right and so copy her answer.

> Two boys, the dialogue team, now come to the front of the class and dramatize the football incident.
> Teacher (to the class): Which boy do you think handled the problem in a better way?
> Rupert: Billy did, because he didn't get angry. . . . It was better to play together than to do nothing with the football.
> Teacher: That's a good answer, Rupert. Has anything similar happened to you, Joan?
> Joan can think of nothing.
> Sylvester: I had an experience. My brother got a hat with his initials on it because he belongs to a fraternity, and I wanted one like it and couldn't have one; and his was too big for me to wear, and it ended up that I asked him if he could get me some letters with my initials, and he did.
> Betty: My girl friend got a bike that was 26-inches, mine was only 24; and I asked my sister what I should do. Then my girl friend came over and was real nice about it, and let me ride it.
> Teacher approves of this, and says, Didn't it end up that they both had fun without unhappiness?

Here we note that the teacher herself has gone astray, for on the one hand her aim is to get instances from the children in which they have been yielding, and capable of resolving their own jealousy, etc.; yet, in the instance given by Betty, it was not Betty who yielded, but her friend. The child immediately following Betty imitated her since Betty had been praised by the teacher:

> Matilde: My girl friend got a 26-inch bike and mine was only 24; but she only let me ride it once a month. But for my birthday my mother's getting me a new one, probably (proudly) a 28. (Many children rush in with the information that 28 doesn't exist.) Matilde replies that she'll probably have to raise the seat then for she's too big for a 26.

As we go on with this lesson, we shall continue to see how the children's need for substitute gratification and their inability to accept frustration are the real issues, which even prevent them from getting the teacher's point. We shall see how, in spite of the teacher's driving insistence on her point, the children continue to inject their conflicts into the lesson. While at the same time they gropingly try to find a way to gratify the teacher. *They* cannot give the "right" answers because of their conflicts; teacher cannot handle their conflicts, even perceive them, because *her* underlying need is to be gratified by the children! The lesson goes on:

> Teacher: I notice that some of you are only happy when you get your own way. You're not thinking this through, and I want you to. Think of an experience when you didn't get what you want. Think it through.
>
> Charlie: His ma was going to the movies and he wanted to go with her, and she wouldn't let him; and she went off to the movies, and he was mad; but then he went outside and there were some kids playing baseball, so he played baseball.
>
> Teacher: But suppose you hadn't gotten to play baseball? You would have felt hurt because you didn't get what you wanted. We can't help feeling hurt when we are disappointed. What could you have done; how could you have handled it?
>
> Charlie: So I can't go to the movies so I can't play baseball, so I'll do something around the house.
>
> Teacher: Now you're beginning to think! It takes courage to take disappointments. (Turning to the class) What did we learn? The helpful way . . .
>
> Class: is the healthy way!

Before entering the final section of this paper, we need to ask: Why are these children, whose fantasies contain so many hostile elements, so docile in the classroom; and why do they struggle so hard to gratify the teacher and try in so many ways to bring themselves to her attention (the "forest of hands")? We might, of course, start with the idea of the teacher as a parent figure, and the children as siblings competing for the teacher's favor. We could refer to the unresolved dependency needs of children of this age, which make them seek support in the teacher, who manipulates this seeking and their sibling rivalry to pit the children against each other. Other important factors, however, that are inherent in the classroom situation itself, and particularly in middle-class classrooms, ought to be taken into consideration. We have observed the children's tendency to destructively criticize each other, and the teachers' often unwitting repeated reinforcement of this tendency. We have taken note of the anxiety in the children as illustrated by the stories they tell, and observed that these very stories are subjected to a carping criticism, whose ultimate consequence would be anything but alleviation of that anxiety. Hence the classroom is a place in which the child's underlying anxiety may be heightened. In an effort to alleviate this he seeks the approval of the teacher, by giving right answers and by doing what teacher wants him to do under most circumstances. Finally, we cannot omit the teacher's need to be gratified by the attention-hungry behavior of the children.

A word is necessary about these classrooms as middle class. The novel *Blackboard Jungle* describes schoolroom behavior of lower-class children. There we see the children *against the teacher*, as representative of the middle class. But in the classes I have described we see the *children against each other*, with the teacher abetting the process. Thus, as the teacher in the middle-class schools directs the hostility of the children toward one another and away from himself, he reinforces the competitive dynamics within the middle class itself. The teacher in lower-class schools, on the other hand, appears to become the organizing stimulus for behavior that integrates the lower class, as the children unite in expressing their hostility to the teacher (Hunter, 1954).

Confession

The Vigilance Club would have been impossible without confession, and the children's pleasure in confession. But, as with the other parts of the syndrome, confessing occurs in other classrooms also; it can be elicited when the proper conditions are present, and the children can be seen to enjoy it—to vie with one another in confessing. Let us follow the lesson "healthy thoughts" a little further. We will see how confession occurs as the children seek to give the teacher *precisely* what she wants.

> 20. Teacher asks if anyone else has experiences like that [of two children who have just recited], where they were mean and angry.

Dick: He has a friend he plays baseball with, and sometimes they fight; but they get together again in a few minutes and apologize.

In this first example we note one of the important aspects of the confession element in the syndrome: the culprit must have given up his evil ways, and now be free of impurities.

In response to Dick's story, teacher says: You handled it just right. Now let's hear about someone who had a similar experience and didn't handle it just right.

Tom: His little brother asked for the loan of his knife, but it was lost, and he got angry with his little brother for asking. [This knife story follows a sequence of several stories about knives told by other children. The exuberance of knife stories following immediately on the teacher's approval of the first one suggests that some of them are made to order and served up piping hot for teacher's gratification.]

Teacher: Now Tom, could you have worked it out any differently? (Observer notes that Tom seems to enjoy this confession; certainly he is not abashed or ashamed.)

Tom: Later he asked me if he could help me find it. He found it in a wastebasket, and then I let him borrow it.

Harry: Sometimes I get angry when my friends are waiting for me and . . . (observer missed some of this) and my little sister asked if she could borrow my auto-racing set, and I hit her once or twice (Class laughs.)

Here we see another factor so important to the flourishing of the syndrome: the audience gets pleasure through the confessor's telling about deeds the audience wishes to commit: who among Harry's listeners would not like to have hit his sister, or anyone, "once or twice"?

The teacher then goes on: What would you do now—would you hit her?

Harry: Now I'd probably get mad at first, but let her have it later.

Thus Harry has mended his ways—in teacher-directed fantasy at least—and returned to the fold.

So far we have had confession of mean and angry thoughts

and violence. We shall now see confession to unacceptable fear. In all cases the teacher says what type of confession she wishes to hear, and what the resolution should be of the unacceptable behavior; and the children vie with one another to tell commensurable tales, as they derive pleasure from the total situation—through approval of the teacher, expression of their own real or fantasied deviations, and the delight of their peers. In these situations the pleasure of the peer group is seen to derive not so much from the "happy ending" the children give their stories but rather from the content of the story itself. It is interesting that no carping criticism appears; rather the entire situation is a jolly one. It seems that within unspoken limits the children permit one another to boast of "evil" behavior because of the deep pleasure obtained from hearing it. Thus impulse expression becomes a device for role maintenance in the classroom.

The lesson proceeds:

Two children enact a little skit in which they have to go to the principal to ask him something. One of them is afraid of the principal, the other is not. The moral is that the principal is the children's friend, and that one should not be shy.
Gertrude: Well, anyway, the principal isn't a lion, he's your friend; he's not going to kill you.
Teacher: That's right, the principal is a friend, he says hello and good morning to you. . . . Have you ever felt shy?
Meriam: The first year I sold Girl Scout cookies I didn't know how to approach people; and the first house I went to I didn't know the lady; and I stuttered and stammered, and didn't sell any cookies. By the second house I had thought it all out before I rang the bell, and I sold two boxes. (Triumphantly.)
Teacher: It helps to have self-confidence.
Ben now tells a story, with a happy ending, of being afraid of a principal. Then Paul tells a story, amid gales of laughter, about his being scared on a roller coaster. By this time there is so much excitement among the children that the teacher says: Wait a minute—manners!
John: He was scared to go on the Whip-the-Whirl (scornful laughter from the class); but after he went he liked it so much that he went eight times in a row. (This is well received.)
Many hands go up. Teacher waits. . . .

Michael: He was at Pleasure Park on the ferris wheel (scornful Aw from the class) and a girl kept rocking it, and I started to get green (roar of laughter).
Teacher: Now we'll have to stop.

Certain phenomena not emphasized before appear in this section. Confession is used by the authoritative figure, the teacher, to strengthen attachment to significant but potentially terrifying figures like school principals, and to polish up cultural shibboleths like "self-confidence." For the child storytellers confession becomes an opportunity for bathing in the emotional currents of the peer group, as the child stimulates the group's approval through presentation of group standards, and awakens group pleasure as the peer group responds to its own anxiety about weakness, and experiences resolution of the anxiety through the happy ending. With a perfect instinct for what is right, each child provides catharsis for his peers. By presenting himself as weak, he enables his peers to identify with him; and then, as he overcomes his weakness, he enables his companions too to feel strong.

What this lesson on healthy thoughts may have accomplished by way of creating a permanent reservoir of "healthy thoughts" is difficult to say, but that it helped create solidarity among the students, and between them and the teacher is clear from the fact that when she suddenly shifted ground to say, "Do you think you are wide enough awake for a contest in subtraction of fractions?" the children responded with a unanimous roar of "Yes," as if she had asked them whether they were ready for cookies and ice cream!

Thus in this lesson, in which all have participated more with their *unconscious* than with their conscious emotions, solidarity has been achieved. The teacher thought she was teaching the children to have healthy thoughts, but she was showing them how to gratify her. The children sensed this and struggled to gratify her, while they sought acceptance by their peers also. The essential difference between this teacher and the one who perpetrated the Vigilance Club is that though the latter tended to demolish solidarity among the children while placing the teacher in supreme command, the lesson on healthy thoughts tended to a dubious solidarity among all.

Both teachers organize some of the same elements in the children, but into different configurations, of total feeling and behavior.

Boredom

It seems unnecessary to document the fact that children become bored in class, for much of modern thinking and curriculum arrangement is aimed at eliminating it. The shifts at 15-minute intervals from one subject to the next in the elementary school classrooms is one example of this effort. Boredom, which means emotional and intellectual separation from the environment, is an insupportable agony, particularly if the emotional vacuum created by such separation is not filled by gratifying fantasies, or if it is filled by terrifying ones. To fill this vacuum people in our culture will throw themselves into a great variety of even relatively ungratifying activities. Since in this situation, bored children attack almost any novel classroom activity with initial vigor, the witch-hunt syndrome or any modification thereof helps to overcome boredom: better to hunt than be bored. In a full and satisfying life there is no place for witch hunts. The school system that can provide a rich program for children has no need of Vigilance Clubs, or even of lessons on "healthy thoughts."

Discussion and Conclusions

In this paper I have used suggestions from communications theory in an effort to order the data obtained from direct observation of elementary school classrooms. Information, the central concept of communications theory, refers to measurable differences in states of organization. In human behavior, as seen in the classroom under discussion, we observe *qualitative shifts in state, for different teachers organize the same underlying emotional characteristics of the children to achieve different organizations of the emotions.* One teacher so organizes the children's emotions as to accomplish an intensification of the fear of intra-group aggression, while she turns the children's hostility toward one another. A different teacher may organize the emotions of the children so that a euphoria in which students and teacher are bathed in a wave of emotional gratification is achieved. The great skill in being a teacher would seem to be, therefore, a *learned* capacity to keep shifting states of order intelligently as the work demands. This does not mean the traditional classroom order, where you can hear a pin drop, but rather the kind of order in which the *emotions of the children are caught up and organized toward the achievement of a specific goal.* It is not necessary, perhaps, that even the most prominent emotions of the children, like competitiveness, for example, form part of the organized whole. Yet, on the other hand, it is difficult to see how, in the present state of our culture, competitiveness can be overlooked. It would seem, perhaps, that the important outcome to avoid is that the competitiveness should become destructive of peers, while reinforcing dependence on the teacher.

The phenomenon I have labeled "docility" occurs because of the absolute dependence for survival of the children on the teacher. That is to say success in school depends absolutely on the teacher, and self-respect, as a function of the opinion of others, in the home or among peers, is in part a function of success or failure in school. In these circumstances the child's capacity to respond automatically to the signals he gets from the teacher is bound to acquire somewhat the appearance of instinctive behavior. Although it occurs at a much higher level of integration than instinct, the child hunts for the proper signals from the teacher, and the child's responses take on instinctual quality. They *must;* otherwise, like the nestling who does not open its mouth when the mother arrives with a worm, he will never eat the ambrosia of teacher's approval, so necessary to his survival. In this situation both children and teacher easily become the instruments of their own unconscious processes, as they, like Joseph and his brethren, fall on each other's necks in a shared ecstasy of exuberant dependence. Teacher and pupil will have gratified each other, but it remains an open question whether the children will have learned what the curriculum committee planned.

We see in the organization of the components of the witch-hunt syndrome an important phase in the formation of American national character, for tendencies to docility, competitiveness, confession, intragroup aggression, and feelings of vulnerability the children may bring with them to school, are reinforced in the classroom. This means that independence and courage to challenge are observably played *down* in these classrooms. It means, on the other hand, that tendencies to own up rather than to conceal are reinforced—a development which, in proper hands, might become a useful educational instrument. It means, further, that while many teachers do stress helping others they may inadvertently develop in the children the precise opposite, and thus undermines children's feelings of security. One could come from a very secure and accepting family and yet have one's feeling of security and acceptance threatened in these classrooms. On the other hand, what seems most in evidence from the stories they make up is that the children come to school with feelings of vulnerability which are intensified in the classroom.

Meanwhile we should try to understand that all the teachers in the sample were probably trying to be good teachers,[2] and all the children were trying to be good pupils. Their unconscious needs, however, naturally dominated their behavior. The teacher who organized the Vigilance Club probably thought she was teaching her children to be upright and honest, and to perform good deeds, but her unconscious tendencies caused these worthy inclinations to seek the wrong expression. All teachers need conformity in the classroom in order that the children shall absorb a respectable amount of academic knowledge. But the teacher's (often unconscious) need for acceptance by the children, and her fear (sometimes unconscious) of her inability to control free discussion, compel her to push the children into uncritical docility at times, while they seek her approval.

The creation of stories, and their discussion by the class, are accepted principles of progressive education. But the teacher's own (at times unconscious) need to carp and criticize gets in the way of her adequately developing the creative and supportive possibilities in her charges. Thus these are not "bad," "vicious," or "stupid" teachers, but human beings, who express in their classroom behavior the very weaknesses parents display in their dealings with their children. The solution to the problem of the contradiction between the requirements of a democratic education on the one hand, and the teachers'

---

[2] I am indebted to B. Bettelheim for this suggestion.

unconscious needs on the other, is not to carp at teachers, and thus repeat the schoolroom process, but to give them some insight into how they project their personal problems into the classroom situation.

References

Henry, Jules, and Joan Whitehorn Boggs, 1952, "Child Rearing, Culture, and the Natural World." *Psychiatry*, 15:261–271.
Hunter, Evan, 1954, *The Blackboard Jungle*. New York: Simon and Schuster.
Starkey, Marion L., 1949, *The Devil in Massachusetts*. New York: Knopf.

Solving Problems
Cooperatively:
A Comparison
of Three Classroom Groups[*]

PATRICIA P. MINUCHIN

The behavior of three groups of children in a cooperative test situation—one which called on their ability to work effectively together in solving problems—is described in this article. This behavior is considered in relation to the teaching and learning atmospheres in their schools.

The material is drawn from a broader study designed to assess the effects of different kinds of education on the psychological development of children.[1] In this study, several schools were selected which differed along a "modern-traditional" continuum—differed, that is, in the extent to which contemporary thinking about child development and learning had come to influence their philosophies and practices. All were urban, middle-class schools. One, the most modern, was a private school; the others were public schools, members of the same school system but varying in their educational approach. We studied fourth-grade children, observing classroom behavior, testing individual children and conducting some sessions with

[1] This study, entitled "The Psychological Impact of School Experience," was supported by the National Institute of Mental Health, U. S. Public Health Service, grant M–1075.

the classroom groups as a whole.[2] One of the latter sessions was the group problem-solving task described herein.

As a background for evaluating the reactions of the children it seems important first to describe the practices and values of their particular schools and classrooms. Three fourth-grade classrooms will be considered: one from the modern private school (Conrad);[3] one from a school essentially traditional in orientation but with mixed features (Adams); one from a school with a clear, unembellished traditional orientation (Browning). These classrooms represented quite different concepts of teaching and learning, but to understand the children's behavior in the situation presented it may be sufficient to highlight four aspects of difference:

The Role of the Child Group

The modern private school (Conrad) viewed the child group as an important and serious work group—to discuss and plan, to carry out activities, to serve as a unit with which children identify and within which they forge their roles and work out relationships. Neither of the traditional schools held this view. In these classrooms teaching was often directed to the total class, but performance and evaluation were individual and competitive. Children from Adams worked in committees and subgroups but were also clearly reinforced in competition for achievement. Neither group was encouraged toward responsibility or self-evaluation in a sustained way.

The Role of the Teacher

In Conrad, the teacher was relatively close and personal in her relationship with the children. She acted as a catalyzer of thought and exploration and carried authority in terms of its rational function—to provide a constructive learning atmosphere—rather than in terms of automatic adult prerogatives. In both traditional schools, considerably more control of the process of learning resided with the teacher, who set content

[2] For full study descriptions see . . . [first, third, and fourth items in Bibliography].

[3] School names are pseudonyms.

and pace and served as critic and judge. Control was tightest and authority least open to challenge in Browning.

Conception of Work

In Conrad, work was assumed to be intrinsically pleasurable to children, if appropriately selected; and this pleasure was considered an essential component of mastery and effective learning. Curriculum content and work relationships were geared to this concept. The traditional schools tended to see school work as a necessary part of training and socialization, whether enjoyable or not. These schools, especially Browning, neither geared curriculum primarily to child-level interests nor fostered cooperative relationship around work problems.

Scope of Child Initiative

There was consistent encouragement, in Conrad, to relate ideas to personally meaningful experiences and to carry problems to new levels of thought and activity. Though the teacher acted as guide and resource in helping children extend learning, the child himself was seen as the agent of discovery. The traditional classrooms stressed the child's responsibility to master a definite and authoritative body of knowledge, defining achievement and mastery in concrete terms. Adams, however, more than Browning, allowed some scope for individual research and creative activity.

Let us consider now the task we set the children from these classrooms and their behavior in meeting it.

Procedure

The children were presented with a modified version of the Russell Sage Social Relations Test (Damrin, 1959). In this test, group members must cooperate in building an object that matches a previously constructed model, using interlocking blocks.

The children were shown the first model, a house, and each child was given one or two blocks—enough so that the class held the total number needed for construction. They were told to hold a discussion, make a plan, and inform the examiner when they were ready. They were then given fifteen minutes for actual building. At the end of that time they were shown the model of a bridge, and the same procedure was followed again. The session took approximately one hour.[4]

It is important to note that the number of children in the classrooms varied. In each of the traditional schools there were thirty-four children; in the modern private school there were sixteen. This disparity undoubtedly affected the work process; but it is unlikely to account for all differences in the children's behavior, especially since behavior was different in the two traditional classrooms, though they were equivalent in size.

Group Reactions

Browning School

The Browning group was characterized by the greatest tension and aggressive activity, the greatest rigidity in group structure, the highest proportion of children who did not participate.

At the beginning of the session this group was eager and attentive, but their planning session was short and abortive. They advanced few ideas, did not develop each other's suggestions and decided quickly to go ahead with the building. Two groups formed around the central table, a small central ring of builders and an external ring of watchers. Beyond this there were children who were no part of either. There was considerable pushing, bickering, struggle for position. The children in the center were clearly the stronger ones, both physically and as personalities in holding their own against challenge. At no time during the session were there any girls in this central group, and few were in the ring of watchers. At one point, when the children thought their construction finished, a sustained "victory yell" rose from the entire class. This screaming, repeated several times during the hour, seemed to serve as a release of extraordinary tension and was, for many of the

[4] Thanks are due to the session observers: Joan Blos, Zachary Gussow and Ethel Horn.

children, the only moment they could feel themselves participants.

The group did not complete the first problem successfully within the time limit. Some reacted with joking comments, such as that it probably took the examiners "two years" to make the model or that the model was held together by tape.

The second planning session was short and impatient, and it brought the monopoly of personalities to open verbalization ("You and me will do the whites, Mike . . ."). The building group was smaller but no more peaceful, and the general atmosphere of the performance was similar to the first. This time, however, the replica was accurately completed in thirteen minutes. At the end of the session, the children were wound up and physically spent. The main performers relived their personal roles, stressing individual achievements. ("I did most of it, with Harry." "You did it, but I had to fix it.")

Adams School

In Adams, the performance had mixed features: evident talent, constructive activity, and effective attempts to mobilize a large group for a united effort, combined with processes destructive to the group's efforts and a general deterioration of effectiveness over a prolonged period of time. The first planning session was competent, and both boys and girls participated. They offered varied ideas, developing each other's plans and offering alternative possibilities for dividing and coordinating the work. The building period began effectively, with children actively searching for sections to which they could contribute. Here the group structure was more fluid than at Browning. There were some central and more peripheral figures; there were skirmishes for individual places, but much of the competition was centered in the several subgroups where the children were committed to completing their subsection first. After eight minutes the children claimed they had finished. When the examiner pointed out errors, they could not mobilize to correct them and did not finish within the time limit. Like the Browning group, they rationalized, protesting that their house was more stable than the model and maintaining they had the wrong blocks.

Handling of the second problem was inferior to the first in planning and participation. The planning period was short, and building was carried on by a smaller group of children. The second construction, completed in eleven minutes, was also incorrect. These children seemed in a special hurry to turn their project over for evaluation, as if the *real* decision about whether it was adequate must come from the adult.

Conrad School

The performance of the Conrad children had the qualities of an effective group effort, carried through with considerable *esprit de corps*. Planning was vigorous and relevant; building was self-propelled, effective and technically accurate.

In the planning session the children offered various suggestions; listened to each other; supported, challenged, debated ideas. There were central, active figures here, as in the other schools; but they seemed less destructively aggressive in maintaining their roles. The less active members were also involved in the general effort, and this continued through the building period. The group completed the first building in four minutes, building separate parts first and then combining them. All the children found roles, some to analyze and communicate about patterns, some to spot the current needs and carry the relevant blocks, some to build. The general mood was less tense and competitive than in the other schools. The children were consistently purposeful, and difficulties seemed to induce concentration rather than scatter.

The second planning session was shorter; but this group, unlike the others, dealt briefly with the special requirements of the second model. During the building period, two children drifted away but were deterred by a critical comment from one of the participants, who called after them: "Some people are very good at drawing on boards!" This group saw itself as a working unit, dependent on the cooperative efforts of all members. Furthermore, they accepted the responsibility for reviewing their own work and finding their own errors. After eleven minutes they began a final check. With a mixed sense of fun and purpose, they compared each block with the model. Children marched their fingers up the bridge construction as

the group chanted in unison, "Right! Right!" until all blocks
were checked and the chant ended in a cheer.

The spontaneous activity which followed completion of the
second construction was unique. One child suggested they
combine the two bridges to form something new.[5] Within the
next few minutes, the construction took on the shape of a man,
was likened to George Washington and given a wig, which the
children formed out of cotton available in the room. The activity was characterized as was most of the session, by a sense of
productive autonomy, a flow of ideas that built on each other,
harmonious relations among the children and over-all pleasure
in what they were doing.

Discussion

Is there a logical connection between the concepts and
practices that guided classroom life in these three groups and
the children's behavior in this group task? In general, it would
seem so.

The group at Browning seemed to reflect a classroom atmosphere in which the teacher was dominant; where children
worked competitively against each other for recognition, with
little experience in group cooperation; and where pleasant
personal contacts were not generally interwoven with intellectual activity. These children could not utilize the potential of a
group for effective effort. Their emphasis was on personal
achievement expressed through destructive competition.

The situation in this classroom seemed to support strong
fighters, children who were competent and capable of taking
control. This situation might seem adaptive in a competitive
society, but these children themselves probably paid a price.
In educating the resourceful and effective individual, we still
presumably do not wish to create a person who must always
be central, is tense and uneasy in his position, and must constantly reaffirm himself. For those who were pushed out—the

---

[5] One of the boys at Browning apparently had a similar impulse,
attaching the two constructions together and calling on others to look;
but another child immediately said to him, "Unconnect them!," and the
activity stopped in midstream.

girls, the less forceful individuals—there must surely be an eventual decrease in their sense of competence and their conviction that they could make a meaningful contribution.

In some of the reactions of the Adams group—less rigidity, more effective processes, more relatedness to each other—we may have seen the effects of a classroom not as tightly controlled as in Browning and with more provision for committee work and independent expressive activities. In other respects, however, they seemed hampered by their classroom experiences, perhaps especially in their expectation that adequacy is judged finally by the adult. They could mobilize with intelligence and spirit to tackle a problem but could not take full responsibility for evaluation of their own work. Deteriorating functioning and attempts to downgrade the adult model seemed products of sensitivity to failure and the undue emphasis on recognized successful achievement.

The Conrad group performed in a way which seemed quite consistent with its classroom experience[6]—with the importance of the child group as a functioning and responsible unit, with its experience in relationships geared to work problems, with its relative freedom from authoritative control, and with its sense that child initiative and extension of ideas are encouraged as the core of learning.

These children had a conscious spirit of group identification and an internalized sense of responsibility. Their energy was directed less to aggression, projection or alibis than to responsible, concentrated work, mediated through personal interchange and group identification. In their spontaneous activity at the end, these children went beyond the assigned job, finding new and original uses for the materials in their life-space and working with enthusiasm and confidence in their own ideas. This activity was certainly consistent with the type of creative intellectual extension encouraged in this classroom.

[6] It would be misleading to imply that all behavior could be predicted from the teaching atmosphere. Other findings from the same study (Biber, *et al.*, 1962) have demonstrated the complexity of effects on individual children, and some of these effects have been unexpected. This group situation, however, is one in which the pattern of children's responses did seem to reflect quite directly the nature of their school experience.

In general, this group demonstrated a way of working on group problems that would meet general approval. Most educators—whether or not they value the group as a working medium or stress mutuality of peer relations in a work situation—would tend to acknowledge and sanction the value of the workmanlike techniques, self-reliance and technical effectiveness that characterized the Conrad group.

What are the implications of this material? Without wishing to extend the meaning of this situation beyond its sensible limits, we find it possible to raise a series of questions geared to the re-examination of prevalent values and methods: Do we wish participation and achievement to be the prerogatives of competent fighters? Is the destructively competitive behavior brought to the fore at Browning School operative at a more subtle level in many of our classrooms, with the implicit encouragement of the teacher? Are success and failure made so important that frustration in the work process brings self-criticism, a cessation of interest and the projection of blame rather than concentration and sustained effort? Is there a tendency for teachers to maintain such a strong role in directing and evaluating class activities that the children abdicate their prerogative to extend learning and to evaluate themselves?

If we consider the effective and essentially desirable performance at Conrad School, our questions are at a different level but nonetheless essential for deepening knowledge and advancing educational practice: When children are identified with their group and skillful at working within it, are there conflicts for some between group and individual interests? Are they growing adequately in their capacity to work on their own? How can the teacher balance group and individual activity in a constructive way?

These questions go back to the goals and practices of the educational system and to the teacher within his classroom. How he perceives his teaching role; activates the child group; defines worthwhile intellectual mastery; and understands children's motivation, learning and relationships—all these are important dimensions of teaching related, it is suggested, to the ways in which children will learn to live and work together in school.

Bibliography

A Study of the Psychological Impact of School Experience: A Series of Papers on Selected Findings. Papers by Biber, B., Zimiles, H., Minuchin, P., and Shapiro, E. Mimeo, 1962.

Damrin, Dora E. "The Russell Sage Social Relations Test: A Technique for Measuring Group Problem Solving Skills in Elementary School Children," *Journal of Experimental Education* (1959), 28, No. 1.

Minuchin, P., Shapiro, E., Dinnerstein, D., and Biber, B. *The Psychological Impact of School Experience: Methodological Report of a Study in Progress.* Mimeo, 1961.

Shapiro, E. "Study of Children Through Observation of Classroom Behavior." In A. A. Bellack (Ed.) *Theory and Research in Teaching.* New York: Teachers College, 1963.

Classroom Social Structure as a Mental Health Problem*

RONALD LIPPITT
MARTIN GOLD

One of the two most important and influential environments for the child is the classroom in which he lives during a part of each day. His relations with his teacher and with his peers are two major aspects of his school environment. These relations have a variety of important meanings for the child: "What is expected of me?" "What can I do and what can't I do?" "What will happen if . . . ?" "Who do I like?" "Who don't I like?" "Who likes me?" "Who doesn't?" "Who does the teacher like?" "Who's the strongest?" As clarification emerges about the meaning of such important questions, relations in the classroom develop a stable pattern or structure, which we are calling the classroom socio-emotional structure. Stratification becomes clear about those who are looked up to and down on in various ways. Each child finds he has a position, or several positions, in this socio-emotional structure. This social structure becomes a dominant aspect of his school environment and of his total life situation. His position in this structure becomes a very important determinant of his personal mental health situation, and of his motivation and ability to participate in classroom interaction.

This paper reports a research exploration of the development and maintenance of the classroom socio-emotional struc-

* *Journal of Social Issues*, 15, 1959, 40–49. Reprinted with the permission of the Society for the Psychological Study of Social Issues, a Division of the American Psychological Association.

ture in a sample of 39 elementary classrooms.[1] The paper also explores some of the mental health correlates of the child's position in this socio-emotional structure, which in turn suggest focal points for diagnosis of socio-emotional problems in the classroom situation and formulation of therapeutic strategy in working toward the improvement of classroom mental health.

The Development of the Socio-Emotional Structure of the Classroom

To what degree can we really talk about a social structure in the classroom? How much consensus is there among classmates about who belongs where in the structure? How stable is the structure over time?

All of the children in all of the 39 elementary school classrooms rated all their classmates on a four point scale, indicating the degrees to which the rates was perceived as able to get the others to do what he wanted them to do. The resulting stratification is called the social power structure of the classroom. If we look at the consensus among the group members in making these ratings, we find that in the average primary grade the children in the top third of the power structure received 47 per cent of the high power (number 1) ratings from peers while the bottom third received 18 per cent high ratings and 46 per cent lowest ratings. Consensus is even higher among fourth, fifth, and sixth grades with 58 per cent of the highest ratings going to the top third and only 11 per cent to the bottom third. The agreement on who is liked most and who least is comparable. The most disliked third of the average class received over half of the strong dislike ratings.

Not only is there high consensus about who belongs where in the social structure, but there is high stability of the structure from early in the school year to the middle of the school year and to the end of the school year. Looking first at the social power structure we find that for the first, second, and

[1] The research reported in part in this paper was supported by grant M–919 of the National Institute of Mental Health. Principal investigators were Ronald Lippitt, Robert Fox, and Douglas Blocksma. Sidney Rosen was Project Director.

third graders there is an average classroom correlation (Pearson r) of .73 between the social structure in early October and in the middle of January; between January and May the average correlation is .72; and from early fall until the end of the school year, the correlation in the primary grades is .63. All of the individual correlations are highly significant. For the fourth, fifth, and sixth grades the average correlation between October and January is .77; between January and May it is .78; and between early October and May, .75. The structures concerning who is liked and disliked and who is regarded as expert and inexpert in classroom activities have an even higher stability, with most of the correlations being above .80. The evidence is clear that the interpersonal social structure of the classroom forms rapidly and maintains a high degree of stability throughout the school year. The same children remain in positions of low power and isolation or dislike throughout the year, and the same children stay at the top of the totem pole.

But are the same children at the top and the bottom of all the totem poles? A partial correlation program was carried out for four different social structures in each classroom; the social power structure, the affective (like and dislike structure, the expertness structure, and the coerceability (ability to use physical coercion) structure. These analyses were summarized separately for younger and older classrooms in the elementary grades, and also for the beginning and end of the year. We find that with the other variables controlled there is still a high relationship between the power structure and the affect structure, a correlation of .57 at the beginning of the school year and .65 at the end of the year. The correlation is significantly higher for older than for younger boys (.44 as compared to .69). There is a smaller but significant relationship between the power structure and the expertness structure (.21 in October and .29 in May). The relationship of the coercion structure to the power structure increases from a zero relationship in the fall to an average correlation of .27 in the spring, although there is a great variability between groups in this relationship, and the relationship is accounted for to a great extent by the boys in each classroom rather than the girls. There is a significant relationship (.40) between the affect structure and the expertness structure in the fall which drops somewhat during the school year (.21 in May). There is a scattering of insignificant positive and negative correlations between the coerceability structure and affect structure and between the coerceability structure and the expertness structure. It is clear then that the children are making differentiations in their judgments of one another, and that being highly liked or perceived as expert are both significant paths to social influence in the socio-emotional structure of the group.

But how do the children really think about each other when they have a chance to freely apply their own descriptive and evaluative labels? Are these dimensions we have been measuring really the central dimensions of the interpersonal structure as far as the children are concerned, or have they been somewhat imposed by measurement procedures? Gold (1958) has explored this question in a substudy of 152 children in kindergarten through the sixth grade. In a preliminary study he had fairly lengthy interviews with 21 children representing all the grade levels exploring with open ended questions their perceptions of their peers. From these interviews emerged seventeen characteristics or properties of children which seem to be matters of some concern as peers describe each other. These items fall into four areas: expertness characteristics (e.g. smart, has good ideas, good at making things); physical characteristics (e.g. fighting ability, strength, appearance); socio-emotional characteristics (e.g. friendliness, fun to be with, doesn't tease); and "associational" characteristics (e.g. likes to do same things I do). These open ended interviews clearly confirmed the previous researches in camp settings (Polansky, Lippitt, and Redl, 1950) concerning the salience of the dimensions of socio-emotional structuring studies in the classroom groups. In a second part of the study specific low power and high power children were compared as to their possession of the valued characteristics. Gold found that the children gave the highest value to socio-emotional characteristics, but also placed a high value on expertness and the lowest value on physical prowess. It was also found that highly valued characteristics were attributed significantly more often to children who were high in the power structure of the classroom group. It seems clear that children do perceive each other in terms of these characteristics, and that these charac-

teristics are evaluated in such a way that they become resources relevant to the acquiring of high or low position in the
social structure of the group.

Mental Health Correlates of Position
in the Classroom Social Structure

Let's turn from the perceptions of peers to the judgments
and assessments of adults. Adults in the school environment
who have an interest in mental health tend to perceive children in terms of adjustment and deviancy along similar socio-
emotional dimensions. We might expect, therefore, that there
would be some relationship between perceptions and evaluations by peers and mental health assessments by adults. Two
explorations of this question have been carried out as part of a
larger study. Douglas (1958) conducted a study of the responses of 115 children to frustration in a series of story completion
situations where a child is frustrated by a loved adult. In these
situations children use various types of psychological defenses
against the expression of their feelings of aggression toward
powerful loved adults. Working within a theoretical framework developed by Miller (Miller & Swanson, 1960), Douglas
coded the primitivity or maturity of the defenses used by the
children in coping with frustrating situations. Partialing out
the effects of intelligence and age, Douglas found that the
children who are lowest in the socio-emotional structure of the
classroom more often used the most primitive defense of denial in the face of conflict than those children high in being
liked and influential, who were more apt to use more mature
defenses showing relatively minor distortions of the reality
situation. In terms of clinical judgments, the use of the more
primitive defenses is a symptom of poorer mental health in
coping with conflict situations.

In a study of seven elementary classrooms, Echelberger
(1959) analyzed cumulative teacher ratings of children on the
Haggerty-Olson-Wickman Behavior Rating Schedule (1930).
This schedule yields five scores: behavior problem symptoms,
problems in intellectual functioning, problems of physical

characteristics, social adjustment problems, and problems of emotional temperament. Echelberger correlated the position of the child in the socio-emotional structure in the classroom with the behavior problems scale (e.g. cheating, temper outbursts, truancy), the social adjustment scales (e.g. shyness, relation to authority, assertiveness), and the emotional adjustment scales (e.g. cheerfulness, excitability, suspiciousness). The tabulation below reports some relevant correlations (those .26 and greater are significant at the .05 level or better).

TABLE 1
Correlations (Pearson r) of Sociometric Ratings with
Selected Haggerty-Olson-Wickman Ratings, by Grade

GRADES	N	BEHAVIOR PROBLEMS	SOCIAL ADJUSTMENT	EMOTIONAL ADJUSTMENT
1–3	64			
Power x		−.28	.26	.21
Popularity x		−.46	.36	.27
4–6	72			
Power x		−.31	.36	.41
Popularity x		−.29	.35	.38

In every case it can be noted that the more influential and more popular children impress their teachers with a significantly more favorable mental health picture. They show fewer behavior problem symptoms, greater social adjustment, and more stable emotionality.

Jennings (1943) has proposed that an important dimension of personality health is the ability to make and maintain social connections, to have the capacity for friendships with others. In this context we might expect that the amount of positive affection, as compared to negative affect, which a child feels toward his peers might be considered a mental health criterion. In our classrooms each child indicated how much he liked or disliked other children in the class on a four point scale, with ratings 1 and 2 indicating two degrees of liking the other, and points 3 and 4 indicating two degrees of intensity of dislike. Table 2 indicates that in the older grades the children in high status positions express more positive affect in their ratings of peers than do low status children. (The differences of 8 per cent are significant beyond the .02 level.) Through the course of the school year, this difference becomes greater, the low status children increasing the proportion of negative feelings toward their fellow classmates.

TABLE 2
Comparison of Mean Percentages of Liking Choices (Spring)
Made by High and Lower Power Children, by Grade and Sex

	HIGH STATUS		LOW STATUS	
	Mean	*N*	*Mean*	*N*
Kindergarten to Grade 3				
Boys	60%	(79)	62%	(83)
Girls	60	(82)	61	(67)
Grades 4 to 6				
Boys	72	(103)	64	(77)
Girls	70	(73)	62	(78)

Direct observation of the children interacting in the classroom supports this conclusion about negative and positive affect. We recorded on quantitative behavior schedules an hour of classroom interaction in a standardized situation a few weeks after the school year began. The children participated in four activities designed to maximize the need for cooperation and coordination with others. Each child interacted with every other child in the classroom in at least one of the activities. The data from these observations permit typing each child in terms of a behavioral output pattern. In Table 3 we can see that those behavior patterns which indicate agressive-assertive or passive-hostile activity output are more frequently characteristic of the low power children in the classroom social structure. Low status children tend to behave in ways that are likely to disrupt interpersonal friendships and also classroom functioning. (Differences of 5 per cent are significant beyond the .05 level.)

To summarize, then, we can say that children in low positions in the socio-emotional structure of the classroom tend to have mental health difficulties which are reflected both in inner psychological processes, in interpersonal relationship difficulties, and in behavior patterns which disrupt the life of the classroom group.

TABLE 3
Comparisons of Percentages of Low Power with Other Children in Behavior Output Type Categories

BEHAVIOR OUTPUT TYPE CATEGORIES	LOW POWER	OTHER
	(N = 311)	(N = 654)
1. Active-assertive, friendly	14%	25%
2. Active-assertive, unfriendly	27	22
3. Neutral or mixed	27	28
4. Passive, friendly	22	21
5. Passive, unfriendly	10	4
	100%	100%

The Impact of the Milieu on the Child's Mental Health Situation

It becomes very important to consider the question: do the on-going processes of the classroom tend to aggravate or to alleviate the mental health problems of children low in the socio-emotional structure of the classroom? Looking first at the meaning of the on-going relationship with peers, we find that children who are low in the social structure have a continuing experience of social failure and rejection. For example, the success of each child's attempts to influence his peers during the standardized activity situation proved to be significantly correlated with his position in the social structure. Those low in the social structure experienced more failure of their own attempts and were more dominated by the behavior of others. This correlation increased during the course of the school year. Some of the low status children reacted to these behaviors from their peers by more withdrawal, and others reacted by more aggressive-assertive efforts to improve their position, which only resulted in still more failure.

That the children are sensitive to this incoming feedback from their peers is revealed by the self-evaluation index, which is a combination of self ratings on the social power and liking scales. Table 4 indicates that children's self evaluations tend to correspond to the feelings expressed by peers. (Differences between high and low power means are significant by T-test beyond the .05 level, except among the younger boys.) The younger boys seem to be less sensitive to the feelings of others about them, although their ratings also indicate some awareness of their status. It may be that they are more prone to make defensive self ratings to help them cope with their unhappy position in the group.

TABLE 4
Comparisons of Mean Self-Evaluation Score (Fall) of High and Low Power Children, by Grade and Sex

	HIGH POWER		LOW POWER	
	Mean	*N*	*Mean*	*N*
Kindergarten to grade 3				
Boys	3.47	(79)	3.86	(83)
Girls	3.23	(82)	3.91	(67)
Grades 4 to 6				
Boys	3.76	(103)	4.53	(77)
Girls	3.74	(73)	4.35	(78)

It is quite apparent to the children's teachers that high and low status pupils are treated differentially by their peers. We asked the teachers in the experimental classrooms to rate each child on the relative amount of warmth he received from others. These ratings were significantly correlated with the peer ratings of social power and likeability. The correlations were considerably higher in the spring than in the fall.

But peers are only part of the classroom milieu. The teacher is an important part of the environment. What about her contribution?

Part of our study included observations of a sample of classroom activities by a team of graduate student observers. Each observer watched an individual elementary school child for an hour at a time, recording (1) with whom the child interacted and who initiated the interaction; (2) the affective quality of the interaction, whether friendly, neutral or unfriendly; (3) whether the content of the interaction was primarily social or was concerned with the performance of a learning activity. None of the observers had any knowledge of the pupils' social status in the classroom. Each child was observed by two different observers. There were 318 child hours of observation in the sample of classrooms. Part of the analysis deals with pupil-teacher interactions which can be summarized only briefly here.

It will be noted from Table 5 that teachers pay attention to the social behavior, rather than the performance behavior, of low status pupils more often than of high status pupils. Evidently this aspect of their behavior leads to social evaluation and response more frequently on the teacher's part, just as it does for classmates. How the teacher responds depends on whether she is interacting with a low status girl or boy. Low status boys tend to receive more criticism than their high status boy classmates; but low status girls receive more support. In Table 6 we see that teachers were friendly slightly more often toward low status girls than other girls, but more often neutral or unfriendly toward low status boys. Differences in children's behavior probably evoke these different responses from teachers. Looking at the data on the children's approaches to their teachers, we note that low status girls are not only more warm in their relations with the teachers, but are relatively passive and withdrawing, while low status boys are more aggressive and troublesome than their higher status classmates.

This brief discussion of teachers' behavior should not be construed to mean that the teachers involved in the study were "playing favorites." Rather, we think that teachers, faced with the task of teaching youngsters in classroom groups and necessarily having to maintain order to do so must respond critically to disruptive behavior, and respond quite naturally with affection to little girls who seem to be asking for it and apparently getting little from their peers. But, we must ask, what are the implications of these findings for evaluating the classroom as a mental health milieu? What solutions to mental health problems do low status boys find from the generally critical and rejecting classroom relationships; or low status girls, who depend upon their relationships to teachers in the absence of satisfying give and take with their peers?

TABLE 5
Comparison of Percentages of Teacher Interaction with
High and Low Power Children, by Sex

	N	SOCIAL BEHAVIOR EVALUATION	PERFORMANCE EVALUATION	TOTAL CONTENT TALLIES	SUPPORTIVE REMARKS	CRITICAL REMARKS	TOTAL SUPPORTIVE-CRITICAL TALLIES
Girls:							
High	43	16%	84%	104	57%	43%	104
Low	44	24%	76%	116	73%	27%	116
Boys:							
High	37	22%	78%	102	62%	38%	103
Low	35	30%	70%	176	42%	58%	176

TABLE 6

Comparison of Affective Quality of Teachers' Interactions with High and Low Power Pupils, by Sex

	N	TEACHERS' APPROACHES TO PUPILS			TOTAL TEACHERS' APPROACHES	PUPILS' APPROACHES TO TEACHERS			TOTAL PUPILS' APPROACHES
		Friendly	*Neutral*	*Unfriendly*		*Friendly*	*Neutral*	*Unfriendly*	
Girls:									
High	43	32%	48%	19%	99	29%	66%	5%	111
Low	44	36%	51%	14%	111	49%	49%	2%	100
Boys:									
High	37	36%	47%	18%	118	20%	66%	14%	64
Low	35	28%	52%	20%	167	17%	74%	9%	118

Implications for Diagnostic Focus and Therapeutic Strategy

When we try to close in on the locus of pathology which maintains and aggravates the unhealthy situation of certain children in the classroom group, it is apparent that the difficulties are created and maintained by a circular social process contributed to by the individual child, by his classmates, and by the teacher. If we focus on the individual child who is in difficulty we see that he contributes to the unhealthy situation by (1) his negative self evaluation and his response to this; (2) his hostility toward others; (3) his unskilled and unrealistic behavior output of assertive aggressiveness or withdrawing noncontribution; (4) his insensitive and defensive reception of feedback from others which might potentially give him more guidance for his own behavior.

If we look at the rest of the group as a source of difficulty for the individual child we see that there is (1) a very rapid evaluative labelling of a child and a strong tendency to maintain this evaluative consensus in spite of further information about the individual child as stimulus; (2) very inadequate skills of the group in providing the member with feedback which communicates sympathetic guidance rather than rejection or ignoration; and (3) a lack of group standards concerning the acceptance and support of deviancy.

If we look at the role of a teacher and her contribution to the situation we note (1) a lack of teaching effort focussed on developing personal attitude and group standards about good human relations; (2) a lack of interpersonal grouping practices and other procedures guided by mental health goals; (3) a lack of clear presentation of constructive behavior patterns toward low status children which could be imitated by her other pupils.

The conversion of these diagnostic insights into a mental health strategy is a challenging task. How much can one do by working directly outside the classroom group with the children in need of help, to assist them to initiate changes in the social process? How much can be done by working directly with the high power children who have the most influence on the socio-emotional structure of the classroom? What can be done by helping teachers to initiate curriculum content and training procedures which will have a direct influence on the socio-emotional structure of the class? These are the questions we are exploring with our collaborating classrooms.

References

Douglas, Virginia. *The Development of Two Families of Defense.* Unpublished doctoral dissertation, University of Michigan, 1958.

Echelberger, Edna. *Relationships between Personality Traits and Peer Status.* Unpublished doctoral dissertation University of Michigan. 1959.

Gold, Martin. Power in the Classroom. *Sociometry,* 1958, 21, No. 1.

Haggerty-Olson-Wickman. *Behavior Rating Schedule.* New York: Harcourt, Brace, World, Inc., 1930.

Jennings, Helen Hall. *Leadership and Isolation.* New York: McKay, 1943.

Miller, Daniel, & Swanson, Guy E., *Inner Conflict and Defense.* New York: Holt, Rinehart and Winston, Inc., 1959.

Polansky, Norman, Lippitt, Ronald, & Redl, Fritz. The use of near-sociometric data in research on group treatment processes. *Sociometry,* 1950, 13, No. 1, 39–62.

Teacher Expectations and Friendship Patterns in the Elementary Classroom*

THOMAS H. HAWKES

Increasing recognition of factors affecting learning in the classroom other than the purely cognitive has become apparent in pedagogic theory and practice over the last two decades. Much theory and research has been devoted to such problems as the effects of emotional factors upon learning (Krathwohl, Bloom, and Masia, 1964), the compatibility of teacher and student attitudes and interests upon teacher-pupil relations (Thelen, 1967), and the effects of different kinds of control regimes upon learning in the classroom (White and Lippitt, 1960). Implicit in much of this research is the recognition of the classroom as a social organism with its own norms, values, roles, status positions, and structures (Getzels and Thelen, 1960).

Naturally occurring student friendships and associations have also been recognized as a potentially important factor in classroom operation and learning. Such associations could be facilitative or destructive for learning depending upon the nature of the association; for example whether it is formed as a coalition based on supportive or antagonistic attitudes toward authority, on positive or negative attitudes about school work, or on external school concerns. In this paper we will explore

---

* A revision of "Structural Constraints Upon Interpersonal Communication in the Classroom: A Study of Reciprocal Sociometric Choice Dyads," a paper presented at the American Educational Research Association convention in February 1968. Reprinted by permission of the author.

the implications of a pilot study (Hawkes, 1967) which investigated the nature of friendship and associations in four upper-elementary-school classrooms.

We shall look at a set of responses of children who were asked to name persons in their classroom whom they considered their friends, persons with whom they would like to work on a social studies committee, and persons with whom they would like to go to the movies outside of school. We will take a look at some variables related to how many times a particular person was chosen on these questions (sociometric status) and a special look at those sets of children who chose each other on these questions (sociometric dyads). We will be interested in illustrating several recurring patterns which regularly occur with the use of sociometric questionnaires, and then commenting on the implication of these patterns for the elementary-school teacher.

Background and Instruments

Sociometric questionnaires have had a long and venerable history as attested by literally thousands of studies reported in the literature (Gronlund, 1959). A sociometric questionnaire is a device used by teachers in order to find out about the social relationships in her classroom. By asking children to select a few of their classmates for participation in some type of activity or association either in school or out, imaginary or real, past, present, or future, a teacher can get a pretty good fix on who is popular in her classroom and who associates with whom. A great amount of research has been done over the past four decades concerning the characteristics of highly selected children on such traits as IQ, achievement, social adjustment, physical characteristics, socioeconomic position, race, and spatial propinquity (classroom seating, or nearness of homes). Generally, it has been found that if a characteristic is valued by a class, then those children who are popular in a classroom are likely to possess that characteristic more so than less popular children in the same classroom. Most of the reasearch in the use of sociometrics in the classroom has centered on the question of popularity. Very few studies have investigated the question of what are the characteristics of children who

choose each other, that is, an indication of real association as
opposed to socially desired association. Is it possible when one
chooses someone whom he actually associates with, that he
might be looking for different characteristics than when he
chooses someone whom he would like to associate with but
really doesn't expect to?

Taking as a starting point the theoretical writings of Helen
Jennings (1959)—a pioneer in the use of sociometry in the
classroom—we asked three questions of the children in two
fifth-grade and two sixth-grade classrooms of a school serving
a lower-middle-class suburb of a large mid-western city.
Whom do you consider to be your best friends in this class?
With whom in this class would you like to work on a committee in social studies? And with whom in this class would you
like to go to a movie outside of class? Each student was
allowed to select three of his classmates for each question.
Helen Jennings postulates basically two types of associations
that persons enter into; first, a "socio" association in which a
person chooses another with whom he will work to accomplish
some external task; the basis for choice is the task competence
of the other; and a "psyche" association in which a person
chooses someone with whom he feels comfortable and with
whom the basic purpose of the choice is friendship. Our second and third questions tapped two types of friendship while
the first question was directed at unqualified friendship.

In addition to the choice data collected from each of the
subjects, the author also collected IQ scores, standardized
achievement scores, teachers' perceptions of the social and
academic adjustment of each child, where the children sat in
the classroom, where they lived in the neighborhood, and a
measure of each child's volition to work.

We could ask and answer questions concerning the relationship among the latter traits and their relationship to sociometric status and association.

Results and Interpretation

In response to each of the three sociometric questions, we
found that approximately a third of the students received

two-thirds of the selections, with the remaining choices going to the rest of the class. This is a recurring pattern in the use of sociometric questionnaires in most social situations.

It was also found that the three types of sociometric popularity (friendship, committee, and movie) were highly related to each other, moderately related to teachers' perceptions of adjustment, unrelated to desire to work, and with the exception of committee popularity, unrelated to achievement or IQ. Teachers' perception of adjustment was unrelated to desire to work, but was related moderately to IQ and achievement. We also found that, although desire to work and IQ are moderately related to achievement, .41 and .49 respectively, IQ and desire to work were relatively unrelated to each other (.22).

We believe these last relationships give us a cue for understanding the culture of these four classrooms. Desire to work is a volitional trait of personality. IQ is a cognitive trait. Both contributed to achievement in these classrooms. However, when it comes to teachers perception of academic adjustment, the teachers were aware of IQ but unaware or unconcerned about the volitional measure, desire to work. Students when selecting someone to work with on a social studies committee, also chose persons high on IQ, while also being unaware or unconcerned about desire to work. Students also chose students who were likely to be high achievers. These relationships would suggest that only cognitive traits seemed to be valued or seem as related to achievement. But is there any evidence about how achievement is valued in this group of classrooms? When children were asked to choose friends or someone to go to the movies with, their choices were unrelated to achievement, IQ, or desire to work. However, popularity as a friend or playmate was positively related to whom the teacher perceived as academically and socially adjusted. This would indicate that in this group of classrooms, getting along with the teacher or classmates, and meeting the academic expectations are valued, whereas actual achievement, the ability to achieve, or the volition to achieve, are not valued when choosing a friend.

These relationships seem to us to indicate a classroom culture in which achievement as measured by standardized tests is recognized as important by the teacher; however, when judgment of factors contributing to achievement is made, only cognitive factors seem to be valued. It also seems that although children are aware of who is a high achiever, their selections of whom to work with on a social studies committee are determined by cognitive rather than volitional factors. In addition, it seems that, when it comes to choosing a friend or movie pal, intellectual traits are unimportant, but a person's adjustment as perceived by the teacher is.

This then brings us to the question, when two children choose each other (an indication of real as opposed to desired association) what are the characteristics each is looking for in the person he chooses? With respect to reciprocal choice, we found that 56 friendship, 44 committee, and 52 movie dyads were formed in response to each of the questions. We also found that 60 percent of the dyads formed in response to any one of the questions was also found in response to either one or both of the other questions. This finding would indicate that the conceptual clarity of "socio" and "psyche" association is not nearly as clear when it comes to reality. The distinction between "socio" and "psyche" types of association in the classroom blurs in the sense that there is a great amount of overlap between the two. In this paper we will look at those dyads which were formed as a response to all three questions, dyads which were general in scope.

When we looked at the effect of classroom seat propinquity on dyad formation, we found almost no effect. When we questioned the teachers concerning this finding we were informed by three of the teachers that they purposely separate friends because they find that such friendships disrupt the instructional process. We did find in three of the classes friends were more likely to live nearer to each other than one would expect by chance.

For the general-scope dyads we found that there was little or no relationship between co-choosers on desire to work, IQ, or achievement. There was a positive relationship between co-choosers in these dyads in terms of how they were perceived by their teachers. Children who were perceived by their teachers as academically doing well, chose and were chosen in return by others whom the teacher saw as doing academically well, whereas children doing poorly in terms of academics chose and were chosen in return by others who were doing poor academically. This is interesting when we recall that persons whom the teacher saw as academically successful were popular.

Those children who were popular were chosen by persons whom they chose in return, and also by others whom they did not choose in return. If one were to look at the characteristics of those children who were popular, one might infer that, when one chooses a friend, he is apt to choose someone above himself in the adjustment hierarchy (as seen from the teachers perspective). However, when we look at actual friendship (reciprocal choice dyads) we find that children choose others who are like themselves. Children high in the adjustment hierarchy chose and are chosen by others who are high in the hierarchy, and children who are low in such an adjustment hierarchy chose and are chosen by others who are low in the adjustment hierarchy. Another way to state the same phenomenon would be that when children aspire to friendship they choose persons who have more favorable positions in the teachers' perspective of adjustment. However, when it comes to actual friendships they choose others like themselves in the teachers' perspective of adjustment.

Discussion

When we began our study of sociometric choice behavior, particularly reciprocal choice behavior, we thought that choices would be determined by three factors: first, a person would choose another who valued achievement as the chooser himself did; second, that one would choose others who would compliment themselves on concerns external to the classroom situation; and third, that one's attitude about and relationship to authority would be a determinant of choice. The only one of the factors that seems to have played a significant part in reciprocal choice behavior for the fifth- and sixth- grade children in this study revolved around how one was perceived by an authority (the teacher). One's desire to work, actual achievement, and IQ had little or no relationship to choice. Only whether one was perceived by the teacher as meeting her academic expectations played a part in determining whom one chose. Then one chose others like oneself.

We do *not* suppose for one second that when these children made their choices on the questions that they did so consciously considering how they themselves were perceived by the teacher or how the person they chose was perceived by the teacher. Just the opposite, the reciprocal choices we believe represent already existing associations. What is important in these already existing associations is that one important referent point for the definition of the nature of the association is the teacher and her perception of the individual child's adjustment.

One might postulate that one of the underlying dynamics operating in student friendships in the classroom lies in the objective, socially dependent relationship that each child finds himself. Authority and power is held by the teacher-adult. In most classrooms, the child obtains rewards or gratifications by behaving in such ways which are congruent with the adult authority's expectations. If by chance the child agrees (consciously or unconsciously) with the teacher's expectations, he then is likely to choose others who also agree with the teacher's expectations. However, if by chance (background or temperament) he disagrees with the teacher's expectations, he is then faced with finding rewards or gratifications elsewhere, and possibly finding ways of buttressing himself against such an authority expectation. In the latter situation, he selects or chooses to associate with others who are congruent with himself in not meeting the authority's expectations. This is so even though he might aspire to friendship with those whom the teacher favors.

If one further extrapolates from such a postulate, this would indicate that the development of teacher- and anti-teacher-oriented factions within a classroom have little to do with actual achievement, but rather revolve around other expectations of the teacher.

This postulate would also suggest to us that if something so far removed from the stated agenda of the classroom, such as, informal friendship, is affected by the teacher's perceptions of individuals in the class, one can be fairly certain that the teacher's perceptions, power, attitudes, and influence would be considerable in other aspects of the ecology of the classroom whether it be interpersonal communication, morale, climate, or learning.

References

Getzels, J., and H. A. Thelen, "The Classroom Group as a Unique Social System," *The Dynamics of Instructional Groups, N.S.S.E. 59th Yearbook.* Chicago: University of Chicago Press, 1960.

Gronlund, N., *Sociometry in the Classroom.* New York: Harper & Row, 1959.

Hawkes, T. H., "Emotional Dynamics of Reciprocal Sociometric Choice Behavior." Unpublished doctoral dissertation. University of Chicago, 1967.

Jennings, Helen Hall, *Sociometry in Group Relations, A Manual for Teachers, Second Edition.* Washington, D.C.: American Council on Education, 1959.

Krathwohl D., B. Bloom, and B. Masia, "Taxonomy of Educational Objectives," *The Classification of Educational Goals, Handbook II: Affective Domain.* New York: McKay, 1964.

Thelen, H. A., *Classroom Grouping for Teachability.* New York: Harper & Row, 1967.

White, R. K., and R. O. Lippitt, *Autocracy and Democracy.* New York: Harper & Row, 1960.

Discussion

In some of the previous discussions, it has been mentioned that many significant experiences students have in school are unplanned. A number of classroom practices, although designed for specific purposes, often influence students in unintended ways. One reason teachers are unaware of these hidden school experiences is that they are not always directly involved. Frequently, the effect is felt not in teacher-student interactions but in the relationship of students to each other.

Each article in this section illustrates the above point. Let us take Henry's observations of peer group aggression as the first illustration. Clearly, the teachers he observed were not deliberately trying to encourage students to attack each other. The Vigilance Club, for example, was not organized to teach the value of spying and confession but rather to teach children good citizenship. Likewise, the classwide criticism sessions he reports were not meant for children to be destructively critical of each other but for urging them to be more sensitive writers. Finally, asking classmates to assist a student who does not know the answer was not intended to teach children to gain success from someone's failure but to support a student in a difficult situation. What is happening in these classrooms is that teachers have organized experiences without anticipating all their consequences. In particular, the teachers do not fully realize how vulnerable a student is before a public audience of peers.

Minuchin's study (which is part of the larger project reported in Part I) indicates how teachers in "traditional" schools implicitly encourage destructive competition among their students. In order to achieve the tightest possible control, these teachers direct instruction at the total class. At the same time, they evaluate academic work by comparing the individual performances of students. What is not realized is that a classroom situation is then created in which students must vie against each other for the teacher's recognition. Consequently, there is little incentive to help each other. The most successful students, in particular, must be aggressive in order to maintain their status against students who might challenge it.

Lippitt and Gold discuss how teachers, without intending

to, aggravate the mental health problems of students who have few friends. They do so by selectively attending to the social behavior of low-status pupils rather than their performance on academic work. As a result, classmates' attention is drawn to the teacher's social evaluation of these children. This process is especially harmful to low-status boys since teachers are generally critical of their social behavior.

Of course, there is no logical necessity that the teacher's perceptions of students influence how students act toward each other. Hawkes' study, however, lends empirical support to the hunch that they do. He finds that the only variable which consistently accounts for the friendship choices which students actually make is the teacher's perceptions of students' school adjustment irrespective of how they achieve. Students who are highly rated by the teacher associate with each other while those who in the eyes of the teacher are having adjustment problems associate with others of similar status. Hawkes believes that students guide their choice of friends by this criterion because of their dependence on the teacher's authority. Students who are perceived by the teacher to conform successfully to his expectations choose friends who will help them maintain the teacher's esteem. But, students who are not in the teacher's favor must seek support from classmates who engage in behavior which is antithetical to the teacher's value system. In short, students form associations in classrooms primarily to protect themselves against the teacher's ability to withhold support rather than to help themselves to do more effective work.

Even though teachers do not intend to facilitate negative relations among their students, they cannot dismiss them, as they sometimes do, by appealing to the myth that children are naturally cruel to each other. Actually, the most serious vice of children is their imitation of significant adults around them. Their identification with adult behavior patterns can be seen in the studies presented here since, in each of them, students are modeling an aspect of teacher behavior which has been discussed earlier. For example, in Henry's observations, students are making evaluations of each other which play on one's self-respect. In the group task presented in Minuchin's study, students from the most "traditional" school created the same rigid class structure that their teachers produce. Lippitt and Gold report that students attach rapid evaluative labels to each other. Finally, Hawkes finds that students select friends and reject others without much regard for their personal qualities.

When we think of a man with character and personal strength, we think in part, of a person who recognizes desirable qualities in others, who is loyal to those he befriends, and who is able to give help as well as receive it. We frown on a man who exploits the weaknesses of others, who submits too readily to those more powerful than he, or who envies his peers. The social attributes which students are encouraged, intentionally or not, to adopt in schools are more likely to create the latter man. If we want schooling to help children learn how to build human relationships as well as develop academic skills, we must be careful not to put students in a position which makes it difficult for them to respect and cooperate with each other.

Part VII

STUDENTS' VIEWS
OF SCHOOLING

Is This What
Schools Are For?*

KATHRYN JOHNSTON NOYES
GORDON L. McANDREW

We go to school because it's the law," a latter-day Holden
Caulfield told us. He was sixteen, intelligent, and had hair too
long and eyes too wise for the comfort of either parent or
teacher. "They make you stay until you are sixteen, and by
then you may as well go on since you probably only have
another year or two, anyway. The point of it, I guess, is to get
a diploma so you can go to college."

In the course of dozens of interviews with students from
coast to coast, and many other conversations with teachers,
school administrators, and parents, we have asked the simple
question: "What are schools for?" Oddly enough, there are
many and conflicting answers. Although most people can
agree on the general purpose of a bank, a hospital, a court of
law, or most other institutions in our society, Americans seem
to have very disparate views on the purpose of their schools.

Adults are likely to say that the schools are designed to
prepare young people for full and meaningful lives, to train
skilled manpower for society, to prepare youth for constructive
adulthood or for self-realization or economic self-sufficiency.
But the large majority of students—the consumers of education—are convinced that the purpose of the school is simply to
prepare them for college. And most of them also believe that
the student who does not enter college is, *ipso facto*, a failure
at the age of eighteen. Since less than half of all American

* Kathryn Johnston Noyes and Gordon L. McAndrew, "Is This What
Schools Are For," *Saturday Review*, December 21, 1968. Copyright 1968
by Saturday Review, Inc. Reprinted with the permission of the publisher
and the authors.

young people enter college, and only a fraction of these graduate, it is small wonder that so many students have a jaundiced view of the schools.

"It's pretty stupid really," our "Holden" went on, "Most of what you have to learn isn't worth the time or trouble. It's mostly memorizing, which in this day and age is so much wasted effort. Information is available everywhere, except maybe in the jungle or someplace like that. And if you were in the jungle, you wouldn't be worried about the kind of information we have to memorize. Even my little brother knows it's stupid. The other night—and he's only ten years old—he asked my mother why he had to memorize all those dates about the Civil War when we have an encyclopedia and he could look them up in five minutes any time he needed to know. She couldn't answer him." He shrugged his shoulders and laughed. "Oh, well, I won't put you on. I could give you some pretty spooky answers to what school is for, but the fact is that aside from the college thing, I really don't know. It's a system, that's all."

The interview seemed to be ended and then, quite suddenly, he began to talk again: "It's a system, you have to understand that. I guess it's because there are so many kids and they all have to be in school so many days a year for so many hours. Or maybe it's because the people who run schools finally get to the point where they don't like kids and don't want to have too much to do with them. Anyway, it's a system. It's like a machine. One person . . . can't beat it.

"Let me tell you about it. I'm failing math and science, see? My second-year algebra teacher told me she took the exact same course I'm failing now when she was a sophomore in college. But that was a hundred years ago, and now they won't even let you in college unless you've already had it. I'm in the eleventh grade, and if I fail these two subjects, I probably won't get into college. So I look around and I see that other kids are passing them who aren't any smarter than I am. So I figure the trouble has to be with me. So I need guidance, right? I decide I should go talk with the guidance counselor.

"But you see, that's where the system comes in. The guidance counselor has the whole eleventh grade to worry about in my school—642 students. So he keeps this sign on his door: DO NOT ENTER WITHOUT AN APPOINTMENT. I guess he's in there, talking with some kid who's in trouble or something, and doesn't want to be interrupted. I go down there before school, after school, and during my lunch break. The sign is always there.

"Finally, I go to the main office and ask how I can get an appointment with the guidance counselor. The girl behind the desk, a student, looks at me like I'm not all there and says that I have to make an appointment with him, personally. I explain that I can't get into his office to make an appointment, and she says that the sign's only up before and after school and at lunch period, and that I can get into his office during study hall, if I get a pass from the main office to leave the study hall. Are you following me?

"OK, fine. The only trouble with this is, I don't have a study hall. I'm carrying a full load and I'm in some class or other all day. Well, the girl didn't know what to do about this, so she went and asked the old lady who works in the office. The old lady comes over to me and starts in again at the beginning and tells me that appointments with the guidance counselor must be made during the student's study hall. I ask her what happens if the student doesn't have a study hall, and she says that it always works out all right because students who don't have study halls don't have them because they are carrying a full load, and the only kids who are allowed to carry a full load are the smart ones who don't need the guidance counselor anyway.

"You see what I mean? You just can't beat it. It's kind of funny when I tell it like this, like a comedy of errors or an old Laurel and Hardy comedy on TV. But it's not funny to me because it's my *life*. If I don't get into college, I'll probably get drafted and get my head blown off for reasons I don't understand. I don't know what's going to happen to me. How can I keep my sense of humor when I'm going to get ruined by a damned *system*?"

We couldn't answer his question and didn't try. He let us off the hook by shrugging again and saying, "Oh, well. My mother finally went and talked with my teachers. They don't think I'm trying. She was all right about it—I guess she's as worried as I am. But I *am* trying and I'm still failing and God knows where it will all end."

Two thousand miles away, another boy picked up the "system" theory. This one was slicker than "Holden" and far slyer in terms of "getting through" (a significantly universal term, by the way). "School is like roulette or something. You can't just ask: Well, what's the point of it?" he explained. "The point of it is to do it, to get through and get into college. But you have to figure the system or you can't win, because the odds are all on the house's side. I guess it's a little like the real world in that way. The main thing is not to take it personal, to understand that it's just a system and it treats you the same way it treats everybody else, like an engine or a machine or something mechanical. Our names get fed into it—*we* get fed into it—when we're five years old, and if we catch on and watch our step, it spits us out when we're seventeen or eighteen, ready for college.

"But some kids never understand this, and they get caught, chewed up, or pushed out. I'll give you an example: The other day this other guy and I had to make up an English test we'd missed because we were absent. The English teacher said she'd give it to us at 8 o'clock in the morning before school begins. Well, I knew that if the test made me late for my homeroom period at 8:30, that teacher would send down an absent slip on me to the office. So I went to my homeroom at five of 8 and wrote a note on the blackboard to the teacher, telling her where I was and that I might be late.

"This other guy, though, he didn't know enough to do that. He hasn't studied the system. So we go and make up our test and sure enough before we are through the late bell rings for homeroom period. I can see he's nervous and he doesn't know what to do, so he tries to hurry up and finish the test so he can get to his homeroom before the absent slips get sent down. He tears through the test and probably marks half the multiple-choices wrong. Then he takes off just as the first bell for first period is ringing.

"I saw him later in the day and he was all shook up. He couldn't catch the absent slips so he had to go down to the dean of boys' office to explain that he wasn't really tardy or absent. But the dean's office had a long line, and while the guy's waiting in line, the late bell for first period rings. So now he's half-way out of his mind, you know? By the time he gets up to the dean of boys, he really *is* late for first period and another absent slip about him is already on its way down from *that* teacher. The dean of boys tells him to come in for detention after school, one hour."

Our narrator stopped and laughed uproariously and then went on. "Well, the guy gets all uptight and tries to explain why he now has two absent slips going when he wasn't even tardy. He loses his cool and says some things and the dean says some things and the next thing you know, the guy's got *two* hours detention, for being rude and smart-alecky. But wait, it gets worse. I swear he hasn't got a brain, that kid. Anyway, as it happens, the day he was absent and missed the English test, he also missed a math test. And he's scheduled to make that one up after school, when he's supposed to be in the detention hall. If he misses the math test, it won't be given again, and he doesn't know if his grade can stand a zero for this marking period. But if he misses detention, he might be suspended and have three days' worth of stuff to make up when he gets back.

"I don't know what he did, finally. Probably just had a nervous breakdown. It was really pathetic. But the point is that he should have foreseen all that and made arrangements for it. I'll be surprised if he makes it through school. He just doesn't understand the system."

The speaker obviously did; he had learned well. The only question is, is that what he went to school to learn?

Our last example is shorter and more succinct, but it is one we heard many times from both boys and girls. It goes like this: School was invented to bug kids.

These were high schoolers, and their stories were depressingly the same from one coast to the other. The system syndrome turns up in junior and senior high schools of all shapes and sizes and, contrary to what might be expected, seems as prevalent in relatively small schools as it is in schools with 2,000 or more students. The same two words were spoken in all the regional accents of America: *system* and *machine*.

The elementary schools are no more human in their dealings with students. Although the self-contained classroom allows more opportunity for the teacher to know her students, this is balanced by her determination to "mold" them into what she and the school authorities think they should be. And what they should be, at the end of any given year, is ready for the next year. In the final analysis, the first-grade teacher's aim is to prepare her students for the second grade, and so forth from elementary school to junior high, from junior high to college.

Generally speaking, the typical first-grader is inclined to be outgoing, uninhibited, and candid. He arrives at the schoolhouse door eager and primed for what lies ahead. If he has the verbal tools or inclination to communicate with you at all, he is likely to tell you early in your acquaintance that he goes to school now. It's a big thing in his life and, psychologically speaking, he is probably far more interested in school at this point than he ever will be again.

What happens to him next will be a series of little things, none of them especially traumatic, but all of them together sufficient to turn his enthusiasm down, if not off. By the end of first grade the child is no longer excited and proud to be a schoolboy. By now, he probably doesn't like school half as well as he likes home or the streets, and his favorite subject is recess. And the chances are that he doesn't like school very much because, somehow, he has gotten the idea that school doesn't particularly like him. He is too often corrected and reprimanded, too infrequently challenged, and too consistently bored. The exceptions to these schools that turn off their students so effectively number in the hundreds. But the American public is supporting more than 100,000 schools.

No child can think well of himself if the individuals with whom he comes in contact do not seem to think well of him; no one who thinks of himself as fodder for a machine—or a "system"—is likely to have a comfortably good opinion of himself. Simply because nobody else seems to think he matters at all, he must spend a good deal of time and energy proclaiming that he does. If he is not able to do this, if he cannot make himself believe in his own worth, he will soon be broken.

As presently organized, the inescapable truth is that our schools seldom promote and frequently deny the objectives we, as a nation, espouse. Rather than being assisted and encouraged to develop their own individuality, our children are locked into a regimented system that attempts to stamp them all in the same mold. The student is filled with facts and figures which only accidentally and infrequently have anything whatsoever to do with the problems and conflicts of modern life or his own inner concerns. What he needs and wants are matters of no apparent interest to anyone associated with the schools.

In sum, we run our schools almost totally without reference to the needs of the children who attend them. What we teach, how we teach it, and even when and where we teach it are far too often based upon the needs and convenience of the school, upon the comfort of the administrators, and the logistics of the system. And the students are all too aware of this; in all of our dozens of conversations with students in all parts of the country, not one boy or girl ever answered our initial question with: "The schools are for kids."

High School Students Speak Out— An Excerpt*

DAVID MALLERY

EDITOR'S NOTE: *High* School Students Speak Out *reports a study, carried out under the auspices of the Committee of School and College Relations of the Educational Records Bureau, of the impact of high school experiences on students. Eight high schools cooperated in the study. They were drawn from different regions of the country and represented a wide variety of types of schools. The chapter presented here summarizes the findings of the study.*

I guess most teachers and school heads don't have much idea of these feelings and ideas we've been talking about. Maybe some of them would be interested in knowing about them— maybe some wouldn't. Your study makes me believe that some people think it's worth finding out what *we* think our time in high school is like. But look—you're a teacher—how are you going to walk into your own classroom again after all you've been hearing in these schools?

The eleventh-grader who said this seemed well aware of the challenge he was putting to me. I am conscious of his challenge as I look back on my visits. Faces and voices of many hundreds of high school people remain clear in my

---

* "An Emerging Picture," Chapter 24, from *High School Students Speak Out* by David Mallery. Copyright © 1962 by Educational Records Bureau. Reprinted by permission of Harper & Row, Publishers.

memory. I rather expected these faces to become blurred, forming a landscape full of merging details. I now find quite the opposite: the details are more insistent than the whole picture. Yet a picture does emerge.

In describing this picture as I see it, I will *not* try to make a portrait of the typical American high school student or his school. The aim of this study has been to examine the effects of school experiences on student values in a few schools. Broad generalizations based on the findings are precluded because the sampling of schools is small and by no means nationally representative. Furthermore, the students who spoke out in this study expressed a wide variety of views and opinions, showing that they do not readily conform to a teen-age stereotype. Instead of trying to form a composite profile, I will attempt to summarize the comments given by the students in each of six areas. This may help the reader to gain a perspective of all the voices, impressions, and experiences that have been described.

Curriculum

In some schools I heard little, if any, spontaneous reference to the curriculum. The experiences which seemed to matter most to students in their own growing-up were described mainly as happening outside of school—with friends, jobs, new responsibilities. In other cases, the curriculum was something discussed solely in relation to a determined drive toward an anxiously sought payment in the form of marks. For some students, those marks "were" the curriculum. Some students even described the curriculum as unreal and irrelevant to any of their own concerns, motives, or interests. Examples were given, however, of courses which awakened or challenged what the students believed was their developing vision of themselves and their world.

In virtually all discussions of curriculum, students of widely ranging abilities and aims stressed the need to be able to see some point, some purpose in a course's work. Even those enrolled in the most high-powered courses made hardly any comment about the *amount* of homework, even when it required three or more hours a night and more on weekends.

The students seemed to be most concerned about having to do some course work which was meaningless from their point of view. The courses they singled out for expressions of appreciation were those that made them feel they were taking an active part in the subjects they were studying. Apparently, they did not like to feel that they were just maneuvering answers without having an opportunity to explore, speculate, and come to grips with the subject.

Students in advanced-standing classes were particularly urgent about the need for flexibility and challenge in intellectual exploration. Many of them felt trapped in advanced courses which just required *more* of the patterned, superficial, question-and-answer work that they had criticized in regular academic classes. On the other hand, a problem arose when departments offered work of higher quality and with more stimulating materials in the advanced courses. If this occurred, students in regular courses often felt that the more human, interesting materials (as in the English work with *Death of a Salesman* and *Babbitt*) that were offered to advanced sections would be just as valuable for regular sections, and would be as appropriate to them as the standard fare (*Silas Marner* and *A Tale of Two Cities*), or more so. Some students in regular sections felt that the real challenge to think and to explore was reserved for the advanced sections, and that teachers assumed that the regular sections had no interest or enthusiasm for anything beyond lesson-learning.

Students were divided about what to respect in a course. Some courses that provided a lot of hard work on the learn-the-answer level seemed "better" than those involving more flexibility of organization and more study of problems with solutions which were less readily available, such as certain courses in problems of democracy. This caused a conflict if some students found their major challenge and interest was in a course which was looked down on by teachers or by students as less "respectable."

The same problem of status appeared occasionally where schools provided unusual opportunities in the arts, particularly strong choir, or a challenging dramatics program, for example. The academically respectable courses sometimes challenged the prestige of serious work in these fields or tended to create an aura of superficiality about work in the arts which was actually of genuine quality.

Individual exploration in a subject field often appeared as an extra, something to do if the required work was done. Students spoke of the required work as simply time-consuming, with little or no individual challenge to explore *within* assignments and little opportunity or encouragement to go beyond them. Students who did go beyond the regular work sometimes spoke of this as if they considered it unrelated to the uniform requirements of a course. For example, I heard many discussions of individual reading, but the students usually said that the books they read on their own rarely became a part of any curricular discussion or research. Still, those books often represented considerable intellectual challenge beyond the curricular fare. Students spoke up eagerly in support of courses that did allow for flexibility in reading and assignment, individual research, and student share in planning.

Teaching and Teachers

Teachers were a favorite topic in the interviews. They were discussed with remarkably little personal griping or idolizing, but with efforts to identify personal approaches and professional techniques that the students felt were important in teaching. Many students seemed to see good teaching as something that transcended the subject rather than as something that illumi.1ated it. A teacher's personality was often a focus for discussion, but the students were willing to move beyond personality into an evaluation of effective or ineffective teaching.

Great variety in viewpoints about teachers' classroom techniques appeared. These themes recurred: the need for teachers to build confidence in the students; to explain adequately; to open a subject up for exploration rather than simply present it; and to *allow* students, if not even to challenge the teacher's statements, at least to think on their own rather than just to accept or recite. Students resented having their exploring and thinking cut off either by remarks such as "That's off the subject!" or "We haven't time to go into that!"

Students urgently advocated student-teacher collaboration in identifying topics for research and for individual and group study. The picture of adults determining, mimeographing, and lecturing on Questions of Concern to Young People, without consultation with the persons most involved, came in for some ironic comments. Capitalization of students' interests and abilities, or even the mere recognition of students as people, was illustrated in a number of positive ways in certain teachers' practice.

Student-teacher rapport outside of class seemed important to many students. Many felt that such rapport, whether achieved in activities, guidance, clubs, or individual conferences, had a great deal to do with classroom morale and with the potential influence of teachers on the school climate.

The idea of entering secondary school teaching as a career seemed to many students unthinkable, even ridiculous or contemptible. These students spoke of the teaching profession as requiring dreary repetition, underpaid drudgery, and intellectual death. Other conversations, fewer in number, revealed students who saw teaching in an idealistic light, even though, for financial reasons or because of suspicion of the restrictions of "the system," they might still for themselves, reject the idea of teaching.

Just how these images of the teaching profession developed was described or implied in many comments. The image varied more from school to school than within a single school. It varied with sex, also. A large number of girls seemed to be planning for a teaching career, perhaps because of their own academic success and a feeling of being "at home" in the school setting. Their over-all motivation was less clearly articulated than that of the much smaller number of boys who were motivated toward a teaching career.

When the small group of seniors in one of the schools experimented with teaching younger pupils, these seniors developed a better understanding of the learning process and the teachers' role in it. They became aware that self-discipline is necessary for teaching and for translating knowledge into action. The effect of this experience on the seniors' attitudes toward teaching as a career choice was not determined, however.

The Crush for College Admission

In five of the eight schools, admission to college was crucially important, according to both students and teachers. Competition for marks appeared to be growing in intensity, incentive for individual exploration was becoming more and more restricted, student activities were being decreased or eliminated, and extreme nervous tension was often generated, all in the drive to Get into the Right College. These problems were accentuated by the drive to win scholarships, whether needed or not, for reasons of school or family prestige. Such driving pressure, described more than once as "a neurotic obsession with college admission," seemed to dominate the thinking of many students and to be the central motivation for their school efforts. Even certain extracurricular activities and school service programs became, for some, a college admissions maneuver.

This drive apparently could become so strong within a school that general and vocational students would speak of a lack in their own motivation, even a lack in *themselves,* since they did not have the college pressure to drive them. They regarded the college preparatory student with some envy, not because of the future advantages of a college education, but because of the single-minded purposes which college admission seemed to provide. On the other hand, most college preparatory students agreed that the effects of the intense competitiveness were undesirable. Some students caught in the "crush" spoke of ways of transcending it by themselves. Others spoke of the ways the school tried to help. Still others, outside of the orbit of preoccupation with prestige colleges, demonstrated the kinds of morale and achievement that can be attained when college admission pressures do not dominate a school.

The Need for Responsibility

The present Teen-Age Culture has been portrayed from time to time in a stereotype of the adolescent. The much-publicized characteristics of apathy, rebelliousness, and irresponsibility associated with the stereotype were not present in all the schools I visited, though. In fact, the typical student character-istics were quite the opposite in some instances.

While student responsibility was less *discussed* by students than were the curriculum, teachers, and college admissions, its presence or absence could be detected readily. The student government activities that were described ranged from busy-work to important action from the students' viewpoints. Some-times the student government was permitted to encompass only those activities that adults considered safe. These activi-ties usually offered little challenge to student initiative and effort. A few of the schools visited had evidently found effec-tive ways of enlisting a large number of their students in meaningful responsibilities. How student concern developed and action resulted were demonstrated impressively.

The student's potential role in actual planning for a school, including its curriculum, was illustrated constructively in the case of seven seniors' self-initiated study of major aspects of their school. In this example, the whole matter of leadership, so much discussed on college application blanks, came in for some close examination with interesting results.

Divisive Forces in the School and Community

In a school where social prejudice had been imported from the community, the students appeared to be deeply concerned, but they expressed grave doubts about their ability to break down established prejudice patterns once they themselves had become adults. Social division born within the school itself was apparent in certain high schools that exhibited signs of a split between college preparatory students and other students. Some schools revealed a similar cleavage between advanced and regular college preparatory sections. Efforts to bring about unity were described eloquently by some students. They were concerned with understanding the divisive forces and with discovering ways of meeting them—ways that schools, especially those designed to be "comprehensive," can work toward harmony and mutual respect within diversity.

Values and Growing Up

Can adults communicate through the wall which so often appears to surround the Teen-Age Culture? Can the school be more than simply the setting where students' values develop at random? Can it harness positive forces which will help to shape values? Answers to these questions, even though they were central to the goals of this study, can only be inferred from the samples of talk and behavior given in this report.

When they were faced with a request to compare their own concerns and outlook of three years ago with those of the present, the students responded thoughtfully and seriously. It is important to recognize that they disagreed on whether their schools had any relation to the changes which had occurred. Their self-examination stressed positive values. They sensed that the years had brought increased responsibility and growing independence. But were these the result of school encouragement? Only, apparently, in some schools. Elsewhere, the schools were seen as restrictive influences. Some of the schools permitted or fostered responsible thinking and action, but others appeared to exclude genuine freedom. Students pictured themselves as amenable to guidance, but hostile to indoctrination.

Public affairs did not often arise in the group conversations unless such topics were introduced by the visitor. When asked to name men and women most admired and least admired in public life, students generally gave names of headline political figures. The discussion of the names was generally superficial and indicated far less interest and information than did the discussion of the young people's individual development. Their own social relationships were, perhaps inevitably, a far more exciting topic for consideration than were public or community problems. But it is only fair to say that exceptions were found, and these were the more dramatic by contrast.

What relation does the social structure of a high school have to its scholastic organization? Are students who are strong academically numbered among the social outcasts? Some schools traditionally revere the athlete rather than the scholar. Where this is true, why is student government dominated by the college preparatory group? Students eagerly debated some of the inconsistencies of their own behavior.

What they talked *about* is less important than what they *said*. Their words revolved around dozens of concerns, and highlighted activities from school politics to religious retreats. Yet, because young people's growth in their teens is growth in and through school, what emerged can stand as a portrait of their schools. If they sometimes talked as if the school were a living entity, and spoke of its spirit as if it existed apart from themselves and their teachers, such a view merely intensifies one's impression of the significance of the whole experience. The spirit of the school *can* reach into the lives of its students, and this spirit and morale, the tradition and the values which the students reflect, carry the school into the world outside. The school which makes its students conscious primarily of marks and by-the-book recitation is one that projects a narrow image. The greater the vision of the school, the more it forces its students to be self-directing and responsible in every action of their lives. What the school teaches is what its graduates become.

The View
from the Pupil's Desk *

MARY ALICE WHITE

The curriculum at the elementary school level can be viewed as neatly organized by subject and grade into rational, sequential units. Indeed this is the view probably held by most educational administrators, most parents and many teachers. Of late, this perspective has derived a good deal of theoretical clarity from the particular emphasis that curriculum specialists have been giving to "concepts" in the curriculum, to heuristically powerful ideas which are taught and retaught throughout the school years. This movement was, of course, originally inspired by Jerome Bruner's *Process of Education* in which he first described the spiralling curriculum. By this he meant that generalizable concepts could be introduced quite early to young children, in a simplified yet intellectually honest form, and then returned to in ever increasing complexity at later grades until mastery was achieved. Some of the current enthusiasms have gone far beyond what Bruner either said or intended, such as labelling anything that is taught a "concept." Perhaps the ultimate parody of Bruner's ideas was reached by the teacher who remarked, "now boys and girls, we must work on the concept of skipping."

Nevertheless, it remains true that in discussions of curriculum or of teaching, the key words today are "discovery," "intuition," "structure." It is strongly implied that if pupils are presented with the proper materials, they will discover for themselves the principles involved, absorbing them into "cognitive content." The picture which is often projected is that of a

* *The Urban Review*, 2, 1968, 5–7. Reprinted with the permission of the author and *The Urban Review*, a publication of The Center for Urban Education.

pupil who discovers for himself concept after concept, or principle after principle, and who can build within his mind a symbolic architectural structure of this cognitive content, including the ability to generalize and transfer. The child has become, as it were, addicted to learning. This is the view of the pupil as some would see him. It is indeed, an entrancing view, both of knowledge and of the pupil; it offers a romance of the intellect that is very seductive.

However, a quite different view is emerging from the research that my colleagues and I have been engaged in over the past three years. We[1] have been interested primarily in how children perceive the learning process in school. The technique we have used most frequently is that of "teaching exchanges" in which two or more pupils teach what they have been taught to two or more pupils who have not been so exposed. While the pupils carry on the exchange spontaneously, we observe them and record their efforts. These teaching exchanges have covered all parts of the curriculum, and have involved various groupings of pupils from elementary school through ninth grade in a number of school systems representing national median-income families. The sample involved in these exchanges to date is approximately one thousand pupils.

The view from the pupil's desk, based on what we have overheard, is very different indeed from that of the romantic intellectualism just described.

What the pupil is going to learn is to him far away in time and entirely mysterious. All he knows is what he *has* been taught, and he only remembers parts of that, often in an isolated fashion. Why he is made to learn this and not that, or this before that, is another mystery to him; nor does he know what the alternative choices might be. Since little of what he is asked to learn makes much sense to him, except perhaps the more visible skills of reading, writing, and computation, he rarely asks why he has been asked to learn them. He also senses he is going to be taught whatever the teacher has decided she is going to teach, so the question is useless.

The elementary pupil has *no cognitive map of content* to guide him through the labyrinth of knowledge he is asked to

---

[1] *That is, Ann Bochm, Clare Ceppi and myself.*

master. About the only recognizable signposts to him are those that he studies a second or third time, such as the explorers, bases, decimals, fractions, parts of speech, the colonists, Greece, and the Revolutionary War. But when the pupil is confronted with a return to a topic, a return which the educator may see as the spiralling curriculum, the pupil's reaction is two fold: (1) Why should I study it again? (2) Why should I study what I learned at a lower grade, as a younger child? The usual expression of exasperation is: "That's third grade stuff!" His important status as fifth grader has been challenged.

Further, he has as yet no cognitive map that can help him to see connections within the curriculum among subjects, among grades, among events, or among skills. Presumably the teacher helps him to see these relationships, but his lack of knowledge makes some of these connections nothing more than a superficial repetition of labels which the teacher has demanded. Pupils may parrot, for example, that division is one form of subtraction, but few can demonstrate that they understand the basis of similarity. Their lack of historical time is hard to appreciate until one hears them locating Greece, as compared to Egypt, by the time at which they studied it. (It is fortunate indeed that the early curriculum ordains that Egypt be studied before Greece, else historical chaos would reign.) The jump, for example, from the Colonies to the Old World is exceedingly hard, as few elementary pupils have any knowledge of what was happening concurrently in Europe or anywhere else. When an elementary pupil tries to establish sequence, he utilizes the only large temporal order he is familiar with, and that is his own temporal order, consisting of his experience in school.

The cognitive map that he does use, we are suggesting, is his *map of school experience*. His experiences in school are the organizers of his knowledge, until high school or later, before he makes connections within that knowledge. Until then, the schema that serves him is his school life. That schema in turn, is organized by the way in which school life itself is organized, that is, by grade level, by "subjects," by teachers, and by the daily schedule. Categories are first built upon their location in school life: "We studied that in fourth grade . . . Miss X taught us that. . . ."

The analogy that might make the pupil's view more comprehensible to adults is to imagine oneself on a ship, sailing across an unknown sea, to an unknown destination. An adult would be desperate to know where he is going. But a child only knows he is going to school, that he has absolutely no choice in the matter, and that all the adults in his life have decided he is to make this voyage, together with all the other children he knows. The chart is neither available nor understandable to him. He does not even know how long the voyage will take. Very quickly, the daily life on board ship becomes all important. If it is highly organized, as school life is, this structure serves as a series of cubby holes into which he tucks those pieces of information he retains. The daily chores, the demands, the inspections, become the reality, not the voyage, nor the destination.

And so we think it is with most pupils. Particular knowledge and skills are considered by the pupils to be important, depending upon the workload assigned to them, and the frequency of evaluation. Pupils say, over and over again, that mathematics is the most important subject in the elementary grades. Why? Because, they say, mathematics has more homework assigned to it and more often; it is corrected more promptly; and they have more tests in it. Spelling is important: "we get practice tests on Wednesday, and tests every Friday." To a pupil, the workload and evaluation demands obviously must reflect what the teacher thinks is important to learn. (This view should appear entirely rational either to an educator or a psychologist.) Is it not entirely rational for a child to conclude that what the teacher assigns most frequently must be important in her eyes? If she gives more tests in one subject than another, is it not logical to conclude that this indicates what is important in her mind? The demands made by the captain of the ship, to return to our earlier analogy, is perfectly clear language which communicates what the captain sees as important. (The behavioral demands of the school, like that of a ship, apparently became clear to pupils at a relatively early age to form still another map—one which we have not yet explored adequately enough to describe.)

The converse is also true. Anything the teacher mentions once, but does not repeat, does not assign work in, and does not test for, is dismissed as unimportant. This might well include the following: why we study this subject, what this topic has to do with some other topic, how this piece of knowledge fits into that piece from last year, how this operation relates to another in a different subject, how we can generalize from this instance to other instances, and how the method of analyzing this problem can be used in these other problems.

If what educators judged important to teach were congruent with what pupils saw as important to learn, there would be little problem. We doubt the existence of this congruence, however, because we have heard what pupils view as the high points of the curriculum. They include the following: "you have to have a half-inch margin on your papers . . . you put the heading on the right, and not the left, and line it up . . . the cover should be felt if you want an A . . . you can't hand in papers that aren't neat, she'll really mark you down . . . you got to put the line over here on the right, like this, to do division the right way . . . you have to write out 'remainder' or it's wrong . . . ."

If work load and evaluation are the major criteria in a pupil's mind for discriminating between the important and the unimportant, then it might follow that both the curriculum and teaching should recognize these principles. This would mean organizing the test to repeat and stress the important points; the review section would highlight the major points; and the test would test for these same points. The same emphasis would appear in the length and frequency of homework assignments, the completeness of corrections, and the promptness in returning corrected papers.

Our second impression of the view from the pupil's desk is that *no adequate evaluative map* is available to him. By evaluative map we mean that the frame of reference, criteria, and symbols for evaluation which are used by the teacher are not clear to the pupil. We even doubt that most elementary teachers have a common evaluative map. The teacher who uses this year's class as her frame of reference for evaluation is not using the same criterion as the experienced teacher who is using 20 classes as her frame of reference. This difference is even more marked in classes of varied ability groupings. In addition, some teachers do not think that marks should reflect a human judgment of actual performance, but should be used to motivate for future performance. Even if James is clearly superior, he may be given a B+ to give him "something to strive for." If Sally is clearly below the rest of the class, she may be given a C, instead of an F, so she will be "encouraged." And how often do the criteria refer to the products only? How often do they include a teacher's global impression of pupil behavior, attitude, homework, class participation, promptness, interest, estimated ability, neatness, the willingness to follow the teacher's instructions, or some unstated combination of these?

Since we think that teachers themselves are not clear about evaluation, it is not surprising that we find pupils confused about the evaluative criteria, their standing relative to other pupils in the class, and what they need to do to get better marks. For example, confusion may stem from having a teacher who feels that competition among pupils is either bad or unnatural, and therefore never makes overt comparisons such as posted grades. Yet she makes subtle comparisons almost constantly, whether she's aware of it or not. To pupils that particular evaluation system comes through loud and clear. They know who is in favor or out of it, who is in trouble or out of it. But this classroom pecking order may not correlate exactly with the grades pupils receive because performance on assignments and on tests cannot be ignored by the teacher. The pupils do not know the distribution of grades for a given evaluation, so they do not know if they did well or poorly relative to the class as a whole. They may know the grade which Sammy said he got, and then they make the estimate: "If Sammy usually gets high marks, and I did better than he did on this test, then I must have done well." Unfortunately for the pupil, Sammy may have done miserably on this one test. (Even the simple solution of posting the distribution of scores without names is a rarity.)

There are further complications. The pupil has little idea of what weight is given to what factor. Assuming that he has been getting "mostly B's," he will expect a B on his report card. Imagine his chagrin to get a C+! He thinks the teacher unfair, and his parents hear his howls, unsympathetically. What this pupil did not realize was that a certain test or project would be weighted at three times the value of the weekly tests. Or suppose the teacher graded him according to her impression of his "potential?" How does the pupil know what that impression is, or whether it is even accurate? Should it be a criterion for a mark?

Elementary pupils find it difficult to predict their grades. They find averaging letter grades a rather difficult computational task. (A simple numerical system in place of a letter system might be easier for all.) Their memory and sense of time are not accurate enough for them to remember which marks came before or after this particular marking period. A simple record system kept by the pupil would seem useful, but many teachers would feel this would emphasize marks too much or encourage competition.

The pupils' attitude toward marks, as we have heard it, is quite contrary to what most teachers think. Pupils think marks are extremely important, even though they may have difficulty understanding them. They realize that their marks make a definite impression upon their families, but marks also establish their reputation among their peers. If they are assigned to sections based upon ability grouping, their marks are vital, for ability grouping is a public pecking order.

The matter of public performance is a great deal more important to pupils than we may realize. The view from the pupil's desk necessarily means that some things are visible to him, and some are not. In the primary grades, for example, he and his classmates will usually agree on who is the best writer. This is often taken as their mark of the best pupil. Why? Because handwriting is visible for all to see, and the best papers are usually exhibited. Who is best at gym? Usually there is concensus in the class on this, again because the performance is clearly visible to all during gym periods. If spelling bees are used, the best spellers are clearly identified. But how does a pupil know what or who is a good reader, a skill the teacher may put foremost in her evaluation? He typically reads out loud in only one of three groups, so his experience is often limited to one third of the classroom. Further, this one third is usually homogeneously grouped, so that if a particular pupil is placed on the "Bluebirds," and the "Bluebirds" happen to be the bottom reading group, it is quite possible that he does not hear an example of good reading out loud from his peers. The ability to read out loud is not all of reading in any event, but how would a first or second grade pupil develop recognition of good comprehension? He knows who giggles instead of answering, but he would be unable to discriminate between good and bad comprehension answers, based on their cognitive content. Instead, he will take his cues from the teacher who either approves or amends the answer, and, in subtle behavioral ways, indicates what and who she thinks is good. In arithmetic the same invisibility problem occurs. A particular pupil may be doing very poorly in arithmetic for a variety of reasons. He may never see what a good performance is, or where his performance stands in relation to the class distribution. If classes are homogeneously grouped, the problem of invisibility is intensified because the range of observable behavior is even further narrowed. How can a pupil observe a sample of the kind of performance which would move him into a higher ability grouping?

Pupils show ingenuity in trying to translate symbols into an evaluation system meaningful to them. At different elementary grade levels, they will describe their underground codes, such as "three wrong is a B+ . . . ," ". . . five wrong would be a C." In the lower grades, it is very hard for them to understand that the grade is also related to the number of examples assigned or completed, so this concrete code is inadequate as a means of translation.

If this impression of our data is correct, it indicates that elementary school pupils lack two important maps, a cognitive one in terms of the curricular content, and the other, evaluative. We think these two deficits are extremely important in the learning process. On the one hand, pupils have no content schema at this stage which helps them to organize knowledge. Instead, they develop a schema where they have the most data, and that is their life in school. We think considerable mislearning and miscategorization occur because of the lack of fit between the pupils' schema and the curricular one. A great deal more attention needs to be paid to the ways in which pupils categorize information if we hope to have them build up relationships, much more "concepts."

Second, we think that their lack of an adequate evaluative map leads pupils to create their own map, based on cues and misperceptions, which in turn lead to various misjudgments in their attempts to raise their performance. This lack of clarity between the teacher's evaluative criteria and those of the pupils may be a serious source of difficulty in school. We would propose that it might be one good principle of pedagogy that a pupil understand, first, how he will be evaluated, and second, that he be able to see or experience those samples of behavior which he is expected to produce and upon which evaluation will be based.

There are those who might say that the view presented here is a discouraging one, certainly not romantic, and apparently not intellectual. Some might feel that this situation is due to the social system of the school which should be reorganized forthwith. Others might feel that teachers do not listen enough to how children learn, and would propose radical changes within the teaching profession.

We do not share the discouragement nor elect such solutions. We find it neither discouraging nor suprising that children may learn in the ways we have described. What we would propose is not at all romantic; it is that we should learn still more about how children learn, and how different children learn differently, before any solutions are proposed. When we have enough data, we think it may be possible to construct a better fit between the objectives of the curriculum and the pupils' perceptions; and certainly, a better fit between those objectives, the evaluation system, and the pupils' evaluative map. Despite the current lack of fit that we have reported, we are also aware that children do learn, that as a whole they are reading better now than a few years ago, and that national achievement tests have to be constantly restandardized to take these absolute gains into account. We prefer the option of knowing a good deal more before advocating changes which could become still another educational crusade.

Teaching and Learning
in City Schools–An Excerpt*

ELEANOR BURKE LEACOCK

EDITOR'S NOTE: *The excerpt presented here is part of a chapter from the book* Teaching and Learning in City Schools. *This chapter is entitled "Classroom Goals from the Children's Point of View." The book reports the findings of a comparative study of elementary schools in four contrasting urban neighborhoods— middle-income white, middle-income black, low-income white, and low-income black. The study is particularly concerned with the socializing aspects of schooling.*

In a brief interview, each child was asked a number of short direct questions about his school experience, such as, "Suppose tomorrow someone told you it was up to you as to whether you wanted to go to school any more? What would you do?" "Why?" and, "Do you think you'd miss anything if you didn't go?" They were questioned about the kinds of things children do that made their teacher happy, the kinds of things the teacher did not like, and what she did about both. They were also asked simple questions about their occupational goals, their school work, and their friends and classmates. Examples of the last topic were: "If you could choose all by yourself, which child in the class would you like best to sit next to?" "What children in class don't you particularly like?" "How

---

* Excerpted from Chapter 7 of *Teaching and Learning in City Schools* by Eleanor Burke Leacock, Copyright © 1969 by Basic Books, Inc., Publishers, New York. Reprinted by permission of the publisher and the author.

come?" "What kind of things do children in your class do that annoy you most?" The interviewers were well aware that answers to questions such as these would be influenced by the children's desire to say the right thing to someone who, despite assertions to the contrary, would doubtless be identified with their school. This was no drawback, however, since a major aim of the questionnaire was precisely to find out what the children thought the "right things" to be, that is, how they defined the expectations their teachers and their schools held for them.

Interviews were distributed across classrooms as follows:[1]

	NO. INTERVIEWED	NO. IN CLASS
Second Grade:		
Lower-income Negro	23	30
Lower-income white	22	28
Middle-income Negro	34	36
Middle-income white	29	32
Total	108	126
Fifth Grade:		
Lower-income Negro	26	30
Lower-income white	32	34
Middle-income Negro	38	40
Middle-income white	36	38
Total	132	142

The deliberately vague and open-ended phrasing of many questions afforded the children the opportunity to interpret

[1] Since up to six or seven children were absent on the day interviewing was undertaken in the low-income second grades, children who were absent in the fifth grades were interviewed on a later day. It was decided that if changes in responses of previously absent children occurred due to conversations with other children, they would be very slight and would be offset by the advantage of a more complete interview series. The smaller number of interviews in low-income classes, with the exception of the white fifth grade, should be noted, since in and of itself it might affect the range and variety of answers relative to the middle-income classes. However, as shall be seen, it is not sufficient to account for the kinds of differences we shall be discussing.

them freely. This allowed the researchers to ascertain the extent to which children interpreted school-related or teacher-defined goals in terms of behavior rather than academic performance, how they defined standards for behavior, and whether academic performance was seen as a matter of simply meeting more or less arbitrary requirements, or whether some feeling for *true learning or understanding* might be involved. As analysis proceeded, it soon became apparent that responses to the questionnaire related as often to the school differences we have noted as to the children's presumed home and neighborhood experiences.

The set of questions pertaining to peer relations was subjected to further analysis in an effort to explore relations between teacher attitudes and child responses. Patterns of response were compared both with observational material on classroom interactions among the children and with children favored or disfavored by the teacher in her interview or through her distribution of praise or criticism in the classroom. The aim was to explore the relation between teacher attitudes and child responses by comparing the children's perception of the goals for their behavior with those the teacher either stated directly or implied through her treatment of them.

Children's Attitude to Work in Relation to Their School Experience

In order to see how the children perceived expectations for their behavior, they were asked what their teachers liked and disliked and what the teacher "did about it." In all the classrooms, children saw their teachers as being more concerned about good or bad behavior than academic work and performance. From 12 to 32 per cent of the second-grade children mentioned good work among the things that made their teachers happy, while from 73 to 88 per cent mentioned good behavior. In the fifth grade, more children referred to work (56 to 69 per cent), even though the range of responses dealing with behavior (65 to 88 per cent) was similar to that of the second grade (see Table 1).

The emphasis on behavior was even sharper when the children were asked what their teacher disliked. One suspects that

TABLE 1

Work versus Behavior Responses to What Does and Does Not Make the Teacher Happy

	BEHAVIOR[a]		WORK[a]		NUMBER
	No.	*%*	*No.*	*%*	*Interviewed*
Low-income Negro school					
Second grade					
Teacher likes	19	76	8	32	
Teacher dislikes	16	69	2	9	23
Fifth grade					
Teacher likes	17	65	18	69	
Teacher dislikes	25	96	1	4	26
Low-income white school					
Second grade					
Teacher likes	16	73	5	23	
Teacher dislikes	17	76	3	14	22
Fifth grade					
Teacher likes	25	78	18	56	
Teacher dislikes	28	88	4	12	32
Middle-income Negro school					
Second grade					
Teacher likes	30	87	4	12	
Teacher dislikes	26	77	1	3	34
Fifth grade					
Teacher likes	25	66	25	66	
Teacher dislikes	33	87	11	29	38
Middle-income white school					
Second grade					
Teacher likes	25	88	7	24	
Teacher dislikes	20	70	10	35	29
Fifth grade					
Teacher likes	28	88	24	68	
Teacher dislikes	34	94	12	33	36

[a] Totals exceed 100 per cent since a child's answer that mentioned both work and behavior was counted twice. A common practice of using the first response only and not counting the rest was not felt to be appropriate for present purposes.

questions about what the teacher likes draw the more formal answers—the parallel to the teacher's overtly stated goals in the classroom—while questions about her dislikes draw responses about those actions which, in fact, make the children fearful of drawing her active displeasure. While from 69 to 77 per cent of the second-graders included some mention of behavior in their answers, only from 3 to 35 percent included references to work. For fifth-graders, the answers on behavior run from 87 to 96 per cent and on work from 4 to 33 per cent. Even these percentages give the teacher the benefit of the doubt. References to what are essentially work-related routines, rather than actual work achievements, are included in the work category, which would decrease even more if they were dropped out.

Educational ideologies hold that the maintenance of discipline should be a means to academic learning and not an end in itself. However, the effort put into enforcing discipline and "proper" behavior in the study classrooms was such that the children saw this area as the more salient for teacher approval and disapproval. Other writers have considered the structure of the school as an institution and have commented on the fact that its custodial nature is in constant conflict with its professed educational function.[2]

Children's responses on teacher likes and dislikes reflected the pattern which was found in our observations and which deviated from our original expectations—the strong emphasis on behavior as well as work in the middle-income classrooms when compared with the low-income classrooms. The negative sanction against poor work in the middle-income Negro and white fifth grades was more strongly felt than in the low-income classrooms (29 and 33 per cent mentioned teacher disliking poor work, in comparison with 4 and 12 per cent). It was also more strongly felt in the middle-income white second grade than in the others (35 per cent mentioned teacher disliking poor work, in comparison with 3, 9, and 14 percent). However, the stronger sanction against poor work did not

---

[2] C. E. Silberman writes: ". . . it is overwhelmingly clear that one of the principal reasons children do not learn is that the schools are organized to facilitate administration rather than learning—to make it easier for teachers and principals to maintain order rather than to make it easier for children to learn. Indeed, to a degree that we are just beginning to appreciate as the result of the writings of such critics as Edgar Z. Friedenberg, John Holt, and Bel Kaufman, schools and classrooms are organized so as to *prevent* learning or teaching from taking place" [C. E. Silberman, "Technology in the Schools," in P. C. Sexton, ed., *Readings on the School in Society* (Englewood Cliffs, N.J.: Prentice-Hall, 1967, p. 246].

mean a dropping off in the perception of a strong negative sanction against bad behavior in these classrooms. (Eighty-seven and 94 per cent of middle-income fifth-grade children mentioned the teacher disliking bad behavior, which is the same as the 88 and 96 per cent of low-income fifth-grade children who answered similarly. For second grades, the figures are 70 and 77 per cent in middle-income classrooms, and 69 and 76 per cent in low-income classrooms.)

Thus the children's responses further emphasized the inadequacy of our initial assumption that greater emphasis on work would involve lesser emphasis on behavior and vice versa, and that classrooms could be evaluated in terms of their relative stress on one as compared with the other. Instead of a greater or lesser emphasis on behavior as such, it was the *qualitative definition of behavior* which was significant. The differences in definitions of behavior which emerged from the child questionnaires paralleled those which were observed in the classrooms, and it was easy to match the children's reports with their counterpart in the teacher-interview and observational material. The second-grade children in the more "permissive" low-income classrooms spoke of such things as sitting quietly and being good as pleasing the teacher and "not hollering," "doing what told," "listening," "not making the teacher scream." In the middle-income Negro classroom, where formal and rigid behavior was stressed (behavior required for successful competition in a highly critical white society), there were ten explicit mentions, out of thirty-four answers, of sitting or standing "up tall." In the white middle-income second grade, there were eight mentions, out of twenty-nine answers, to "self-control" which was stressed in the classroom and which is part and parcel of the training for an authoritative social role.

Good peer relations were referred to as pleasing the teacher by several children in the fifth-grade middle-income white classroom. They stated she was happy when "we get along with other children," when "we are good sportsmen—when we lose, some of the kids start to cry," and when "we try to help everybody . . . [and are] courteous to each other." In another fifth grade, "getting along with each other" was mentioned by one child but, apart from an idiosyncratic answer, "when they aren't afraid to dance with a girl," there were no mentions of good peer relations as pleasing the teacher in the other fifth grades or in any of the second grades. There were but one or two mentions of friends in most classrooms, or none at all, in response to the question about what a child would miss if he did not go to school. However, four children in the middle-income Negro fifth-grade classroom and six in the middle-income white fifth grade spoke of missing friends or social life.

Although answers about peer relations are so few as to be suggestive rather than definitive, they afford a good example of the way in which school-defined goals can tie in with neighborhood social patterns and the way they reinforce one another; this contrasts with the view that sees the school as simply responding to independent neighborhood differences. In a middle-income school there is more likelihood for a child to have visiting relations out of school with some of his school "colleagues" than in a low-income school. Parents have more time and facilities for and interest in the children's social life in and out of the classroom. In the middle-income neighborhood, there are parties for school friends and acquaintanceship with other parents through the PTA, in contrast with the low-income neighborhood, where friends are necessarily on the block or at least nearby, and where they are not as likely to be in the same classroom, given the greater number of classrooms in a grade in the larger low-income schools. The structuring of the learning situation to involve closer peer relations in a middle-income classroom can both use and strengthen existing social patterns.

The marked variations in the degree and extent to which children refer to work in their answers about what the teacher likes or dislikes are illustrated graphically in the following compilation. As can be seen, in the fifth-grade middle-income classrooms there is (1) an increasing explicitness in the references to subject matter, (2) more references, not just to completing work, but to its correctness and to doing extra work, and (3) the emergence of references to attitudes toward work. The fact that the children are here reporting what they see their teachers to be asking of them casts new light on the commonly held assumption that a presumably greater motivation for success in school among middle-class children derives solely from their home backgrounds. An examination of their content shows the children's answers to reflect the kinds of practices which were observed in the classroom and discussed in the teacher interviews. On the whole, the children are apparently repeating what their teachers have said or done, rather than expressing their own attitudes. For example, the middle-income white fifth-grade references to speaking up and engaging in good discussion, correcting the teacher, and pausing to think about a problem before answering are recognizable as characteristic of that classroom. The few references to work that occurred in response to the question, "What does school teach you about how you should act?" also reflect classroom differences. In the low-income fifth grades these took the form of not interrupting or talking when someone else had the floor. A child in the middle-income Negro fifth grade said, "Not to talk and how to be quiet—when you first start school, you can't sit still for a long time and work by yourself." An equally explicit remark from a white middle-income fifth-grader was, "If somebody talks to you, don't answer back unless it's to get what assignment they missed or something," and a classmate's answer, unique for this question, was, "Always know your facts."

Contrasts among the classrooms with regard to the emphasis on work were even sharper in answer to what the teacher did *not* like. Here the second-grade middle-income white classroom and both fifth-grade middle-income classrooms stood out, with considerably more references to poor work. As a corollary, in the question about how the teacher acted when she did not like something, there were no mentions of bad marks in either of the low-income Negro classrooms, while in the other classrooms from 19 to 41 per cent of the children made some reference to grades, conduct marks, or report cards. The weight of threatened negative sanction was little felt for poor work in the former classrooms but strongly felt in the middle-income fifth grades and the white middle-income second grade. Again, one could argue that this was differential perception on the part of the children, according to their previously held value scheme if the interview material did not tally so well with the classrooms as observed. As a humorous example, one child in the middle-income white second grade sagely answered that when his teacher was displeased by a child, she "pretended to put 'U' on the report card."

In short, the children's accounts of how the teacher rewarded and punished closely paralleled and in some cases filled out the picture of the teachers' classroom management techniques. . . . To be sure, the picture given by the children is more lively than that observed, with teachers "hollering" and "screaming" and getting red in the face. One would expect a teacher not to lose her temper with observers present and would assume that she did at other times. However, there were only two specific practices mentioned by the children which were not recorded in the classroom observation or teacher interview or which might not have readily been inferred from these materials, and these fitted the comparative picture of differential controls and expectations we have been presenting. They were the threatening "list" for nonpromotion, supposedly kept by the middle-income white fifth-grade teacher, and hitting as a form of punishment in the low-income Negro fifth grade.

In response to the question, "What would you like to do in school that you don't do now?" the children's stated desires for more and harder work increased with income level:

	SECOND GRADES		FIFTH GRADES	
	No. of Children Mentioning Work	% of Respondents	No. of Children Mentioning Work	% of Respondents
Low-income Negro	5	22	7	27
Low-income white	3	14	6	19
Middle-income Negro	8	26	17	45
Middle-income white	8	23	18	53

In all classrooms, however, and in the fifth grades as much as the second, the responses of the children reflected their reaction to the restrictions of the school day. Some 50 per cent or more of the children in every class expressed the desirability of more time for pleasant activities such as gym and various kinds of games, art, music and craft activities, and school trips. References to the desirability of academic activities were as follows, with most answers implying a child would like more of a subject already given:

Second Grade: Low-income Negro: Read, write, number work, "read books that James reads"

Low-income white: Real writing, number work, learn mathematics, homework

Middle-income Negro: Read, write, write like third-graders, write stories (3 responses), arithmetic

Middle-income white: "Read for fun," more math, homework, spelling harder words (3 responses), "arithmetic where don't have to write," geography, history, sciences, "study big reptiles like dinosaurs"

Fifth Grade: Low-income Negro: "Individualized reading" (actually the system in this class), write, "easy arithmetic," more science, do arithmetic and spelling better, do work better, "work all the time—write to authors"

Low-income white: Lot of math, science (2), social studies (2), French, algebra, "get ahead in my work"

Middle-income Negro: Reading, math, spelling, French, Spanish, science, social studies, "a book with paper that I could write stories in," "be good in math," "catch up in math," "take general course," "get a higher reading and learn higher math and do what sixth grade do," "study geology and astronomy," "engineering, electric shop and woodwork shop," nursing

Middle-income white: Math, algebra, social studies, language (5 responses, including some French, some Spanish, some simple language), spelling, chemistry, "harder work," "find out about dinosaurs," "spelling bees—learn more from them," "sixth-grade math or higher subjects," "more nature working with animals"

Relations among Teacher Attitudes, Sociometric Preferences, and Achievement

Other questions showed the same "fit" between the children's answers and observed differences in teaching, classroom management practices, and teachers' expressions of goals and expectations. Questions about the children's attitudes toward their peers indicated the way the children accepted teacher goals and attitudes as they tried to please her. They were asked what their classmates did that annoyed them, whom they would like to sit next to in class, and whom they did not like and why. As might be expected, 50 per cent or more answers to the question as to what annoyed a child concerned

noise, talking, fighting, and teasing of one kind or another. The
number of answers that referred explicitly to disturbing work
varied from classroom to classroom as follows:

	SECOND GRADE		FIFTH GRADE	
	No.	*%*	*No.*	*%*
Low-income Negro	5	22	3	11
Low-income white	9	40	8	25
Middle-income Negro	4	12	7	18
Middle-income white	9	31	12	33

These figures have to be considered in relation to how
much confusion and disruption of work was in fact allowed in
a classroom. In the second grades, the frequency of responses
varied from the relatively low percentage in the highly controlled middle-income Negro classroom, through the somewhat
less controlled classes to the highest percentage in the most
"permissive" setting. By the fifth grade, however, differentially
perceived goals entered in, for while degree of control may
have contributed in part to the relatively low percentage in
the highly disciplined middle-income Negro classroom, it cannot account for the considerable difference between the low-
income Negro and middle-income white classes. Furthermore,
answers in the former referred only to talking going on while a
child was working; in the latter they also referred to another
child looking at one's work and copying, to talking during tests
and, in a unique reply, to making "fun of me because I'm not
so good at math." The fact that there is a slightly greater
variation in the second grade than in the fifth grade in the
low-income Negro school is interesting. Mentions of copying
and of "noise disturbing the speed of work" occur in the second grade. The number of answers involved are far too small
to make the variation significant in any technical sense, but the
trend is suggestive of the widening gap between the classrooms with respect to academic goals as the children move up
the grades.

Variations from second to fifth grades in the pattern of
sociometric choices, that is, preferred and disliked children,
conformed to the findings of other studies in that fifth-grade

positive choices were directed toward a wider range of children than were second-grade choices. Studies of classroom favorites typically show "stars" in the lower grades, with more stereotyped answers directed toward a few children, in contrast with greater individual selectivity by the fifth grade and a "clique" pattern or two or three definable clusters surrounded by a periphery of less popular children and "isolates." Variations among the study classrooms in the present case, however, were suggestive of other differences across social groups (see Table 2).

TABLE 2
Patterns of Sociometric Choice

	AVERAGE NO.	CHOICES PER CHILD	% CHILDREN CHOSEN	
	Positive	*Negative*	*Positive*	*Negative*
Low-income Negro school				
Second grade	1.6	0.5	62	20
Fifth grade	1.7	0.6	87	33
Low-income white school				
Second grade	1.5	0.7	71	43
Fifth grade	2.0	1.0	82	21
Middle-income Negro school				
Second grade	1.9	0.4	53	38
Fifth grade	1.8	1.0	67	42
Middle-income white school				
Second grade	1.5	0.7	44	30
Fifth grade	2.0	1.0	76	45

Children could give several choices to the question which children they "did not particularly like," or they could answer "no one," and in all classrooms they found it easier to make positive than negative choices. This was the more true in the second grades and particularly in the Negro classrooms. In the fifth grades, negative choices increased considerably, but less in the low-income Negro classroom than in the others. They averaged little more than one choice for every two children, while in the other classrooms they were about one per child. Positive choices, in part due to their greater number, were wider ranging than negative. In the second grades they were wider ranging in the low-income schools, with the star pattern most pronounced in the white middle-income classroom.

The sociometric questions put to the children were placed in the classroom context: "What child would you like best to sit next to?" and "Who would you choose next?" Sociometric questions may be phrased in terms of accompanying a friend to a movie, inviting a friend home, and so on, but our purpose was to stay close to the school situation and examine school-related goals and attitudes toward peers. The assumption has been that the clash of "values" leads to a lower-class pattern of peer alliance vis-à-vis the teacher by contrast with the greater identification of middle-class children with the middle-class teacher. We have questioned the simplistic formula of "value clash" and have examined the role played by the teacher in the influencing of children's motivations and identifications. Therefore, the questions raised by the sociometric material were: who were the favored and disfavored children; to what extent did choices seem independent of teacher preference; or to what extent did they mirror her attitudes?

The rating of the affect shown by the teachers in their descriptions of individual children was described in . . . [Leacock *Teaching and Learning* . . . , Chapter 5]. The distribution of these ratings for the fifth grades was as follows:[3]

	LOW-INCOME NEGRO	LOW-INCOME WHITE	MIDDLE-INCOME NEGRO	MIDDLE-INCOME WHITE
Very positive	1	1	2	2
Mildly positive	7	10	5	10
Neutral	7	12	18	25
Mildly negative	11	9	11	1
Very negative	4	1	3	0

As can be seen, the teachers' evaluations of the children parallel the children's status as groups in the eyes of society, with

[3] The total of thirty-three and thirty-nine, instead of thirty-four and forty children in the low-income white and middle-income Negro classrooms, respectively, is due to the transfer of children to other schools.

Negro lower than white, low-income lower than mildle-income. Nor can the more negative teacher attitudes expressed toward the Negro children be considered a result of simple race prejudice, for both of the teachers in these classrooms were themselves Negro women.

Not only was there a general downgrading of Negro and low-income children, but it was directed more sharply toward the *more* able children in these groups. As stated in . . . [Leacock, *Teaching and Learning* . . . , Chapter 5], the teacher-favored children in the middle-income white fifth grade had an average IQ score that was eleven points higher than those toward whom the teacher felt negative, while in the low-income Negro fifth grade those about whom the teacher felt positive or neutral had an average IQ score that was almost ten points lower than those toward whom she felt negative. Given this situation, an alliance of peers might well follow from a defensive attempt on the part of low-income children to preserve their self-respect. In the middle-income white fifth grade, there was a meshing of teacher and peer favor, ability and achievement; the better readers were more popular with the other children than the poorer readers who were more unpopular. In the low-income Negro fifth grade, the better readers with average IQ's, or those children who were presumably the more school achievement oriented, were more unpopular than the mediocre readers with higher IQ's, or the more able but nonconforming children.

The following figures show teacher affect ratings viewed in relation to reading achievement and IQ in the middle-income white and low-income Negro fifth grades:

	TEACHER RATING	NUMBER OF CHILDREN	AVERAGE READING ACHIEVEMENT	AVERAGE IQ
Low-Income Negro:	Positive	8	4.3	84.4
	Neutral	7	4.0	84.2
	Negative	15	4.1	93.2
Middle-Income white:	Positive	12	8.4	122.8
	Neutral	19	8.7	118.3
	Negative	7	7.0	111.7

These figures dramatically indicate the effect of the teacher's negativism toward the presumably more able children in the low-income Negro classroom. Despite an average IQ almost ten points higher than that of the positively and neutrally viewed children, scores of the negatively viewed children averaged slightly lower on reading achievement. This is in marked contrast with the positive correlation between IQ and reading achievement in the middle-income white classrooms.[4]

	TEACHER RATING	NUMBER OF CHILDREN	AVERAGE READING ACHIEVEMENT	AVERAGE IQ
Low-Income white:	Positive	11	6.2	96.7
	Neutral	12	6.1	95.4
	Negative	10	6.1	98.7
Middle-Income Negro:	Positive	7	6.9	103.2
	Neutral	18	5.6	92.6
	Negative	14	6.5	93.1

A study of Rosenthal and Jacobson, which focused directly on the effects of positive teacher expectations on children's performance, reinforces some of our own conclusions about the significance of teacher attitudes.[5] Rosenthal and Jacobson found that children who were, in fact, randomly chosen but who were believed by their teachers to be potential "spurters" who would show considerable gain during the academic year, did on the whole make greater gains than their classmates. The teachers also described these children more favorably in relation to their disposition, curiosity, and chance for success in life. The gains were particularly marked in the first and second grades, then tapered off, and, interestingly enough, did

[4] The figures for the low-income white classroom show an almost neutral relationship, in contrast with the above two classrooms. The interesting figures for the middle-income Negro classroom cannot be compared with the others because of the complicating factor that the "reading track" system in that school meant the children shifted classrooms for the reading lesson.

[5] R. Rosenthal and L. F. Jacobson, *Pygmalion in the Classroom: Self Fulfilling Prophecies and Teacher Expectations* (New York: Holt, Rinehart and Winston, Inc., 1968).

not affect the fifth grade, where child roles were presumably more firmly established, until the second year of the study.

When Rosenthal and Jacobson inquired more closely into teacher attitudes and children's performance, they found *an unfavorable response to children who progressed when they were not expected to.* They comment, "It would seem that there are hazards in unpredicted intellectual growth." Where this unfavorable response to intellectual growth was most marked, however, was in the "slow-track" classrooms in a school which was attended by some middle-income children but mostly by low-income children, including Mexican-American families and families on welfare. Rosenthal and Jacobson write:

> When these "slow-track" children were in the control group, where little intellectual gain was expected of them, they were rated more unfavorably by their teachers if they did show gains in IQ. The more they gained, the more unfavorably they were rated. Even when the slow-track children were in the experimental group, where greater intellectual gains were expected of them, they were not rated as favorably with respect to their control-group peers as were the children of the high track and the medium track. Evidently it is likely to be difficult for a slow-track child, even if his IQ is rising, to be seen by his teacher as well adjusted and as a potentially successful student.[6]

The authors speak of the need for more research into the nature of teacher-child interaction and the means by which a teacher may unwittingly communicate her expectations to a child and influence his conception of himself and his "anticipation of his own behavior."[7] Our study has thrown light on some of these means, though we would assume there are many more.

[6] R. Rosenthal and L. F. Jacobson, "Teacher Expectations for the Disadvantaged," *Scientific American*, CCXVIII, No. 4 (1968), 22.
[7] *Ibid.*, p. 23.

Discussion

Verification that schooling is experienced the way the authors in this volume have portrayed can only come from students themselves. But, it is not an easy job to get students to talk about school. The query "How's school?" is answered as mechanically as the question "How are you?" After all, school is such a daily event that stating feelings about it is an impossible as summing up one's view of life itself. For this reason, the interview studies which were selected for this section approach the task by asking students what they see as the basic goals of schooling. The views expressed in these studies suggest that school is not always experienced in ways we would like to believe. Students' perceptions of what is important in school are especially uncomplimentary to the school's official intentions. This is because the institutional requirements of schooling often appear to students to be more essential than its educational aspects.

High school students are, of course, veterans of several years of schooling. According to Noyes and McAndrew, they feel that schools are for learning how to "get through the system." The "system" to which they refer depends on a set of rules which communicate to students what actions the school rewards and expects. Students claim that only by knowing how to play by the rules can you be successful in school. Otherwise, you "get caught, chewed up, or pushed out." The system appears to students as a calculated plan for insuring social control over large masses of students. They would most likely disagree with the view that the school administration is largely unaware of the hidden curriculum it has created.

Mallery also finds that high school is perceived by many students as a restrictive force rather than a liberating one. It is a place, they claim, where you primarily contend with the requirements placed upon you rather than explore how you can use its resources for greatest personal benefit. Schooling is additionally a "rat race" for grades, while the academic curriculum is of little significance. When students get together to discuss school, they rarely mention the courses of study they are taking. Talk about teachers and institutional procedures arouse students in ways in which the curriculum never does.

Elementary-school students appear more confused than cynical about their experiences in school. According to White, they perceive the learning process to be an amorphous, unconnected experience, structured more by grade level than by concepts and principles. They have little notion of why they are learning something nor where the present learning leads to in the future. The picture is one of students immersed in the routines of daily school life, oblivious to its central purposes. What is important, students reason, is what the teacher stresses most—school virtues such as neatness, quietness, and punctuality. The importance of evaluation is also recognized by the children, but, as White suggests, they are unsure about the criteria on which it is based. Young students have a vague sense that evaluation is tied both to the academic and the institutional curricula of the school but are still puzzled by their teacher's judgments.

When it comes to deciding which of the two curricula is more important, elementary-school students interviewed in Leacock's study believe that good behavior is of more concern to their teacher than good work. In their experience, violations of classroom regulations are more likely to draw the teacher's active displeasure than academic deficiencies. They also dislike the "restrictions of the school day." Despite these negative views of their school experience, Leacock finds that elementary students readily accept their teacher's admonitions concerning how to act. Moreover, they are quick to adopt the teacher's attitudes toward certain students. As we have seen previously, young children learn in the classroom the value of perceiving their classmates the way the teacher does. Their dependence upon adult acceptance makes it difficult to oppose the teacher's perceptions, not only in regard to who is worthy of praise and recognition but also to what is worthy to learn and to believe.

Many of the views expressed by students in these studies run contrary to our hopes and expectations. We tend to assume that children really understand the purpose of what they do in school and the reasons why we insist on certain ways of doing them. We also are inclined to discount their complaints by arguing, in a contradictory fashion, that students really do *not* understand the necessity for our rules, standards, and objectives. Our own confusion and cynicism begets that of students.

If schooling is going to make sense to children, let alone appeal to them, we must assume certain responsibilities. First, we should carefully examine the experiences students undergo. The examination of experiences which result from institutional aspects of school life is especially urgent because they have received superficial study up till now. Second, we must make a conscious decision to alter conditions that create undesirable experiences. Third, we must communicate clearly to students the goals and expectations we believe make sense. And, fourth, we should affirm the right of students to negotiate our purposes and demands so that the activities we undertake with them have greatest possible meaning to all.

At first glance, these recommended actions appear simple to do. But, our reluctance to undertake them suggests otherwise. What has held us back? One obstacle may have been the sheer complexity of students' experiences in school. What happens to children in classrooms is not easily reducible to a few general categories and thus is difficult to examine. Another obstacle may have been a belief that children do not know what is meaningful to them. And even if they do know, we may have had serious doubts whether they can communicate their thoughts in terms adults can understand. Despite these apparent obstacles, however, we cannot continue to ignore the problems schooling poses to children. To help make school a basically positive experience for students, we will have to cut through its complexity and risk that students are capable of taking an active part in it.

Index